Quang Tri Cadence

*Memoir of a Rifle Platoon Leader
in the Mountains of Vietnam*

by JON OPLINGER

McFarland & Company, Inc., Publishers
Jefferson, North Carolina, and London

British Library Cataloguing-in-Publication data are available

Library of Congress Cataloguing-in-Publication Data

Oplinger, Jon.
    Quang Tri cadence : memoir of a rifle platoon leader in the
mountains of Vietnam / by Jon Oplinger.
        p.   cm.
    ISBN 0-89950-873-1 (sewn softcover : 50# alk. paper) ∞
    1. Vietnamese Conflict, 1961–1975 — Personal narratives, American.
2. Oplinger, Jon.   I. Title.
DS559.5.065   1993
959.764'38 — dc20   92-56676
                                                         CIP

Manufactured in the United States of America

McFarland & Company, Inc., Publishers
  Box 611, Jefferson, North Carolina 28640

CONTENTS

CHAPTER 1

In the fall of 1965 I flunked out of college. This did not go unnoticed by my draft board. Although at the time I undoubtedly agreed that "somebody had to do it," I did not agree that it had to be me, so my interest in recruiters increased. I got no further than "the nearest army recruiting station" and enlisted to repair or do something with, anti-aircraft rockets. I would—and this was my plan—spend three years waiting in the United States, or possibly Germany, for Russian bombers that would never come. My recruiter assured me that the night life in Muskogee, Oklahoma, was better than originally supposed and showed me a brochure of Fort Benning, Georgia, where I would be going through basic training. Fort Benning seemed to have many swimming pools.

May I say that I spent almost a year at Fort Benning during which I went swimming just once—in the Chattahoochee River, during Ranger training, in February. But that was not my recruiter's fault. During basic training I volunteered for Officers Candidate School and that meant the infantry. True enough, I didn't request Infantry OCS; I put as my first choice Army Intelligence (mystery, adventure, air-conditioned offices) but was not surprised when I was assigned to the Infantry School at Fort Benning.

Informally known as Benning School for Boys, Infantry Officers Candidate School is entirely geared to the manufacture of that commodity which the wartime army expends quickest—rifle platoon leaders. Quickly expended, quickly produced. OCS lasts only six months

1

and a lot is crammed into that period, leaving little time for quiet reflection; none, in fact. And what the army is pleased to call harassment has over the years developed into high art. In addition to running everywhere, doing hundreds of push-ups a day and learning to function while someone was shouting in your ear, we also attempted such esoteric skills as doing the manual of arms with a footlocker and getting dressed inside a wall locker.

In the chow line you stood a precise stride behind the man in front of you. When he moved up, you called yourself to attention, marched two or three paces forward and then went back to parade rest. With a hundred men in line, the overall effect is a curious rippling movement that proceeds from front to back. Seen from a distance an OCS chow line resembles a huge undulating python that seems to be eating its way into the mess hall. We ate by the numbers, while sitting at attention: one, lift fork vertically with morsel of food; two, move fork horizontally to mouth; three and four, reverse the process. The traditional first meal at OCS is fried chicken. But after a couple of weeks, etiquette was relaxed to avoid general malnourishment. When behind schedule, we might be granted "gobbling privileges" and encouraged to eat with our hands. This was all standard. "Extra Curricular Activities," a variant of harassment, were more physical and closely followed an unsatisfactory performance.

It is at OCS that the army's fetish for highly polished surfaces is fully expressed. We took our boots off before we entered the barracks so as not to scuff the "highly polished" floor and one of the first sights I saw when I arrived in the battalion area was a harried candidate sprinting past me with a box of sanitary napkins under his arm. I had no ready explanation for this spectacle, but soon discovered that the pads were glued to the bottom of your footlocker so as not to scuff the "highly polished" floor. We walked only on the narrow strip of rubber that ran down the middle of the hall, so as not to . . . My tac officer (tactical training officer) demonstrated the correct method of entering your room: you swung from the doorjamb onto the bed. Ideally you didn't walk on the floor.

Lieutenant Contee was an ex–artillery sergeant who, unlike many tac officers, did not confuse himself with Jehovah but it did not do to displease him, either collectively or individually. One early problem involved scrambling down a rope from a thirty foot tower. No one had any trouble with this, except for one man who was terrified of heights.

He refused to leave the tower. Lieutenant Contee's face grew sad. We double-timed off to lunch leaving Contee alone with the, by now, trembling candidate. When we returned Contee called us to attention and we watched as the man sprang from the tower and flew down the rope like a gibbon.

Many of our field problems were run by the Ranger School. The Ranger cadre did not like candidates and when bored or annoyed were perfectly capable of stretching out a candidate between two saplings with communication wire or binding him hand and foot to be dumped into an icy stream. This was to "provide realism" which, in my case, it surely did. But such high jinks aside, these exercises were by far the best training we got. Some of our instructors had recently returned from Vietnam and we thought them spooky.

Military history seldom made its way into the curriculum. There was not enough time. We left such frivolity to West Point, an institution, in our view, of Ottoman luxuries. OCS, by contrast, made a cult of practicality. For instance, the same venerable joke circulated through every barracks. Side by side (goes the joke) an OCS man and a West Point graduate addressed the urinals of some forgotten officers club. The "ring knocker" (West Point) tarried to wash his hands; the OCS man headed directly back to the bar.

Ring Knocker: "Don't they teach you OCS guys to wash your hands?"

OCS: "They teach us not to piss on our hands."

We came to accept the punch line as our motto: "Don't Piss on Your Hands." It does suffer from ambiguity in concrete situations, unless you are urinating, but taken in the abstract it is good advice. The official OCS motto is "Follow Me," the emphasis being on leadership, and in front of the main classroom building is a statue of a platoon leader done in the tradition of U.S. Army neo–Tupperware realism, of which it is a fine example. It looks like a gigantic Ken doll. Platoon leader Ken has his arm upraised, sweeping forward. "Follow Me" is on the pedestal. If there is a statue anywhere at Fort Benning appropriate to the unofficial motto, I'd be surprised. But there should be.

OCS then provided a fair cross section of middle- and lower-middle-class Americans, both black and white. One of my classmates was the son of a physician but that was rare. Our class was perhaps unusual in that we had a large number of former NCOs who were

3

willing to accept the torments of OCS, and the near certainty of a second tour in Vietnam, to obtain a commission. To a man, I'm sure they made good officers. Some men, small and very tough, came from Special Forces. I distinctly remember one man who was utterly nerveless; during graduation, someone had to wake him up so that he could accept his commission. Several men, and maybe more, graduated as young as 18 and without exception they were as enthusiastic and obedient as hunting dogs. Two of them volunteered for immediate combat duty and went lolloping off to Vietnam to be swiftly killed.

But they were not the first. During our eleventh or twelfth week, one of our tac officers left for Vietnam. His platoon, feeling obligated, gave him a present and a party. His division patch—Twenty-Fifth Division—was painted on the side of his car. Bon Voyage! Home for two weeks and then off to Vietnam. He was dead before we graduated. It says more than I can convey about OCS that many in his platoon were pleased that he had been killed. Benning School for Boys does not hold reunions.

After graduation I was ordered to Fort Wolters, Texas, which was the army's school for primary flight training in helicopters. With what can be described as minimal foresight, I had married a month before Officers Candidate School, and to a woman that I had known only for a short time. Six months of OCS and several hundred dollars of long distance phone calls later I was still married. So, in July of 1967, I found myself in the unexpectedly agreeable situation of driving across country in the company of a partial stranger to whom I was wedded. She proved to be a most interesting stranger. Our destination, Mineral Wells, was a West Texas spa of decayed reputation chiefly known for its Crazy Water Hotel. Fort Wolters was a few miles outside of town.

Alas, the Crazy Water Hotel had closed and we checked into a motel at rates that would have exhausted the funds in a few days. I was not in a position to be choosy about housing and I was not; our first house was a "shotgun house." What it lacked in charm, it made up in ventilation. In theory, a shotgun blast fired through the front door would pass through the living room, bedroom and kitchen and out the back door without doing any damage. The neighborhood was poor, but the people were friendly and it was safe. It was, to be precise, the kind of neighborhood that attracts vacuum cleaner salesmen. Elsa and I lived there comfortably until base housing was available.

4

Fort Wolters was dominated by refurbished wooden structures that had been erected early during the Second World War in days, if not hours, by gangs of construction workers. The result was a sort of wood frame tentage: long, narrow, two-story barracks; squat headquarters buildings; huge wooden circus tents of mess halls braced and tied together by doubled two by tens and turnbuckled iron rods an inch thick. In a few places there were newer, three story concrete block structures. These represented Vietnam and housed student pilots.

The air above the scrub landscape surrounding Fort Wolters droned, night and day. Off toward the flight line dozens of tiny toy-like trainers circled. Everything that flew at Fort Wolters was painted day-glow orange giving the place a carnival air; but that was deceptive. Most of the officers on base were pilots who had already completed a tour in Vietnam, and, if the war continued, could look forward to a second tour. Few did so with enthusiasm.

I was assigned as the executive officer of the Headquarters Company for a training battalion of warrant officer candidates undergoing basic flight training. Any warrant officer candidate (unfortunately called a WOC) who flunked out was bundled off to us and we housed them until their orders arrived.

The most serious species of screw-up that did not necessarily result in death was an attempt to fly a machine that had been grounded by the mechanic. A big X was lined on the maintenance record: not to be flown. I can remember seeing two shaking and incredibly lucky candidates shortly after they had twice circled the field in a helicopter which had been X'd because the rotor blades were not properly attached. They were hardly attached at all and no one could figure out how the two men had gotten the machine into the air. Every month, every week, I think, there were fatal accidents. Unless the candidate dove the little trainer straight into the ground, it would roll and by the time it stopped there was a crumpled ball of plastic and metal small enough to put on the back of a pick-up truck. This was a common sight.

Any orderly room in the United States Army will provide three things in abundance: paperwork, popular music and a sort of oral history. I sat behind a desk, filled out forms and, when the company commander was not around, I signed forms. That was one of my jobs; I was the back-up signer. If I left the orderly room, it was often to count things. I counted wall lockers, foot lockers, blankets, and men to see if we had the correct number on hand. We seldom did. I told one of our men who kept women's clothes in his wall locker that he was better advised to keep them in the trunk of his car. That saved us a tremendous amount of paperwork.

A sort of oral history? I mean by that war stories. You heard them often and they were usually told in a way that was unrevealing of any investment of emotion or courage. Such sidebars you had to provide yourself; you were just supposed to know.

An insurance salesman regularly visited our orderly room. He was a retired officer who was living off his pension and really didn't care if he sold any policies. His true reason for showing up on our doorstep was to trade war stories with the company commander and the first sergeant. Germany, Korea, Vietnam — the first sergeant had been with the First Cavalry and during a firefight had been shot through the mouth. "Lost my teeth," he said, obviously recalling the sadness of the moment.

"Well they certainly did a fine job of reconstructive surgery," I said. "That must have been rough."

Sarge looked at me from beneath lowered brows. "No Sir, not hardly; but I had to go all the way back to An Khe to get a new set."

Eventually the stories would get around to the Louisiana Maneuvers of 1942. Having been in combat was one thing, but the Louisiana Maneuvers — that *was* something.

The company commander, a captain, had come into the army by way of the National Guard and for a time — longer than most — had flown for the 1st of the 9th, the First Cavalry's recon battalion. He still limped from having had his legs and buttocks carved up during a mortar attack. His office was the usual setting for these war stories. Framed citations for medals hung on the wall and a shell-base ashtray and a chrome hand grenade cigarette lighter decorated his desk. In what may have been an attempt at humor, someone in his old unit had sent back the pants he had been wearing when he was wounded. Stiff with dried blood and minus the legs, these went on the wall too and nicely complemented his purple heart.

The company commander's favorite activity was trying to locate an old stage coach route from the air. He often took me along to help, and to keep an eye out for Kamikaze WOCs. We would plod along in an old H-23 (he flatly refused to fly in the army's new trainer), and land on the tops of mesas to look for arrowheads, or chase deer through

6

the chaparral, or try to find the stage route. Now and again, he allowed me to saw away on the cyclic until it looked like I was going to stick the aircraft into the sod. We landed once in a dried out pothole that didn't have five feet of clearance at any point. "I gotta pee," announced the captain, cranking down on the collective which controls the pitch of the rotor blades. "Don't touch anything." Fat chance.

"Can we get out of here?" I asked after he returned. I didn't see how we could.

"Oh sure. Think up." And with barely perceptible movements of feet and hands, he guided the ship above the scrub—a Zen take-off.

With large numbers of men constantly coming and going, it was hard to keep track of who was assigned to the company. We never really did, and detected some men only when they made the mistake of showing up on payday. The local sheriff occasionally would pay us a visit; usually the offense was minor and could be smoothed over (patriotic boy about to go to Vietnam, etc.). But one of our men was engulfed by the Texas prison system for writing several thousand dollars worth of bad checks while impersonating a major in the Air Defense Commandos, a branch of service that does not exist.

Our company was the base version of Manpower, Inc.. There is trash along the main road through camp; call us. The shrubs around the officer's club need to be trimmed; call us. The officer's wives club needs live oak leaves and cattails for a centerpiece; call us. Your son has been killed in Vietnam; call us.

Call me. I ran the funeral detail. Eight men (usually) form the firing party and six pallbearers carry the coffin and fold the flag that covers it. In the company supply room was a "practice coffin." I presented the flag.

Almost always, it is a woman who receives the flag. There were times when they, wives more often than mothers, would refuse to take it. Then a man—brother, father, uncle—would step in and I would give the folded flag to him. Small towns that had already lost a number of men were sometimes cold, hostile. "Sir, I think you better tell somebody," I was told by one pallbearer who couldn't decide whether to laugh or throw up. It was late summer and the parlor-chapel must have been pushing a hundred degrees. "You should tell somebody . . . the wax is running out of that guy's head!" I got the funeral director to close the casket. I learned that families would ask for the expended cartridges used to fire the volleys. In a cold, rain-darkened stand of trees, I watched a softly mewling man crawl on his hands and knees into his son's muddy grave.

My orders came in January. A gambler's shuffle of computer cards somewhere in the Pentagon assigned me to the June allocation and I received 50 copies of Special Orders No. 3 to prove it. The number of copies did not compensate for the lack of clarity. I glanced at the first line: "212. TC 240 Fol rsg dir. PRAP AR 55-28 W.P. T.D.N.," I read. (I still have a copy, so that is exactly what I read and in a print so dense and tiny that it resembles Carolingian minuscule.) It was several incomprehensible lines further along before I came to: "Ind will arr Vietnam wearing khaki trousers and short sleeve shirt, . . . Dress unif not req." Some happy soul at battalion had already called down to say that I should "go ahead and buy some green underwear," so I knew I was on orders to Vietnam but I was still stunned to see that confirmed in print.

I asked First Sergeant Randolph to interpret the remainder of my orders. He angled his head back slightly, aimed his bifocals, and began to read aloud, mumbling through the bafflegab, enunciating what was important. "Mumble, mumble, Fort Jackson, mumble, Canal Zone, Jungle Training, mumble, not later than 30 May, mumble, San Francisco, mumble, Vietnam, mumble, mumble, . . . Ninth Division, mumble, mumble," is close to what he said. This saved me some confusion and forestalled any temptation to look for the USAOSREPLSTA in Vancouver, Canada.

My day became complete when the battalion executive officer dropped by to congratulate me on my orders. He was sincere but that did not prevent him from being amused at my reaction, which was not joy. Then he told me not to worry—the war would probably be over before I got to Vietnam.

The burial business picked up during the Tet Offensive. We had to train a second burial detail and often both would be out at the same time. The emotions of many of the young men who performed this task soon crusted over and on a bus ride back from a funeral, I heard them chant a salute to the man we had just buried.

You, You, You
Better YOU Than Me
Fuck YOU

In March my replacement arrived and after that I no longer had to go out on funerals which was good because by then I was presenting the flag with a ridiculous tic of a smile on my face. I was conscious of it but that made no difference. On my last burial, I handed a woman the flag as though it was a box of candy and was sick about it for days.

When I heard that Martin Luther King, Jr., had been murdered I simply climbed in my car and drove off post. Three hours later I found myself in Fort Worth entering a black Baptist church. I think it was Baptist. It was black; I was greeted with courtesy—and suspicion. Towards the end of the service I was asked to stand and give a testimonial. The request was totally unexpected (white middle-class Methodists don't give testimonials) and I managed to do no more than identify myself in a crow-like voice and express my sympathy. Then I shook my head and sat down feeling sad, drained and foolish.

I really had no idea of how I arrived at that church and it took me nearly an hour to get back on the road to Fort Wolters. And, as you usually do when you have neglected to say something, or said it badly, I kept conjuring up images of myself saying something memorable. I could think of nothing. I was nearly home before I realized that the only person who could have made sense of that tragedy had been its victim.

I was back in the orderly room the next morning feeling angry and disoriented. The night before, a dozen senior pilots had disappeared from Fort Wolters, called away on verbal orders in the army's anticipation of full-scale urban warfare. They did not return for several days and none of them would say where they had been.

My leave began in April and I departed Fort Wolters in a used car that was an advertisement for the half-carny existence of an infantry lieutenant. Khaki shirts hung from a bracket above the side window; a footlocker containing boots, blankets, web gear, and my personnel file, sat on the back seat. My upper arms were swollen to the size of cabbages by immunization shots, and sitting beside me was my pregnant wife. Two more footlockers and several pieces of Texas Gothic furniture—heavy pine, stained to the color of lead—had preceded us in a moving van.

Dallas, and a great deal more, soon receded behind us. It was sunny, flowers were blooming beside the highway, and before us lay a long, leisurely route—east, then northeast—back to my parents' house in Ohio. The car radio was tuned to the only station in Texas that

9

did *not* regularly play "These Boots Are Made for Walkin'." I was content.

My wife, who was from Argentina, had over the past year adapted to a foreign pattern of life. After a couple of tearful misadventures with American food—I once manfully crunched my way through a dinner of Shake 'n Bake patties because the illustration on the box had clearly indicated instant drumsticks—she developed an encyclopedic knowledge of the Post Commissary. We saved money; I don't know how. The mandatory folderol associated with the Fort Wolters Officer's Open Mess (the "Fawoom") did not intimidate her at all. She sailed through receiving lines while I clomped behind her as stiff as Frankenstein in dress blues. She was no more than bemused by the ragged behavior that sometimes ended these grand affairs. The army of that time drank; and it drank heavily. Wives, left alone and in less control of their fate, did the same. I vividly remember a major making his courtly goodbyes and all the while with his paralytically drunk wife slung over his shoulder.

I married my wife for the second time at Fort Wolters; this time in the Catholic Church. As an admitted Methodist, no paperwork was required of me, the principle being that there is no point in documenting error, but Elsa lacked essential records (baptism, first communion). All of that was in Argentina. A letter was hurriedly written to a person identified as Tia Julia, by her picture a large and very stern Indian woman, and to whom, it developed, I was now related. Tia Julia came through and six weeks later the ceremony was performed by the chaplain who was drunk right down to his brain stem. Red eyed, red nosed and swaying gently, this kindly man made it through the ceremony on Jungian institutional memory alone.

At the time of wedding, Elsa was five months pregnant. Now she was nearly eight months pregnant and due to deliver our child about two weeks after I was scheduled to arrive in Vietnam. We did not speak of this. For months I had been burdened by hearsay of a regulation allowing a six week deferment of orders to Vietnam if your wife was due to deliver on or around the time you were to leave. I should add that I had also heard that there *had* been such a regulation but that the resulting spike in fertility had caused it to be rescinded, which seemed more plausible. But I had never pursued it, nor had I told my wife.

Our car broke down before we were out of Texas. It was swiftly

10

repaired by a man who kept a javelina in his backyard. The javelina's name was Sam Houston and it had been trained to clatter its tushes together whenever the man said "San Jacinto." Then Sam Houston would get an apple. I had to tell him—the man, not Sam Houston— that if I paid his bill, I would probably not have enough money to get home which is a hard admission to make to an individual whose idea of a pet is a fearsome little pig. For about a minute, the man stared at the top of his can of Lone Star beer. Then he looked up. "My address is on the bill, 'lootenant'—and good luck."

In Louisiana, because of my wife's very dark complexion, we received a salt and pepper glare from a waitress who did not think we should be eating at her restaurant. I am not mistaken in this because the woman retreated to the kitchen and began emitting squawks of racial purity. We left. The woman had the purest of Southern-belle complexions that would, in about twenty years, provide her with every advantage in the competition to become "Miss Melanoma of Central Louisiana." We had crossed the Mississippi before I was no longer wishing her well in that contest.

We stopped at the Vicksburg battlefield. Grant's siege, I remembered reading, had lasted many months before the starving river port had finally surrendered on July 4th, 1863. For the remainder of that century there had been no celebration of Independence Day in the city of Vicksburg, in consequence of which the Mississippi River had abandoned the city, shifting miles to the west. So Vicksburg had languished, never overgrowing the encircling, zigzag ridges thrown up by its defenders more than a century before.

Many of the children and a few of the adults walking the top of the enormous, grass-covered earthworks were wearing blue or grey kepis that seemed to be made out of pressed blotting paper and resembled party hats. An elastic chin strap held the little hats firmly planted on more than one bald pate like a suction cup. Young couples boosted strollers containing sleepy infants through the grass; someday to be my role, I thought—if I were lucky. People marvelled at the size of the earthworks, took pictures and, in one instance, commented on the battlefield's potential as a golf course, which was not obvious to me.

On our way out of the park, we drove through the battlefield cemetery. There were acres of gravestones, cool under trees hung with Spanish moss. A year before, I would have stopped.

11

We spent the night in Demopolis, Alabama. That uninteresting tidbit resides in my memory because the movie *Sergeant York* was on local television. Elsa immediately recognized Gary Cooper, although, naturally, she didn't have any idea who Sergeant York was and she watched the first part of the film with declining satisfaction. I don't think she liked seeing Gary Cooper in bib overalls.

It was shortly after that point in the movie where Gary Cooper, having just gotten religion, says, "I ain't agoing [to the war]," that Elsa asked, "Who are these people?" I explained, in very bad Spanish, which I won't attempt to reproduce, that Gary Cooper was supposed to be a poor boy from the hills of Tennessee and that he didn't want to go to the war against Los Alemans.

"La guerra mundial?"

"Yes."

"The one your father was in?"

"No, the one my grandfather was in. My father was in the Second World War."

"There were two?"

"Of course!"

"What war was Sergeant Randolph in?"

"He was in the Korean War and in Vietnam."

"Cuatro guerras," she snorted, "que barbaridad."

Then she rolled on her side, braced her vast belly with a pillow, and entered an iron cage of Argentine privacy. She had had it, temporarily, with me and my country which she had come to regard as cold, barbaric and half mad (actually, medio tonto—half stupid). I did not mind that attitude on her part; what bothered me was the incisive manner in which she defended that attitude.

Gary Cooper did go into the army after all and, as I watched, he seemed to be having a pleasant time of it. Who could blame him with such jolly companions—all played by actors in their thirties. And his officers, Biblical scholars and moral philosophers to a man, were sympathetic. Send a man overseas to kill Germans when his heart wasn't in it? Gosh! We couldn't do that. So Gary Cooper had been given leave to go home and make up his mind. None of this corresponded to my experiences in basic training and I knew that if I had been sent home to commune with my deeper identity, I would have decided that I could best serve my country by selling insurance in Akron.

But basic training had been long ago. Now, I would surely go.

12

Why? If anyone had asked me why (no one did), I would have said I was going because I had been ordered to go. And if they didn't understand that, then fuck them. But I knew there was more to it than that.

Assisted by mountain solitudes and his trusty hound dog, Gary Cooper does decide to return to the army and go to France. Next scene: the Americans are attacking, "Yankee Doodle" is playing, and now the Americans are pinned down. Gary Cooper flanks the Germans and gobbling like a turkey to attract their attention, he shoots them down one after the other. The Germans surrender. (I have since read the citation for Alvin York's Medal of Honor and, indeed, much of that is true, although the citation makes no mention of gobbling.)

I could not sleep. The movie bothered me. It had contributed to one of life's little epiphanies. I was lying beside a pregnant Argentine girl in a motel room in Alabama having just watched Gary Cooper gobble like a turkey and shoot Germans through the head. And, as was seldom far from my mind, I was going to Vietnam.

When I was in college, which then seemed a decade past, it was said to be humanly impossible to fail a course in cinematography. That is not true; I know because I failed one. What I remembered of that course, and probably all that I ever learned, was this: Nations use film to send messages. Not, the instructor had taken pains to say, films such as the *Flying Leathernecks* (his current example was doubtless the *Green Berets*) but more potent, deeply cultural epics. *Alexander Nevsky* was directed by? Who was it? I couldn't remember (it was Eisenstein) but I recalled that it had been made in the late thirties by the Russians. Message? Invade us and the happy proletariat will destroy you — again.

If there is any American film that fits this category (I learned this in college so it must be true) it is *Sergeant York* which was in the theaters during the months before Pearl Harbor. Americans are God-fearing, peace-loving and nice. They are good shots. Threaten them, get them riled, and they will all (but as individuals) do the right thing; take the old long rifle down from the mantle and drill the forces of wickedness . . . something like that. So, you might ask, by 1968 were there many men who believed that, who *felt* that way? The truth is: It is no accident that there is a long rifle on the Combat Infantry Badge and that there were a lot of men who felt that way, who held to that simplehearted belief which was as compelling as a brain tumor — and, often, just as fatal. I didn't get much sleep that night.

The next morning Elsa had her first and, to my certain knowledge, unrepeated experience with grits. An hour on the road and we ran into a tremendous cloudburst. There was nothing to do but pull over and sit. In the still air behind the storm we drove on, billowing the steam that came off the highway as it wound through yellow-green, shack-dotted countryside and bridged overflowing streams. Snakes fled the high water. I thumped over one and left it writhing in the rearview mirror. In bright sunlight, we swung northeast across Georgia heading toward the plowshare of North Carolina and the Great Smoky Mountains. Three hours later we had traveled back into springtime and discovered that the Smoky Mountains really are smoky—only it's not smoke, it's pollen. We stopped at Cades Cove inside the national park and there, a hundred years back in time, the war was entirely absent from my mind.

Our final night on the road was spent somewhere in a thicket of motels outside of Gatlinburg. I told my wife that Sergeant York had been born near there (he wasn't but I thought so at the time). "Here?" she asked pointedly. You couldn't see anything from our motel but billboards and neon signs. On toward Kentucky the next morning and by noon we had crossed the Ohio River. Within an hour the Wisconsin Maximum was behind us and the land flattened and grew richer.

Late that afternoon I pulled off Route 71 and drove a short distance to the small town of West Lebanon, the home of my grandmother's brother, Arthur Youngman, a timeless bachelor who had from the age of 14 worked in the coal mines that wormed beneath much of North Central Ohio. By the 1930s the mines had played out. Thereafter, Joe (he was never called Arthur) lived by his savings, sporadic employment, and by hunting and fishing. He was a locally renowned mushroom hunter and celebrated expert at that illegal depression skill of "looping fish." He had been the perfect uncle to my father and his brothers.

Joe always had a garden in his backyard where he grew green peppers ("mangos"), strawberries, tomatoes and corn, none of which he would eat. For as long as I had known him, Joe had subsisted on chewing tobacco, beer, homemade wine, eggs and summer sausage. To this may be added an occasional rabbit, squirrel, sunfish or chub. It was a diet that would have killed a Masai warrior but Joe, of middle height and still powerful, looked much younger than his seventy-some years. A shock of steel gray hair contributed to that deception. In summer or winter, he wore a heavy wool suit coat and from a distance might have been mistaken for a British officer in mufti. That resemblance broke down at close range because of Joe's leathery face and the enormous bulge of chewing tobacco under one cheek. If Joe had encountered a British officer, a circumstance he would have avoided, he probably would have been addressed in Urdu.

As a boy I can remember being excited to learn that Joe's house was really a shingled-over log cabin and that my father had been born there while my grandfather was in Europe during the First World War. My grandmother, no romantic, was not nostalgic about that period. Somewhere in Joe's house among the old shotgun shells, ancient and seldom used shaving gear, pocket knives, horn buttons, and packages of Beechnut chewing tobacco, was a German Army belt buckle. "Gott Mit Uns," it said around the Imperial Crown. Joe claimed to have once met (but not socially) General John Pershing and described him as "standing so straight, he could split a bird turd." The occasion of Joe's brush with greatness had been a regimental inspection. Pershing said that Joe looked like he *had* been lying in the mud. Joe, by his account, replied that he *had* been lying in the mud; someone had been shooting at him. "Get that man a new coat," roared Pershing. Joe had been twice wounded in France (neither time seriously) and then had nearly died of diphtheria. He viewed all travel in the light of that experience. If you left home, people fed you strange food, shot at you, and then you got sick. Not even my grandmother could coax him beyond the confines of Wayne County, Ohio, and so far as I know, my grandmother had left Ohio only once. I'm sure that my grandmother would have preferred riding on the back of the diving donkey at the county fair to braving the crowded wartime trains but she had done that in the fall of 1944, traveling all the way to New York City to say goodbye to her rifleman son as he boarded a troopship to France. He arrived just in time for the Battle of the Bulge.

We found Joe at home (he would have been at home or in nearby Mount Eaton buying beer). I introduced Elsa, explained to her that "having meat on your bones" was a compliment, and we settled into Joe's porch chairs to a stream of gossip. An Amish buggy had been rear-ended; a local farmer who would not turn away stray dogs had been required to get a kennel license; an abandoned building had burned down because "mice had been chewing on matches." According to Joe

15

it had been "two-legged mice." A great aunt of mine had died. A relative by marriage, I used to hunt on her farm. Anything I shot was subject to confiscation but I did not mind because of her stories. She could remember her great grandmother telling of how as a girl she had gone with her family each night to Mount Hope because of Indian raids. That had been in the War of 1812. You could still see the outlines of the original cabin in her lawn. From time to time as we sat on Joe's porch, Amish buggies would clop by, the people inside waving.

I finally got around to telling Joe that I was on orders to Vietnam. He showed no surprise but remained quiet, ruminating tobacco. After a time he imparted to me his central insight on the First World War. "All them goddamn Limies ever fed us was mutton," said Joe.

We arrived at my parent's house late that night, exhausted and tense now that we no longer had travel to distract us from what lay ahead. My wife had no relatives in this country and faced the prospect of living with her in-laws for a year. In a little over a month she would have her first child and I would be gone, as far from my home as she was from hers. We were both scared and for the remainder of my leave we alternately fought and made up, making my parents miserable. I left a day early for Panama.

The U.S. Army Overseas Replacement Station (USAOSREPLSTA) at Fort Jackson was a cluster of one-story wooden buildings upon which transient infantrymen had for the past three years taken out their frustrations. Holes had been punched, kicked or, evidently, head-butted through the sheet rock. There were no screens on the windows. I had this setting to myself the first night.

By the following afternoon the replacement center had filled. Many of these men I knew from OCS. Some had married, some had divorced, nearly all had gained weight. One man had married, divorced and gained weight. With only a few exceptions, we had all spent the last year sitting behind a desk. One man had been in the Detroit riots which he described as being "fucking awful."

"When they pulled us out, I was so tired I pissed myself—was laying in my cot, had to urinate, said fuck it and pissed in my fatigues."

He was 21 years old, in temperament and appearance a regular young Westmoreland, and I knew him as the perfect OCS candidate, the guy who stays in the barracks over a (rare) weekend pass in order to spitshine his boots.

16

The state executioner of France has somewhere written of his method of getting people to the guillotine with minimal fuss. It is this: Just as the condemned man catches sight of the apparatus, the executioner punches him in the stomach. The condemned man's head is not finished contemplating this unexpected indignity before it is detached and in the basket. Jungle training is like that; it is distracting, and useful.

Our arrival in Panama was memorable. We were met by a wall of heat and humidity and were sweating through our khakis by the time we entered the terminal. Inside we saw 150 men sitting on their duffle bags, staring at the exit with stony intensity. Their arms and faces were covered with scratches and pebbled with insect bites. At the announcement that they would be boarding for the States, they let out a collective bray of joy and began trampling over one another in a mad rush to the plane. We all took this as a strong hint that Jungle School does not operate on a relaxed schedule.

The bus ride to the Jungle School provided a brief tour of Panama City and, as we crossed the canal, a glimpse of the water boiling tremendously out of the Mira Flores Lock. It was dark when we arrived. I could see a series of three-story concrete barracks, probably built during the twenties, fronted by hundreds of yards of immaculate lawn. A persistent, scratching, rustling sound pervaded and was soon traced to small scuttling shapes. The lawn was a playground for hundreds of crabs.

We filed through the supply room to draw a sheet, poncho, canteen, machete, and a large nylon mesh net from which you could construct a hammock. "Go to the third floor and pick a bunk. Reveille at 0500." Additional information: "There's no officer's club, so you have permission to use the NCO club. Be advised—the Fleet Marines are also going through school training and they're at the club. We suggest you avoid it." A few went and came back an hour later. "What was it like?" I asked. "War," they said. The principal contribution to this ambiance had been made by a dozen marines who were smashing land crabs with bats.

The first two days were spent learning how to make thatched roofs, animal snares, and other useful things. It filled our time as we acclimatized to the heat. We ate portions of monkey, sloth, snake and lizard. We sampled edible plants and were shown plants to avoid, strychnine bush for example. We petted a boa constrictor.

17

Then we went into the jungle to get used to being in the infantry again. We were allowed only one bottle of insect repellent per week to insure that we were bitten more or less continuously. There were two things that we heard repeatedly. One—"You're lucky this is not the rainy season." In fact, it rained for days on end and several men got themselves sent home early with immersion foot. Two—"The jungle is neutral." This was the official wisdom. The army had once insisted that "The jungle is your friend," but since no sane person would believe that, it no longer did. We said, "The jungle is out to get you."

We spent a great deal of time crossing and recrossing the Chagras River which runs parallel to the Panama Canal for much of its course and was said to be a haven for caymen. We never saw any. A rope was stretched over the river and we crawled across it doing the "commando crawl." We made "Australian poncho rafts" (brush and clothes tightly wrapped by three ponchos) and pushed them across the river. We practiced riverine assaults in the few rubber rafts that had not been bayoneted by the marines.

We took a rope slide (melodramatically called the "slide for life") over the Chagras. A heavy rope was anchored high on the ridge above the river. It stretched down the ridge and across the river and was attached to a tree on the opposite side. The first man in line was put into a harness that slid along the rope and was sent hurtling to the opposite shore. About ten feet from the tree there was a knot to prevent those taking the slide from smashing into the tree. The man hit the knot at terrific speed, upended and dropped into the mud. He picked himself up, woozily climbed the river bank, sat down and threw up. We watched this with alarm.

The sergeant in charge turned to the next man in line. "The marines came through yesterday," he said in an off-handed way. "You shoulda seen it; we had every bit of slack outta that line. We was really knocking their dicks stiff! ... O.K., your turn."

The same thing happened.

The sergeant called across the river for the rope to be slackened using the army's universal increment of fine adjustment. "Let - The - Rope - Out - About - Two - Cunt - Hairs," he boomed. The man on the opposite bank waved, fiddled with a knot and allowed the rope to slacken perceptibly.

For some of the older NCOs, those much the worse for cigarettes and alcohol, Jungle School was brutal. A few simply could not make it. In every instance, they had to be carried out, actually weeping with frustration. Nothing is more revealing about the army of this period than the fact that a sizeable percentage of American infantrymen could not swim. The ghetto is not replete with Olympic pools. In the space of two weeks I must have seen a dozen young men fished out of the water in a state of gasping panic. To them the course was a series of potential drownings.

A few training areas were linked to headquarters by land line. We soon discovered that it was possible to call directly into the base commander's office which we several times did to convey an obscene message. This gave us a surprising amount of satisfaction. We were stretched out one day, munching mangos and enjoying the sun's reappearance, when the phone gave a dull buzz. Someone picked it up and was told that Bobby Kennedy had been murdered.

The final two days of the course were for "escape and evasion." We were to sneak through the woods, avoiding the school cadre who represented the NVA, and arrive at the mouth of the Chagras River. It was all pretty tame. We didn't have to go very far—five miles at the most—and in order to get lost you would have had to miss both the river and Caribbean Sea. We were told not to move at night because the chance of falling was too great and not to try to swim the Chagras. A month before, several Navy SEALs had tried to do that and drowned.

The group I was in made it in about 12 hours which was quicker than most. After reporting in, we boarded a small boat and chugged across the Chagras close to where it flowed into the Caribbean. This area was marked by the dorsal fins of cruising sharks that we were sure were still burping the undigested remains of sailors. "Debriefing" took place on the far shore in a shack furnished with long tables. Spaced along the table tops were cans of burning motor oil which filled the top half of the shack with dense black smoke. Mosquitoes still ruled the bottom half. Our names were checked against a roster to determine who was still wandering around in the forest. Inevitably men did get lost but rarely for more than a few days. The record for getting lost, set months before, was claimed by a group from an unnamed Latin American country. They had been located after a week-long search: they were trying to navigate *around* the Caribbean Sea.

Once back at Fort Gulick , we were given a pass and also a handout listing places of cultural interest in Colon, Panama. It was a short list. The list of places that were off limits was considerably longer and included the Zamba Bar. My impression has always been that this was the first place everyone looked for. I don't know that for sure because I heeded the advice that the Guardia Nacional tended to shoot Americans in uniform and stayed on post.

In the next building over the marines were celebrating and by nightfall had started to attack the crabs. There would be a sickening crunch followed by a high cackling laugh. Evidently the crabs were attracted by the remains of their dead predecessors so their numbers never diminished. The sounds of this crustacean massacre—Karuuunch! "Hey, heh, heh, mutherfucker ha"—drifted upon humid breezes through the windows of the barracks and made sleep difficult.

Sleep became impossible around 2:00 in the morning when the bus from Colon returned. Someone claimed to have rescued a crab from the marines and then to prove it produced the animal from his hat. He released the hapless creature and it scuttled back and forth across the barracks floor menacing anyone who came near with its big claw. I endured a lachrymose and amazingly detailed confession of infidelity by a former gospel singer. "God is merciful," he concluded and "Lord only knows what my wife is doing." Another man fossicked through his duffle bag, located a large bowie knife and began to throw it at a concrete pillar. It would clang noisily off the pillar and skitter along the floor. Outside the marines were still smashing crabs.

Morning and graduation arrived early. The marines who were all undoubtedly hung over and puke sick were marching in impeccable formation to their singing cadence call. The army, on the other hand, looked no better than it felt. The marines had even flown in a band for the occasion. It only played one tune: "The Halls of Montezuma."

We left Panama looking just like the men we had seen two weeks before. But we did not celebrate. Most of us were going to Vietnam.

The army in its wisdom returned us to Fort Jackson which was a surprise because there was nothing in our infinitely detailed orders to suggest that we would not be transported directly to Vietnam. We had 48 hours to get to the West Coast by means of, and these were the only instructions provided, "anything leaving Columbia [South Carolina] that smokes."

Forty-eight hours was just enough time to get home to say goodbye, again, and the airport at Columbia was jammed with men desperate to do that. Men bought tickets to anywhere and, often, to anywhere else, before they made connections to one of the major airline hubs, Atlanta, Chicago, New York—it didn't matter. Then came the tense standby wait for the flight home and another hideous parting. I flew from Atlanta, to Chicago, to Cleveland and caught the last limo home. "I had to see you." I was back in Cleveland four hours later to catch a flight to San Francisco. Hundreds took similar drunken, desperate, zigzag, pilgrim's routes to the West Coast.

San Francisco: six hours to kill. Stow duffle bag in bus station locker. Bars.

Retrieve duffle bag. Cab to Travis Air Force Base.

"See you in a year," I said to the cabbie when we arrived.

"That'll be twenty-five dollars," responded the cabbie.

CHAPTER 2

"We are now being vectored
around artillery strikes.
When they tell us to change
course, we do so immediately."
—*Pilot, Army charter flight, June 1968*

Including layovers in Hawaii and at Clark Field in the Philippines, our flight over the curve of the Pacific consumed a night and a day. The only points of interest outside the aircraft had been a few flyspeck ships trailing tufts of white yarn and, once, a sooty-brown blotch identified as the island of Guam. We slept, or tried to, read without concentration, and we talked, each man trying to appear calmer than the others. I remember nothing of these distracted conversations. I do remember that on the last leg of our journey a sergeant who had been coaxed into a frilly pink cap and apron by a stewardess served us drinks. Probably every flight had a similarly heroic victim. It cut the tension and made us laugh. The man could have stuffed straws up his nose and dropped his pants and we would have laughed at that too.

Over Vietnam we gaped like children at the landscape not far beneath us and within minutes we were tailing into Bien Hua Airport to an uneventful landing. The stewardess at the door wished each man good luck in some variation as he emerged from the plane in rumpled khakis, blinking owlishly against the heat and bright sunlight.

Dancing a little on the blistering tarmac, we formed up, answered to our names, and boarded buses for the short trip to the replacement center at Long Binh just outside of Saigon. These were ordinary Blue Bird school buses except that the windows were covered with thick, close-meshed screen as protection against grenades. In the natural

23

progression of things, the VC had taken to putting hooks on satchel charges and our driver informed us, by way of conversation, that several days before one of these devices had caught the screen beside an army colonel. While everyone else clawed toward the rear of the bus, he had picked the bomb free. Along the road to Long Binh a squatters settlement had sprouted of which the most durable memory is the smell of urine. Its inhabitants ignored us as we stared at them through protective mesh.

Life at the replacement center consisted of lounging around and consulting lists, one of which would provide you with an assignment. Recreational sallies beyond the perimeter were forbidden, but no one minded that restriction. Dusty armored columns clanked by just beyond our compound and in the evening we gaped at flares dropping in the distance. That first evening we were joined by a hollow-eyed infantry lieutenant who was evidently being reassigned in-country. Everything he owned was in a battered NVA pack. He commandeered an empty bunk, slept like a stone for 12 hours and left the following morning, never having said a word to anyone.

Because my orders had assigned me to the 9th Division, I had reconciled myself, in small ways, to the Mekong Delta and a life of gunboats and swamps. On the afternoon of the second day I found that I had been reassigned to the First Cavalry Division. Why? I could think of only one reason, but I can remember someone who had given the matter less thought than I congratulating me on my good fortune.

Those of us who were headed north to I Corps and Quang Tri Province where the First Cavalry then operated were roused early the next morning, while it was still dark, and transported by truck to the airfield. In the early dawn a mortar round (probably) crumped in the distance and, to the enjoyment of some onlookers, we all looked around in confusion. The man beside me who, like myself, was also an infantry lieutenant, gestured grandly toward a nearby garbage can and suggested immediate action for mortar attacks: "Invert same and cower within." He told me that he planned to be a doctor and that his girlfriend wanted nothing more out of life than to work her butt off putting him through school. This was said with both conviction and commitment. He was assigned to another division so I did not see him after that. I wondered how he ended up in the infantry.

It was mid-morning before we were herded into a C-130 and arranged in rows on the floor of the cargo bay by the crew chief. He informed us that due to atmospherics it sometimes misted inside the aircraft, which it did for much of the flight. A C-130 from the perspective of its passengers is a flying terrarium. We arrived at An Khe sore and soggy.

An Khe (more properly, Camp Radcliff), in the Central Highlands, had once been the base camp of the First Cavalry Division and a few logistical connections still existed. Our gear and clothing was stored in footlockers and we were issued an M-16, flak jacket, helmet, jungle boots, and three sets of jungle fatigues. Everyone emerged from this transition feeling awkward and stiff in new boots and, literally, green in bright new field clothing.

An afternoon was spent on the range sighting in our M-16s. I was glad for even this little experience with this new gadget, because I had trained on the M-14 and had fired an M-16 only once before — a grand total of 20 rounds. We were told that the M-16 is reliable when correctly maintained, a half truth, and that at close range it is devastating, an understatement. On the range my first impressions were confirmed. An M-16 doesn't feel like a rifle; all alloy and plastic, with a long coil spring that rides back into the stock, it feels like you're shooting a pogo stick. It really is a gadget more than it is a rifle; but it is a very lethal gadget. And, in many ways, it is a very practical one. It doesn't easily corrode, the magazines especially, and the 22 caliber ammunition is light, so a "basic load" which is 300 rounds is readily carried. An M-16 is not very accurate but where I was going that wasn't important.

An Khe was a sprawling boom town with dozens of mess halls and clubs, enormous warehouses, an airfield capable of handling all but the largest aircraft, and a PX that rivaled just about anything that I had seen stateside. I visited this once and mostly gaped at the delicate Vietnamese women behind the counters. Just outside of An Khe was "Sin City" about which we were warned; it was off limits.

The perimeter around An Khe ran for miles and was now and again penetrated by NVA sappers. Hundreds of Vietnamese worked at An Khe and NVA knowledge of the base was therefore very good but the sheer size of the place defeated them. On one occasion, at least according to the lieutenant in charge of the transport depot, a pilot aborted his landing and then called the tower wanting to know the identity of "those idiots milling around on the runway." The tower wanted to know too; they were NVA. The lieutenant also gave us very specific instructions in case our part of the base was attacked. "Get up," he said (the attack would surely come at night), "put on your flak jacket, sit down on your bunk, and stay there." In other words, keep out of the way.

After three days of drawing equipment and processing, we were awakened on a grey and dismal morning and trucked to the flight line to await the plane to Camp Evans, the division base camp in I Corps. Everyone kicked around disconsolately until a smiling, grey-haired lady in her sixties appeared with mugs of hot coffee. She reminded me of the lady who, two years before, had thrust a cup of coffee into my hand as I boarded the bus to the Cleveland Induction Center to be sworn into the army. So strange that she could have beaten me to Vietnam.

An hour later an army caribou landed. I buckled into one of the plane's canvas seats just behind the cockpit. There was a small brass plaque above the co-pilot's seat: "You are now being flown to where you should have gone in the first place by the [something] Air Transport Group." Part of our route was along the coast which from the air appeared to be absolutely tranquil. Villages peaked out from beneath copses of green trees and in places the countryside was dotted with myriads of burial mounds. Briefly, and with some enthusiasm, we examined a thin column of grey smoke but it told us nothing.

We were soon over Camp Evans. The pilot yawned, said something to the co-pilot, and then shoved the yoke toward the instrument panel. A short, metaled runway appeared in the windscreen and rapidly grew in size. The pilot pulled up at the last instant, thumped the plane onto the runway and brought us to an abrupt, vibrating halt.

Camp Evans was a shock. I had expected a survival of the First World War complete with trenches behind thickets of barbed wire. It was nothing like that, not then, and appeared to invite attack. The perimeter was defined by widely separated guard positions (or so they seemed to me) and I could see no real impediment to just walking into camp aside from a few sections of cyclone fencing that stretched here and there beyond the "green line." Such was the appearance but it was deceptive. Camp Evans was located in the middle of open rolling grassland and at night gunships ghosted low over the landscape and ambushes were out. That much I knew. But I had no understanding of how difficult it would have been for a large enemy force to get near Evans without being detected and I was wholly ignorant of just how welcome such an attempt would have been.

The division training center, where I would be spending a week, was located on the edge of Camp Evans and consisted of a row of large GP tents along a dusty road, a mess hall, also under canvas, and a few bleachers. If you wanted to, no one did, you could stroll down the road and out onto the grassland.

Division training covered predictable topics: booby-traps ("dirty trick devices"), ambushes, medical evacuation (always give the map coordinates in the clear), combat assaults, and so forth. It was clear that our instructors spoke from experience. One of them, a lieutenant who had spent most of his tour with the 1st of the 9th, opened a lecture on ambushes with a casual reference to the third time he had been wounded. After the lecture there was a timely call for volunteers for the 1st of the 9th. "You have," said our instructor, with something like a smile, "an opportunity to become a real barbarian."

Instruction was lively, to the point, and sometimes humorous. One story dealt with the confrontation that an infantryman had with his malaria pill — which tastes like chalk, is as big around as a dime, and almost a quarter of an inch thick. Usually you had to break it in half to get it down. Time in the field is the enemy of table manners and when confronted with this formidable pill in the mess hall, the man laid it on the table and slashed at it with his machete, provoking a stampede for the exits.

We sat in bleachers and watched mock combat assaults (Charlie Alphas, i.e. helicopter assaults) complete with artillery preparation. I had forgotten how loud artillery is. During one of these demonstrations the lead chopper came in so low that the rotor blades clipped the tip off the long whip aerial on the field radio that was being used to control the maneuver.

Various types of ordnance were demonstrated and some of it was new to me. One new, and especially nasty device, was the "firecracker round." This was an artillery round which disgorged a dozen or so little bomblets attached to a mousetrap-like spring. When a bomblet hit the ground it popped back up into the air and exploded about head-high. Clever. The problem, and this too was mentioned, was that the mousetrap didn't always work so anyone moving through the area was likely to spring a little bomb loose and it would go off in your face.

We were told point blank that NVA equipment was very good. The AK-47, the standard Russian assault rifle, was praised. It is accurate, very reliable and has a 30 round magazine. An AK-47 does

27

have some liabilities but they are minor; it is heavy and the safety makes an audible metallic noise. The thrice wounded lieutenant held up a captured weapon and demonstrated: "When you hear this sound," he clicked the safety on and off and it went, "tick, tick," "hit the ground fast. That's how they give away their ambushes." He seemed to believe that we would be comforted by that information.

There was a graduation ceremony. We were lifted a few miles from Evans and landed on a low grassy hill. Our instructors, two lieutenants and a sergeant, looked the area over, designated positions and then retired to the top of the hill to chat. We dug elaborate holes and watched as the FAO (forward artillery observer) called in defensive targets around our perimeter. The rounds were landing over 200 yards away, but they seemed very close.

Well after dark we were provided with one firm order. "If you *really* see anything or hear anything, come and wake us up." We took turns staring at animated, noisy bushes but throughout the night no one reported *really* hearing or seeing anything. When not on guard, we clustered together like nervous baboons and talked in low tones about, among other things, scorpions (they just make you sick), home, the monsoon (it was coming; it had just ended), and, of course, women. "Show me a man who don't eat pussy," said a young staff sergeant gravely, "and I'll show you how to break up a marriage." It's an old joke, old enough to have made its way into James Jones novels. But we had never heard it before, we didn't even know that it was a joke, and decided that the sergeant was wise beyond his years. Well after daybreak, our instructors awoke refreshed and cheerful. Division training was over.

A few other recollections of Camp Evans are worth mentioning since they set the tone for the division. I saw no Vietnamese civilians while at Camp Evans and only once a South Vietnamese soldier. It was, I believe, a firm policy—"no gooks inside the perimeter." The tale I had heard at Long Binh and then again at An Khe about the friendly Vietnamese barber found dead among a party of sappers did not circulate at Camp Evans. There were no Vietnamese barbers at Camp Evans, friendly or unfriendly, nor hooch mates, laborers, or bar maids. No gooks.

"Shitburners" made up an established social category at Evans. The army's method of disposing of excrement was to burn it. The most functional parts of a U.S. Army latrine, the holes, were directly over

28

cut-off 55-gallon drums which daily had their contents burned. A shit-burner's task was to pull the sawed-off drum out from under the latrine, douse it with kerosene and set fire to it. At Camp Evans, shit-burners did this with surprising joy and spirit. They were career shit-burners I gathered, and their entire demeanor suggested they were under the protection of some occult charm. We speculated that they really had one; a voodoo doll of varnished turds buried deep beneath the floor of a bunker. As long as it was unharmed, they would live. For whatever reason, their behavior carried a message: "I may be burning shit, but I'm going to live and you're going to die." I do not know, but firmly believed at the time, that one became a fulltime shitburner for an act of cowardice—a category of behavior that the division defined in the broadest possible terms.

It was also at Evans that I was informed by a young infantryman in ragged fatigues—after months in the field, he was going through squad leaders training—that "gooks don't bleed" and that American captives would sometimes be killed by having their heads encased in a rat-filled cage. Blond, rail-thin, and burned by the sun, the man resembled an anorectic Hitler youth. "The gooks have this special fuck-ing cage," he elaborated. "They clamp it over your fucking head," he put his hands up to his throat, "and then they stick in a fucking rat." It was also his opinion that when you were killed (he said "when," not if) the army freeze-dried your body for shipment home. "That way they save space. Just before your parents see you, they fucking add water."

"No they don't," said his companion, "too fucking expensive. Freeze drying is too expensive." That settled the issue. Both men seemed perfectly willing to believe that the army would, at its convenience, freeze-dry your corpse but not if it cost the army extra money.

I was assigned to the Second Battalion of the Fifth Cavalry, First Cavalry Division which operated out of Landing Zone Juliet. Along with six or seven others destined for the 2nd of the 5th, I was put aboard a chinook and, after a flight of only a few minutes, deposited on a grassy field about a hundred yards outside of Juliet's perimeter. I hadn't ex-pected a color guard but had supposed someone would be there to meet us. There wasn't. I eyed the distance to the camp with suspicion, decided it wasn't mined, and we all sauntered past an unmanned bunker and into the camp. After a few minutes we were noticed.

"You the new guys?"

Things quickly fell into place. I learned that I was in Delta Company (D/2/5), to which I gathered I properly belonged, although I never saw a copy of the orders, and met with the executive officer who said that the company was short two officers. He called the company commander in the field to tell him of my arrival. The CO, from what I could overhear, was momentarily uplifted. "What kind [of officer], double banana?" The company commander was a first lieutenant, long in the field and anxious to be relieved. He had hoped I was a captain. The XO then turned me over to the supply sergeant and returned to his sunbath which I had interrupted.

The supply sergeant, at least, was pleased to see me. My extra sets of jungle fatigues were badly needed to supplement the common pool from which everyone from the company commander on down was infrequently issued a change of clothes; I was left with what I had on my back. I soon learned that the entire Delta Company establishment at Juliet consisted of one large tent strewn with cots and gear, a couple of smaller tents, a bunker, a latrine and jerrybuilt shower. This, in sentiment, was home to Delta Company but actually housed only a few men (plus transients, such as myself) who handled company supply and administration and at night manned a bunker which marked the company's segment of the perimeter. Delta Company was "in the field" and there it lived.

That afternoon I was trotted over to a neatly sandbagged hive of bunkers topped by a dozen aerials to meet the brigade commander. A guard, in full combat gear, stood impassively at present arms as the general emerged from his bunker. The general, a lean, very intense man, spoke to me briefly, insisting that "the maps are good" (the rumor was that they were hopeless) and then fell silent provoking a stiff salute which I held for perhaps thirty seconds while he glared at me intently. Satisfied, apparently, he turned and left. I felt as though I had been granted an audience with Oliver Cromwell and forgotten to zip up my fly.

Juliet had a shrapnel-splashed PX not much bigger than a house trailer which sold cigarettes, cigarette lighters, a limited variety of canned food, and tabasco sauce. If the Roman Army marched on grain and diluted wine, the American Army in Vietnam marched on C-rations and tabasco sauce with infrequent infusions of powdered eggs, carrot sticks, and melted ice cream. Juliet's PX, as nearly as I could tell, existed to provide some relief from that diet.

There were other ways, I would soon learn, of escaping the boredom of C-rations which came in cases of 12 individual meals that had popular designations—"beans and muthafuckers," for example. Some meals were highly prized and some could not be eaten unless drenched in tabasco sauce. By combining various meals, new and palatable dishes, such as pizza, could be prepared (when there was time). The recipe for pizza and other exotic forms of C-ration cookery could be found on the jar of tabasco sauce. The typical infantryman in the field consumed between 3,000 and 4,000 calories a day (and sometimes more) and on this most men rapidly lost weight.

The morning after I arrived at Juliet I joined several new lieutenants for a tour of a nearby fire base. It was a tiny affair with, as I recall, less than a full battery of 105 howitzers positioned on a small dusty knoll. Scrub trees grew to within a hundred yards of the perimeter. The base was guarded by a company of infantry most of whom had burrowed into their bunkers to get away from the heat. I could not at the time imagine a more dreary existence. The battery commander, just the same, was as cheerful as a game show host and ushered us around the base with enthusiasm. He even fired a "beehive" round for our entertainment although I don't think that was supposed to be on the bill of fare since the only way the base could be resupplied was by helicopter.

A beehive round is nothing more than a refinement of canister which has been used since the days of smoothbore cannon. In essence the artillery piece becomes a gigantic shotgun and as such is used for close defense—when, in other words, the base is about to be overrun. The modern round contains thousands of flechettes—little metal darts about an inch long—which when fired will produce a cloud of tiny lethal projectiles that can kill people out to about 300 yards. We were told of NVA soldiers being pinned to trees by this thing. No one believes this. First, a shell casing was hammered to warn the infantry. The two or three men outside the bunker to our front gave a long-suffering look in our direction and scuttled like badgers to cover. Without the slightest hesitation, the cannon was fired directly over their position, the tracer element in the round missing it by only a few feet, and the scrub trees quivered.

The base, whose name I've forgotten or was never told, was utterly dominated by a range of naked, grey hills to the west. Anyone on those beetling ridges with a set of binoculars could have determined what we

31

were eating for lunch. What, I asked myself, was it like to be among the infantry that patrolled those dead hills?

The following morning I was told to report to battalion headquarters at eight — "bring your gear." Along with another new lieutenant, I arrived early, entered the largest bunker and was greeted in half light by a beer-sipping first lieutenant sitting behind a desk. A hand grenade from which the fuse had been unscrewed served as a paper weight. The fuse was holding down another stack of papers. The lieutenant, slightly drunk, was in a chipper mood and hoisted his beer in mock toast to announce that another unit had a battalion of NVA trapped "near the beach."

"They're in the process of dumping a shitload of artillery on them [the NVA]. They can't get out," he said contentedly.

They did, though, I later heard.

The lieutenant finished his beer and immediately levered open another. I brought up the rumor that the 2nd of the 5th was slated for search and destroy missions in the mountains. "Search and evade," corrected the lieutenant, "if you know what's fucking good for you." Conversation stalled. At the sound of approaching voices the lieutenant slipped his beer into a desk drawer, a gesture which telegraphed the colonel's arrival.

The colonel, trailing a captain in his wake, stalked through the entrance of the bunker, chatted briskly with the lieutenant about some sort of report, and then turned to me. "Ready for some local color." It did not sound like a question and I came to understand that I was to accompany the colonel in his command helicopter, which was parked just outside.

I buckled into one of the jump seats along the outer edge of the huey's open cargo bay and watched as the door gunner fed a belt of ammo into his M-60 and clamped the feed tray shut. The sunvisor was down on his flight helmet which gave the appearance that he was looking at the world through opaque, bulbous fly-eyes. The colonel climbed aboard, put on a flight helmet so he could talk to the crew and we lifted off. As we soared over Juliet's perimeter, the colonel leaned forward and began to scrutinize the land directly beneath us like a satisfied farmer, as though it had been in his family for years. After a short flight we dropped in on a small group of engineers who were cutting shrub trees beside a brown sluggish river. The VC, it developed, were moving supplies by boat and the colonel did not like that.

Bone-dry rice paddies distorted in the heat on either side of the river and in the distance a weaving column of dusty, grey infantry took shape. The weaving was for security. In a land where booby-traps were part of the flora, the normal pattern of dispersal invited death so a rifle company in the open snaked towards its destination, each man following in the path of the man in front, and, if he were wise, in his footprints. The sinuous column closed on our position and the two commanders conferred. From the situation I guessed that an ambush was being discussed otherwise the small notch that the engineers had cut in the underbrush would have been little more than an inconvenience. On the other hand, it seemed to me, if it was to be an ambush the VC would obviously know its exact location. I was mystified by the whole business; everything seemed casual to the point of being aimless. The engineers had obviously been out here without security for some time and the infantry was paying no noticeable attention to their surroundings which I assumed must be crawling with snipers. I stood around with the other lieutenant feeling useless and out of place.

Having already whistled up his helicopter, the colonel walked toward us smiling. "You might," he said, "give some thought to taking off those bars," which we immediately did. The huey landed in a swirl of dust and the colonel climbed aboard. We followed at his heels like two beagles.

I saw this man on only one other occasion—he was soon reassigned—but again his amiability and self-confidence held true. He seemed to both enjoy and believe in what he was doing. He was respected, obeyed, and, after his departure, missed. As with most commanders he had his quirks, some doubtless cultivated. One of these, or so it was said, centered on his bayonet: he wanted it used for its intended purpose.

"The colonel always hoped some guy would kill a gook with a bayonet. He'd always check your bayonet and you best not let him see you using one for a tent peg."

From the colonel's huey, the country beneath us looked mottled and sandy. I could see a two lane road, Highway One. In minutes we were on the ground near an old French headquarters building. Not a classic of colonial architecture, it was basically a very large concrete box penetrated by two doors and several small windows. It resembled a bunker and it seemed likely that that was what the French had in mind when they built it. All four sides were deeply pitted by small arms fire. Everyone called it the "Alamo."

"Delta Company," announced the colonel, and I trudged behind him in sand so hot I could feel it through my boots. My company commander, First Lieutenant Timothy Bannerman, dressed in skivvies, flip flops and a T-shirt, emerged from the grey, shabby building, snapped the colonel an incongruously sharp salute and then advanced with outstretched hand to greet me. I was introduced around: to Ogletree the Second Platoon leader, to his platoon sergeant, and to Bannerman's RTO — the only men who were awake. The Second Platoon had just returned from a night ambush and everyone else was sprawled sound asleep in an astonishing chaos of men, equipment, weapons and beer cans.

The colonel talked briefly with Bannerman, Bannerman nodded, and then the colonel left. Bannerman lit a cigar and retreated to his corner of the room where he had a desk (a thick plank laid across two stacks of sand bags) and a chair. The Alamo had no other furniture apart from air mattresses. Propped against the wall behind Bannerman were three field radios (PRC — naturally "prick" — 25s) on, respectively, the company, battalion and artillery frequencies. Bannerman had been listening to a tape recording from his family and it was to this, utterly absorbed, that he returned. It was impossible not to catch snatches of this and a lot of it was halting and strained. A woman's voice — "Grandma why don't you say something"..."Aaah...Hi, Tim, I hope you're doing fine...we get your letters...(*sotto voce*) I don't know what to say, you talk some more..." And so on for perhaps half an hour. He rewound the tape and listened to it again.

To Bannerman's right was a window covered by a billowing poncho; behind it, mounted on a pile of sandbags, was an M-60 machine gun wrapped in plastic to protect it from the sand. From time to time the various radios crackled and brought messages but most of the time emitted steady sibilant static which I soon learned to ignore.

Ogletree and I chatted. They had been at the Alamo for about a week. The First and Third platoons were some miles to the south along Highway One and guarded bridges. I would almost certainly be put in charge of the First Platoon which was then being led by a staff sergeant, although, Ogletree added, the mortar platoon also had no officer.

Towards mid-afternoon I walked with Ogletree across the dunes to test my rifle which I had not fired since An Khe. I was about to cut loose when a group of children appeared. "Well that's no damn good," drawled Ogletree. We looked in another direction which was clear. I ran through two magazines, the last one on full automatic, pleased that the weapon did not jam but still conscious of its curious rattling recoil. Ogletree, a stocky Missourian, more than kept up his end of the conversation. The heat did not seem to bother him. He had rejoined the company a few weeks ago after two months in an army hospital in Japan. A red puckered scar lanced over the back of his hand.

"Dude shot me," explained Ogletree.

The Second Platoon had been investigating a village when one of the villagers had darted into a hut. Ogletree had followed only to be greeted by an automatic weapon. He described how a round had caromed off the flash hider of his car carbine and through his right hand. Later, when I took over Ogletree's platoon, I was told much the same story but with embellishments.

"Inside that little hooch was a big ol bunker...rat, tat, tat... ouch, ouch, Jesus, he's still in there." The storyteller danced around waving his hand to demonstrate Ogletree's reaction. Because Ogletree had not been seriously wounded, by their standards, they treated it as a comic episode. There was a pause. "He walked all the way back to base with us before he called medevac . . . bleeding like a pig. You gotta give him credit." Ogletree had not mentioned that. He did mention that his father had been an infantry officer during the Second World War and that, like Ogletree, he was an OCS graduate.

When we returned, Bannerman was on the radio. The Third Platoon had taken a few scattered rounds, probably from a single sniper, and the platoon leader was going after him. "All right," said Bannerman, "but don't Gomer Pyle it." No one seemed very excited by this report. The sniper vanished.

Towards evening I sat on the Alamo's front steps drinking beer and watching the traffic along Highway One; foot traffic most of it and mostly women and children. Everyone seemed to be carrying something. A little distance away, and on the opposite side of the road, was another beat-up concrete structure which housed a jail for VC prisoners. A barbed wire enclosure was attached to the building and I could see a few small drab figures walking around inside it. Bannerman and Ogletree announced that they were going to visit there to play cards for a while. They knew one of the advisors.

They walked down the road carrying their rifles. About an hour later and just after dark, they came pounding up the road, legs churning. I did not appreciate being left in charge of the company six hours after joining it and made a point of asking them how their card game had gone.

"OK," said Ogletree after a little reflection.

The nighttime routine begins as the platoons respond to calls for situation reports ("sit reps"—sit rep negative is the response) and the men on guard relieve each other every two hours. Around three in the morning several rounds are fired at one of our ambushes from about 150 yards away. But the rounds are wide, probing, and the squad does not return fire for fear of giving away their position. Bannerman sits by the radio cupping his cigar so that it cannot be seen through the doorway. Nothing more comes over the radio. Dawn.

In the morning, Bannerman rocketed me by Jeep to the First Platoon. Isolated vehicles attracted sniper fire and so the usual practice was to drive as though possessed. For ten minutes Bannerman careened in and out of traffic and around clusters of pedestrians. I was amazed at how spread out the company was. Just before we came to a bridge, Bannerman turned up a broad footpath that led into a Vietnamese village and skidded to a halt.

The First Platoon was not so much dug in as camped on a sandy beach next to a small river. A wall of sandbags, evidently designed to repel an attack by Red Coats, extended across the beach at right angles from the river. No more than 50 yards beyond the sandbags, tangled undergrowth and a few rolls of concertina served to catch paper. Hooches, ponchos snapped together like shelter halves to make a pup tent, were pitched behind and in front of the wall of sandbags. On the other side of the river which was no more than 40 yards wide the undergrowth extended to the river bank.

Bannerman introduced me to my platoon sergeant, Staff Sergeant Edilio Aguirre, a short, wiry, gravel-voiced Puerto Rican, and said goodbye. Aguirre called the squad leaders over, introduced me, and then took me across the bridge to the mortar platoon. More introductions. The mortar platoon was positioned on a low grassy area beside the river and was protected, but only symbolically, by barbed wire entanglements which had long since fallen into disrepair. As I talked with the buck sergeant in charge, I could see a boy of eight or nine twist his way through the wire with barely a break in stride. One of the mortarmen tossed him a can of C-rations.

On the way back, Aguirre and I stopped at Mama San's, located just across the footpath from the First Platoon. Mama San (a term which identified all Vietnamese women over thirty who were not carrying a weapon) ran a thriving establishment that sold beer and sundries — mostly beer. Mama San was friendly but also hard-nosed when it came to business. Any Vietnamese who objected too strongly to her outrageous prices ran the risk of being accused of being VC. Because her figure was ample, she was reputed to be part French. "I'd like to fuck Mama San between the titties," said Aguirre wistfully. From early morning until dark, Mama San's stereo blared rock and roll; after dark, the music was Vietnamese and it was not hard to figure out why.

Aguirre was a career soldier who had spent half his life in the infantry including a tour in Korea. There wasn't a spare ounce of fat on him and his entire aspect suggested that he had been constructed out of jerked beef. He obviously knew what he was doing and I had the good sense to let him alone for the first week. He ran the platoon; I watched, tagged along on ambushes, and took out small patrols just to get some feel for the area.

I learned a lot from Aguirre including, that first night, the deeper meaning of "simulation." "Tonight," said Aguirre with a note of finality, "we're going to simulate." I nodded sagely. At the time, I was mostly preoccupied — dumbfounded would be a better word — by the platoon's defensive arrangements and I believe that the first order I gave in Vietnam was that no one should sleep in front of our positions. It seemed untidy. To *simulate* means to fake an ambush. I knew, of course, that the company frequently ran night ambushes, but I didn't know they *always* ran them. In fact, as was typical, Delta Company had a standing ambush requirement of one squad-sized ambush per platoon. Simulation consisted of simply faking the radio traffic that an ambush would produce; no one actually left the platoon perimeter.

While this fraud proceeded, Aguirre and I talked into the evening, mostly about his experiences in Korea which he described with unfeigned nostalgia. These had included several highly successful ambushes. Long after the Vietnamese music from across the footpath stopped, Aguirre turned in and was soon snoring.

I tried to sleep but could not. Well before dawn, I joined the guard who was standing stock-still, a picture of vigilance, behind the wall of sandbags. He was sound asleep.

From Cleveland Hopkins Airport, to Travis Airforce Base, to Long

37

Binh, to An Khe, to Camp Evans, to LZ Juliet, to Delta Company had taken, I believe, 12 days. Exactly at what point I had fallen down the rabbit hole I couldn't decide but for the first time I had doubts about being able to climb back out of it.

CHAPTER 3

*"Don't touch anything,
not even a fucking twig."*

Two engineers lived in the platoon area and from the look of the stuff they had accumulated (cots, radios, poncho liners, a cooler) had been there since time immemorial. I never saw any evidence that they were subject to higher authority. It was part of the platoon mission to provide security for these men each morning as they checked a section of Highway One for mines. The engineers rose early, accomplished this same dangerous task which took them several hours, and then returned to their cots. At intervals during the afternoon they would get up, stretch, and walk over to Mama San's.

That first morning the First Squad leader returned from the mine sweep steaming mad.

"Those engineer assholes wanted us off the road . . . on the berm, you know, where we'd trip every fucking booby-trap from here to Hai Lang."

Aguirre supported him. "Fuck that shit," he said. He repeated himself, slowly emphasizing each word in case the engineers hadn't heard him the first time. "FUCK THAT SHIT."

The First Squad leader was a tall, willowy man of 21. His name was Luger; Aguirre called him alternatively "Flacco" or "Bitch." He didn't seem to mind. Luger ran his squad easily, with real authority, and was never careless. He was devoid of bravado. Bravery he had in quantities. Aguirre respected him and told me of the time Luger had been caught in an open field by a VC mortar. He held his position until the second round dropped and then as the third round left the tube took off running in the direction opposite to the line and the mortar was being adjusted along. Aguirre said he ran right by the smoke from the second burst. Maybe so. Anyhow, by the time the VC gunner had recovered, Luger had gone to ground. I had heard of that gambit before; the navy calls it "chasing salvos," but it had never crossed my mind that anyone would try to do that on foot.

Second Squad was assigned that night's ambush and as the afternoon progressed I looked for preparations. I had assumed that there would be some visible preliminaries; a discussion of tactics in a huddled group, camouflage, a check of weapons, just as at Fort Benning, or in the movies, which no doubt still provided basic images. But I could detect nothing like that, nothing at all beyond the ordinary heat-laden, daytime routine. Finally, I confronted Aguirre only to be told, as though a child, that such obvious behavior would be certain to be communicated to the VC. What actually happened was far different. In the transition from day to night, which doesn't take long in Vietnam, Second Squad put on its gear and without a word filed out along the footpath heading away from the designated ambush site. That much I could figure out; when it was completely dark, the squad would shift location and take up its assigned position, which that night was only about 700 yards away just on the other side of the village. Mama San was now playing Vietnamese music, I noticed.

Toward midnight and under a quarter moon, a whispered transmission came over the radio.

"This is One Six Delta [the ambush], we have movement, some people moving around — two hundred meters, can just make them out."

Much closer than that and the ambush would have already opened fire. As it was, they would have just given away their position without much chance of hitting anything. Aguirre pounced on the radio like a jumping spider.

"This is One Six Mike, where are they? Over."

No answer. Aguirre did not repeat the transmission. The radio maintained an empty hiss for two or three minutes before the ambush responded.

". . . can't see them anymore — they were just outside the ville."

Gone, maybe. The mortar crew wanted to shoot a fire mission. I didn't because I was afraid of hitting our own men or the village. The VC escaped, if they were VC.

On several afternoons I took out small patrols to "familiarize myself with the terrain." Actually, I was sightseeing; I nosed across the dry paddies — "We don't walk on paddy dikes, sir" — and poked around the villages. Curious, I entered one hut and was greeted by a terrified child, a little boy of perhaps two, sitting bare bottomed on a tamped dirt floor. I backed out and peered behind the hut: no one there. Was this child alone, unattended, unfed maybe, for much of the day? Probably. The village was half empty during the daytime, usually you just saw old people and young children. Most of the men were gone — dead or serving in one of the several armies.

I found it impossible to avoid the impression that left alone, left free of landlords, government officials, VC, NVA, and Americans, the villages would have been very happy places. I am quite sure that those living in them felt the same way and probably had for centuries. I thought about that a few weeks later when I learned that part of the village next to the bridge had been bulldozed away to provide a better field of fire. "The gooks were sure pissed about that," I was told.

The local children, dark eyed, vexatious and engaging, visited us daily. C-rations were exchanged in return for filling sandbags, or just begged, and as with all hungry children they stole with ingenuity and persistence. When things got out of hand, a burst from an M-16 was fired into the air and they scattered like gazelles. On the assumption that it is not hard to bribe a hungry child I kept a close eye on them and once went into a roaring, vein-bulging tantrum when a little boy reached for a can of C-rations — or the fragmentation grenade beside it which someone had carelessly left in the open. The kids backed off, silently studied my face for perhaps 15 seconds, and sized me up for a paper tiger. All of them that is except for one little girl who ran in terror down the footpath. For an hour I scuffed around feeling like an ogre until she returned.

Every afternoon, I believe on his own initiative, the medic held sick call. The kids, but none of the adults, would line up to have cuts and sores cleaned and daubed with antiseptic. We gave out GI soap freely and they were as happy to have that as C-rations. In return for this, Mama San's old father spliced together C-ration cardboard with bamboo and wire into a six by eight foot sheet and presented it to us. He figured that we could use the shade and that we were too ignorant to make practical use of the building material all around us. He was right on both counts. It made life a little more comfortable.

One afternoon the medic was unaccountably absent. The children were lined up and . . . no medic.

41

"Where's Doc?" I asked.

"I dunno."

"Tell Sabalch to get some people together and find him."

"He's just down the road. He should be finished in a few minutes."

"What! Well go get him."

The squad soon returned with Doc who was peevish for the rest of the day. I may have frustrated a liaison, but visiting the villages alone, night or day, was dangerous. You could get "krokodiled."

That same day, a few of the older boys asked to go fishing. They needed our permission since they lacked the proper tackle, which was a hand grenade. A couple of frags were dropped off the bridge while the boys waited expectantly downstream. After a few minutes a large black and white catfish floated to the surface and was collected. Smaller fish were ignored. One of the boys, a Vietnamese version of Tom Sawyer, brought the fish around for us to admire and then went proudly home.

Third night: "Don't touch anything," lectured Aguirre, "not even a fucking twig." He was running this night's ambush and since I was tagging along, he was anxious that I didn't get them all killed. The VC booby-trapped everything: trails, branches, paddy dikes, fences, the dead, old fox holes. You never used old fox holes. If you did, I was told, "You'll be popping right back out," that is, blown out. Aguirre showed me on the map where he intended to position the ambush. It was over two miles away in an area that he called "the sands." From the look of the map, it was open country, well away from the nearest village.

Third Squad, resigned and quiet, formed up quickly and we left while it was still daylight so that we would be in a position well before midnight. I tacked onto the column towards the rear, without my RTO because the other radio would be needed at the bridge. The column crossed the highway and continued down the footpath beside the river, at one point stepping over a fallen branch as though it was a high tension wire. Aguirre kept chattering away happily. "Boom boom Mama San?" he said by way of a greeting to one old lady who was tending her pig.

As we left the village behind, Aguirre pulled off the path; there was less foot traffic beyond the village and therefore more danger from booby traps. Away from the river the country turned into scattered scrub and then to grass-tufted sands. I was having trouble following our course on the map; Aguirre didn't seem to need one. We came to an old railroad bridge that spanned a dry stream bed, guarded by two ARVN soldiers who waved to us out of sheer loneliness. If the VC were going to blow this bridge, it was clear that it would have only been for the practice because much of the roadbed leading to it had long since disappeared. We passed by without stopping and did not cross the bridge; but clambered down into the stream bed and up the other side. By now everyone was laboring heavily and soaked with sweat.

Aguirre stepped out from the front of the column, his face a storm cloud.

"Spread out!"

The column stretched out so that there was an interval of four or five yards between each man. There was no need for a reminder from Aguirre and if there had been, it would not have come in that form. Sabalch, the Third Squad leader, a short, sandy-haired man whose speech had overtones of Eastern Europe, later told me with detectable awe that, "If you bunch up, Aguirre will shoot right over your head."

We stopped, smoked, and took long pulls on our canteens as it grew dark. Then we set out again on a different course which took us onto rolling grassland dotted with grave mounds. The night was clear and the moon revealed this landscape in shades of blue grey. Aguirre seemed to be navigating from grave to grave. We moved more slowly now and with frequent breaks, during which we sat quietly on our haunches, listening. By soft stages we came to a region of scrub-covered dune and stopped by a large grassy hummock. The hummock is a very old grave mound and is to be our ambush position.

Aguirre and Sabalch conferred in sibilant, accented whispers. Aguirre wanted Sabalch to take five men and set up about 300 yards distant; Sabalch didn't want to go because the position was exposed. He went.

By splitting the squad, Aguirre had more than doubled the area under surveillance, and if one of the fire teams sprang an ambush, it might have driven the VC directly into the other fire team's position. The danger was that we could fire on each other. Aguirre pointed out Sabalch's position. . .or where it should have been since he was far enough away that we couldn't see him.

Three two-man fox holes were quickly dug. While one man slept, the other would be on guard. We settled into the ambush; it was past

43

midnight before anyone slept. The radio was turned down and hourly calls for sit reps answered by keying the handset. I needed a cigarette and poured some tobacco from a crumbled up smoke on my lower lip like snuff. In five minutes I spat this out and reached for my canteen. Empty. Two a.m., three a.m., asleep, awake, four a.m., a noise...no it's nothing, dawn; and we returned to the bridge.

A small unit of ARVNs, less than a platoon, also guarded the bridge. Towards evening, when the spirit moved them, they pulled a roll of concertina across the footpath and set out trip flares behind Mama San's. One afternoon, in return for some C-rations, there was a general sampling of dog stew by the platoon. At least we thought it was dog stew. The previous night someone had taken a shot at a dog which night after night had been scavenging near our position, tripping flares and scaring us half out of our socks. Badly wounded, the animal ran howling through the village leaving a trail of burning flares to gales of laughter on the part of everyone including, some said, VC outside the wire. Grunt humor is not complicated. The next day the ARVNs were cooking stew.

We had other cultural exchanges with our South Vietnamese counterparts which were less convivial. Sabalch's camera was stolen. Using some clumsy charades and a few English words — camera, click, click — I communicated this to the Vietnamese lieutenant in charge and the culprit was identified. After a few preliminary shouts, the lieutenant slapped his man full force across the face, knocking him down. The man got up, went to his bunker and returned a few minutes later with part of the camera. "That's not all of it," said Sabalch. I indicated this to the lieutenant who again knocked his man down. This time a lens was produced; but the process had to be repeated twice more before all of the camera was recovered.

I had a son. This news came over the radio: "Mother and baby are doing fine." No other particulars were provided, but that's all I really wanted to hear. A bottle of local firewater — brand name "Silver Fox" — was purchased and passed around. Two weeks before I had sat with my wife at the airport, both of us numb, unable to speak. I had not said goodbye — maybe afraid to. Now, I thought, all I have to do for the next eleven and a half months is stay alive. The afternoon sun, the untamed Vietnamese alcohol, and this new simplicity of purpose combined to produce a feeling of raw, sweaty contentment. The mood did not last.

Shots rang out. I caught sight of a burly, red haired American, one of the mortarmen, racing across the bridge in hot pursuit of a much smaller ARVN. Another ARVN was shooting his carbine just over the American's head. At the third round, the American, drunk and long in the field, dove headlong off the bridge missing the water by ten feet. The sandy river bank broke his fall but I still don't understand how he escaped serious injury. Unconscious and bleeding, he rolled into the river. He was immediately fished out and revived.

The medic was already painting his cuts and scrapes with antiseptic when I got to the other side of the bridge. Someone else applied a cigarette to a huge bloated leech adhering to his stomach; it plopped to the sand and was stepped on. I asked what happened.

"Leave me alone, sir."

"What happened?"

"Sir, get away from me."

"What happened?"

"Fucking gook fruit tried to steal my beer."

Aguirre was hot for a fight and stalked back and forth across the bridge raving at the ARVNs in both English and Spanish. "Bastards, hijos de putas, maricóns." The ARVNs, some of them with weapons in their hands, stood in an angry gaggle watching this performance. In the end the situation lost momentum. Aguirre stopped bellowing and the ARVNs returned to their stew pot. The weedy smell of marijuana began to drift from their bunker.

The village children who had scattered in the excitement returned and lined up for sick call. Mostly it was just minor cuts and scrapes that they wanted tended (some so minor that it was clear that the attention was valued as much as the treatment) but one little girl shyly held out her foot which had an evil-looking, suppurating sore. The medic cleaned it, smeared it with some sort of antiseptic salve and tried to make her understand that she should come back in a couple of days which, as I recall, she did.

Sick call that afternoon was interrupted by more excitement over at Mama San's. A half dozen GIs were gabbling around a Vietnamese man who was croaking in terror. Everyone was shouting. Mama San yelled "VC, VC, VC," from her doorway and then retreated inside. The man struggled against the grasp of several pairs of hands. A .45 was produced and its muzzle jammed against his temple. His knees buckled; vomit and spittle slid down his chin. The children stood by open mouthed, eyes wide, transfixed.

45

The man's eyes were rolling. "No VC, no VC," he squealed, convinced he was about to be killed. I was appalled. Christ, I thought, he'll be dead before I find out who he is. The shouts began to sort themselves out. "The dumb fuck wouldn't pay for his beer...everything was fine and then she starts screaming 'VC...'"

"Let him go," I said.

"What?"

"Let him go; get him the fuck out of here."

Released, the man sank to one knee, got up, backpeddled a few steps, and then turned and walked slowly away. When he got to the highway he couldn't resist looking back at us before he continued on with his life — whatever that life was.

Who was he? I don't know. The ARVNs didn't seem to think that he was VC; or, perhaps they didn't care. Anyway they had paid little attention to the scene as though it was just so much more chaos to be ignored. I was satisfied with the outcome, a living minor enigma as opposed to a certified corpse, but did not report the matter since I was sure the people at battalion would have preferred things the other way around. Besides, I couldn't say it was my son's birthday, and I just didn't want to see anybody killed.

We were visited one afternoon by a delegation of Vietnamese Popular Forces. They somehow made it known to Aguirre that they were running an ambush that night and wanted an FO team to go with them. The lieutenant in charge of the company's forward observers agreed to this and detailed a sergeant to go along. Shortly before dusk, off they went, a garrulous column of twenty or so pajamaed Vietnamese accompanied by two tall Americans, the long-whip aerial of the RTO's PRC 25 twitching above everyone.

The FO team returned the following morning with tales of woe and radiating indignation. The Popular Forces were on the move all night long to a constant clatter of equipment, including tea pots. Periodically they would stop, smoke various kinds of cigarettes, light a fire and brew tea. Then, said the sergeant, "They'd all have to take a motherfucking leak. They're fucking ka-razy. I'm never going out with those people again."

Amazingly, they ambushed a VC carrying party which was transporting supplies to the NVA in the mountains. Sergeant Tanner, the FO, graphically described the "green fucking tracers" going over his position and moved his hands like a dog digging, evidently his reaction

46

at the time. The VC immediately broke contact and escaped, leaving behind several bags of rice and the body of an adolescent girl.

Some days later, Two Niner Mike India, Sergeant Tanner's RTO, asked me to exchange a handful of tattered piasters, which Mama San would not accept, for military currency. Knowing that he was broke, I did this. It was not until later that I realized that the piasters had been taken from the dead girl's body.

If there are people around a million years from now they will know of the war in Vietnam as a well defined geological stratum. The hard pieces of modern warfare are everywhere: bits of shrapnel, big chunks of shrapnel, the tail fins of mortar rounds, wire, dud shells, dud bombs, burned out rocket motors, plastic, brass, tiny little flechettes, copper jacketed bullets—billions of copper jacketed bullets. Out to a distance of several miles the perimeter of every American base was seeded by tens of thousands, often millions, of spent rounds.

Mines and booby-traps are the worst of these left-behind things; often they were set out and then forgotten leaving behind a potential for random tragedy. After a shattering explosion (at first I thought we were being mortared), I can remember whooping across the bridge and down the highway trying to warn people in a crowded market that the grass fire 100 yards from them was cooking off claymores (mines) any one of which could have turned the market into a slaughterhouse. I was about to start shooting over their heads, although I doubted that would do much good, when the men from the mortar platoon spilled into the grass and among the claymores. Ponchos flailing, they got the fire out before any more of the mines exploded. Aguirre gave them hell for not doing that in the first place, but I was impressed that they had done it at all. I thought it a very brave thing to do. Set weeks or months before, the mines had evidently fallen over and instead of scything through the crowd of women and children at the market had gone off harmlessly into the air or into the ground. As far as the Vietnamese were concerned, the entire episode represented nothing out of the ordinary and they never gave it the slightest notice.

Now word came over the radio "to keep our eyes open." A group of VC had been spotted close to our position and might try to cross the river nearby. In the middle distance two cobra gunships circled around a column of dark smoke. Hanging from invisible rotor blades, noses slightly down, the gunships looked to me like bottom-feeding fish.

Periodically one of them would dart down and release a brace of rockets, hoping that one of the VC would be foolish enough to fire back and give away their position. Then a whole school of fish would arrive. After an hour the gunships went away. No one tried to cross near our position that afternoon nor did our night ambush, which I kept close to the village, intercept anyone.

The next day a woman in her late thirties was carried to the bridge in a hammock slung underneath a pole. The two old men staggering at either end of the pole put her down and left without comment. The warheads on the 2.75 inch rockets used by our gunships have a reputation for exploding into long, evil shards. The woman's condition seemed to confirm this: one foot was sliced off and her chest looked like it had been cut open by a butcher knife, leaving one breast attached only by a shred of skin. Her color was ashen and I found it hard to believe that she had not already bled to death.

An old lady, probably the woman's mother, was with her. A cot was commandeered from the engineers and the woman carried down to the open field next to the mortar position. Medevac arrived in minutes. As the ship flared for a landing I could feel the old woman begin to shake uncontrollably. The machine obviously terrified her. The shattered daughter was placed aboard the chopper then her mother somehow willed her feet toward it. An arm caught the old woman around the waist and pulled her aboard. The huey swept low across the field, nose well down, its big sweeps digging the air for speed.

Was the woman among the VC attacked by the gunships or did she just happen to stray into the wrong field at the wrong time? Maybe, after all, she had just triggered a mine. It is impossible to say.

That night Juliet, some miles distant, was hit with a dozen mortar shells and responded with a storm of red tracers. Seconds later we heard the distant forest fire crackle of the hundreds and hundreds of rounds that produced this spectacle. Sometimes an LZ or a firebase will stand to, all guard positions doubly or triply manned, and then at a set instant everyone cuts loose on full automatic. This is called a "Red Splash" because at night that is exactly what it looks like from a distance—a crashing, incandescent surf of red tracer rounds. Squad sized ambushes when they make contact erupt briefly into something like a spiky red flower followed after an interval of seconds with the sound of automatic weapons. Then comes the urgent, brittle call over the radio for artillery or mortar support.

Bannerman, somehow, got wind of the "incident" with the ARVNs. I pointed out that it is difficult to keep men from drinking when they are stationed 50 feet away from a bar but did not mention the bottle of Silver Fox.

"It's your platoon, damnit, control them," was the message. "I've had nothing but shit since we came to the villages."

The Vietnamese in the villages could have said the same thing; "nothing but shit since we arrived." We weren't there to protect them; we protected the bridge which the local Vietnamese could have done without. The bridge invited attack and the only certain outcome of an attack would be the destruction of much of the village. I think that's how they saw it. That's how I came to see it, especially at night as I listened to Mama San's stereo play Vietnamese music and tried to peer past her darkened house. The most likely avenue of attack was through the village. Therefore it made perfect military sense to bulldoze away part of the village to provide a better field of fire. And so, after all, by the peculiar logic of events in Vietnam, the bridge claimed part of the village even though there had been no attack. Mama San's had been among the houses destroyed.

Mama San's children we all enjoyed: a boy of about 14 who kept asking me if I were honcho and a girl of 11 or 12 who spoke a little English. When I noticed one afternoon that her brother was crying, I asked her why and was informed that it was because he was being sent away to school, to Hia Lang which was all of six miles distant. I was mystified. I did not at the time have the slightest glimmer of the Vietnamese concept of XA: the consuming attachment to the self-contained world of the village, which was everything. From the boy's point of view he might as well have been going to Arabia.

A chasm separated us from the Vietnamese. We were culturally alien and lived at cross purposes to the people in the village. We communicated by means of a crude pidgin concocted of English, French, Vietnamese, and, on the assumption that all gooks speak gook, a few Japanese and Korean words. It was a language that filtered out all emotion and sensitivity. "G.I. souvenir me bookoo [beaucoup] chop chop," that's about all there was to it.

"G.I. eat water buffalo," said Mama San's daughter one afternoon. (As I recall she said "water buffalo" and did not use the Vietnamese word.) This was an encompassing criticism meaning among other things that we were not Buddhists.

49

"G.I. eat chop chop," I countered, pointing towards a case of C-rations.

"G.I. *sat* [kill] water buffalo."

"No, we don't," I blurted in plain English.

"G.I. *sat* water buffalo," she insisted and then she walked away.

I thought of the sergeant who had once told me of how he had plinked away with his M-16 at a water buffalo until it had finally keeled over: ". . . put the whole fucking clip into it. The gooks were really hot over that." He said he wanted to be a mailman after he got out of the army.

A new man has joined the platoon. Big and strong, Aguirre dubbed him the Mountain Man and gave him a grenade launcher because he could easily pack a grenadier's heavy bag of M-79 rounds. Sullen, depressed, bewildered, the man said that he was in the Reserves and did not belong in Vietnam; there had been a mistake. "I only missed a couple of meetings." But here he is and like everyone else he will stay here until he is wounded, or killed, or his tour is up. A new and reluctant mental patient, it would take him, I knew, only a few days to shake the bewilderment, to adjust to the unusual reality of "being in the field," but the depression, like a cold, unblinking constrictor, would never let go.

By the army table of organization a rifle platoon consisted of four squads of between nine and twelve men—three rifle squads and a weapons squad—plus the platoon leader, platoon sergeant, two radio operators, and a medic; as I recall, 45 men altogether. This official arrangement was *never* found in Vietnam. A rifle platoon typically had between 25 and 35 men (and never 45) divided into three squads. Each squad was self-contained and was home to the men assigned to it. They lived together—ate, slept, dug holes, ambushed, patrolled, rode in helicopters, killed people, were wounded, and now and again died, with the same familiar faces and voices around them. A man was rarely reassigned to another squad and it was even rarer that he wanted to be.

The basic armament was the M-16, but each squad was equipped with an M-60 machine gun and an M-79 grenade launcher. In some respects a squad was a bodyguard for the machine gunner and the M-60 he carried, usually balanced on his shoulder, which was the squad's primary offensive and defensive weapon. An M-60 is heavy (about 24 pounds), reliable, and capable of long sustained bursts that gobble ammunition at a ferocious pace. Most squads had over a thousand rounds of M-60 ammo on hand, broken down into 100-round belts which each man draped over his shoulder while on the move. Ammunition carried in this manner tended to corrode. It was a bad practice which I tried to discourage. I was never successful for more than a few days and never knew a platoon leader who was.

A grenade launcher looks like a stubby single barreled shotgun that does not so much fire as "pop" a little 40mm shell in a high arc out to a distance of 400 meters. The weapon has a distinctive signature; a soft report, then a wait of long seconds, followed by a shattering crack and a puff of black smoke.

Hand grenades were carried in profusion. I hated them but carried them on the principle that I couldn't make others carry them if I didn't. The soft metal pin which secures the fuse tended to work loose and eventually would if not checked daily. Then, as I morbidly feared, it would plop at your feet to explode a few seconds later. And, of course, a careless or very frightened man could easily drop a "frag" in the act of throwing, especially at night and especially when they were being thrown simultaneously by five or six men, something that rifle squads in the First Cavalry division did as a matter of routine.

Each squad was responsible for one or two claymore mines. This is an electrically ("command") detonated mine about a foot long, four inches wide and an inch and a half thick. A claymore is slightly curved and embossed on the convex side is a useful bit of advice: FRONT TOWARD ENEMY. An electrical blasting cap attached to 100 yards of wire was inserted in the top. A small hand-held "clicker" generates an electrical charge and explodes the mine. Basically it was just a plastic case containing a pound of plastic explosives. Several hundred ball bearings were embedded in the convex side and when you "blew" a claymore the ball bearings scattered in a broad deadly cone. The North Vietnamese had their own version of the claymore; it was much bigger.

Each night claymores were carefully set in front of the squad's fighting positions. The man carrying one usually set it out. He would take the clicker and put it in his pocket or set it on his position where he could see it. Then he would move out beyond the perimeter, plant the claymore on its short, spindly legs—"FRONT TOWARD ENEMY"— insert the blasting cap and play out the wire as he backed into the squad position. Only then would he plug the clicker into the wire. The

51

blast from a claymore can kill whether you're behind it or in front of it. A platoon or company perimeter was always ringed with claymores and sometimes with frags which dangled head-high in the trees. The fuse was unscrewed and the blasting cap from a claymore inserted. Tracing through all of this was a ragged spider's web of trip wires that connected to small magnesium flares—trip flares. Anyone brushing against a trip wire "tripped" the flare which gave a harsh pop and hissed into life, emitting a cold, arctically white light.

About the only benign thing we carried (trip flares are not benign, if you're not careful when setting them out, they will instantly produce a bad second degree burn) were smoke grenades. Everyone carried at least one smoke grenade which was used to mark your position. Smoke, in colors of red, yellow, violet and green, was "popped" when a chopper came in, otherwise it was hard (or impossible) for the pilot to locate a unit on the ground. Green smoke grenades never struck me as very practical for Vietnam, but we had green smoke. For whatever reason men liked to stand at the base of the thick, coiling plume of smoke given off by a smoke grenade which dyed their boots and the bottom part of their pants yellow, red, violet or emerald green.

We lived by these devices but mostly by our radios, PRC-25s. The platoon leader, platoon sergeant, forward artillery observer (FAO) worked necessarily in tandem with their respective RTOs (radio telephone operators). In brief time I could not imagine a life unattached to this stridently ordering goiter. A rifle platoon could neither function nor survive without its radios. At night or under the jungle canopy an electronically mute platoon was all but impossible to find and could be overrun in the twinkling of an eye. The relieving force would find a standard scene (all too standard in Vietnam): radios inoperable, probably smashed by the same rounds that killed the RTO, and the few men who survived the initial ambush methodically murdered. With a radio, with this umbilical cord unsevered, air strikes, gunships, and murderous sheets of artillery could be called in on the enemy. The response from the company mortar platoon seldom took much longer than the flight of the round.

Virtually all the information that orchestrated the ground war in Vietnam and conveyed its sorrows and miseries was channeled through the insides of a prick 25. We spoke, and thought, according to radio procedure. Even in "normal" (not over the radio) conversation, the company commander was not Lt. Bannerman or the CO but "Six"; I

was "One Six" (First Platoon leader) and Aguirre, "One Six Mike."
Medics were "Bandaids" and the platoon medic, therefore, "One Six
Bandaid." Our maps, appropriately, were "the Funny Papers." Sister
companies within the battalion were identified as often as not by their
call signs—Apache, Cheyenne, Runner, and Commanche. We were
Navaho. Actually, we were Ready Navaho, Cheyenne was Cruel
Cheyenne, Commanche, Brave Commanche, Apache, Lean Apache,
and, naturally, there was Ridge Runner. But usually, the first word was
not used. Unavoidably some archness crept into the dreaming up of
call signs. One company in another battalion answered to "Limping
Scholar," and an artillery unit to "Birth Control." Our battalion headquarters, however, was simply Prescott Arizona; the battalion commander, Arizona Six.

The gadgets that we served, and which served to protect us, keyed
our perceptions. We thought in terms of perimeters, sandbags, fox
holes, tanglefoot and concertina, avenues of approach, radio contact,
smokes, frags, claymores, booby traps, mortars, fire-missions, gunships, slicks, trip flares, sixteens, grenade launchers, sixties, fields of
fire, killing zones, and dead space. Out of such things the mental furniture of our environment was constructed; it was a sort of totemistic
landscape structured according to the cadences of thought imposed by
the prick 25.

Any comprehensive history of the Vietnam War at the ground
level would be a tapestry of lineal accounts with each account restricted
to the operations of a single rifle company. Men knew little and cared
little about what happened to another company. Nor did their knowledge of events within their company extend back in time beyond a
year. I never heard anyone speak of the battles the Cav had fought in
the Central Highlands; those things had happened to other men.
Delta Company spoke of the relief of Khe San and the attack on the
French fort, the Tet offensive ("It rained all the goddamn time."), ambushes, accidents, personalities, and the death and injury of people
they knew. Hearing of these things drew me into the company.

My predecessor had been killed about six weeks before my arrival.
I did not ask and was never told of how he died. Delta Company, no
different from any other, had a catalog of private tragedies. About a
week before I joined the company, the mortar platoon had been
decimated, literally, by one of their own mortar rounds which had,
somehow, gotten into a pile of burning trash and exploded. Aguirre

mentioned this matter-of-factly and did not elaborate except to make it clear that several men had been terribly maimed. Misplacing an 81mm mortar round seemed a tall order but it wasn't hard to see how this could have happened. The endless litter that accumulates mountainously around any American position, if it is not constantly picked up and burned, was strewn all over. Naturally I ordered "a thorough police of this area." Returning to check an hour later, I found four or five men gathered apprehensively around an enormous bonfire of trash. "Get away from the fire!" I yelled, horrified that I might have ordered a repetition of the first tragedy which I did not believe was really an accident.

Many of the men in the company packed NVA rucksacks (which were much better than ours) and often wore the comfortable sandals that both the VC and the NVA cut from old tires. For obvious reasons these sandals were known as "Ho Chi Minh Racing Slicks" and would be confiscated from an enemy corpse before it had started to cool.

The ambush at Dong Ha supplied much of this booty. About a month before I joined the company, it had operated around Dong Ha which was about ten miles to the north and close to the area sometimes known as "The Street" — short for the "Street Without Joy." (Although I didn't know it at the time, the real "Street," the one immortalized by Bernard Fall, ran parallel to Highway One and passed within a few miles of the bridge First Platoon was guarding.) In shimmering heat the company would trudge over dunes and through scrub by day and set up a Forward Operation Base (acronym FOB, but few used it) by night. Delta Company was then commanded by a man named Wright who was nearing the end of many months in the field.

On intuition, or maybe because a few mortar rounds had landed nearby, Wright decided to shift the FOB. It was, by most accounts, not a popular order and it took some encouragement to get all four platoons moved and settled into a company-sized ambush. About two hours later, some said only an hour, an NVA company walked across Delta Company's front. "They were all bunched up, in a column of twos like basic trainees," snorted Aguirre, "Gook CO in front with his little Chicom pistol — Captain Wright always wanted a Chicom pistol." I believe that Aguirre stuck close to the truth, as he remembered it, but it was obvious that I was to accept his recounting as an Aesopian tale, the moral of which is that a good commanding officer is always rewarded by a prized souvenir.

In Aguirre's version Wright triggered the ambush, killing, it was said, his enemy counterpart. Instantly the NVA were caught in a splash of red tracers. One of First Platoon's machine gunners said "that sixty just spit out that sand and started to chug." It was over in minutes.

In the early morning they counted 42 bodies, some within 30 yards of the perimeter. One man from Navajo had to be medevacked because of a mild heart attack; there were no other casualties. That evening, and every evening until Wright left the field, a helicopter would deliver, courtesy of Arizona Six, a bottle of whiskey and a box of cigars.

The French fort was a legacy of the Indo-China War located very close to Khe San. During Operation Pegasus, the relief of Khe San, another company had been butchered by mortar fire trying to take it and Arizona Six asked Captain Wright if Delta Company could make a second assault. Wright, naturally, said yes. What everyone remembered vividly was the forced march to get into position. "Nine clicks," I was told, "Big Man [Second Platoon] humped that 90 mike-mike for nine clicks."

The fort was empty. The NVA had pulled out. "We policed up all kinds of American equipment," said Aguirre. "Sixteens, packs, a car carbine; shit everywhere. There were these built-in base plates [for mortars] with the ranges marked on them; right on the base plate. Every fucking thing was plotted in."

After about ten days at the bridge, (and two big yellow malaria pills—52 pills and you go home) our battalion was given a new assignment. We were to replace the 2nd of the 12th in the mountains. The first reliable indication that this was not just a rumor came in the form of hot chow, flown in by huey and kept warm in insulated cans. Arizona Six also gave everyone in the battalion a present: a sort of water-proof wallet with a Cav patch on it. The rains were coming and everything not in plastic would be soaked. These wallets were thoughtful, practical gifts; into them went photographs and letters, all that documented that we had once lived in another world, and might again. So ended the first week of July.

CHAPTER 4

"How many hordes in a gook platoon?"
—First attributed to an anonymous
private during the Korean War

"We're not fucking around with little people anymore," was the way Bannerman described our new mission. "These people have long-range artillery coming out of Laos: 82mm mortars, heavy machine guns...." It didn't sound very encouraging.

Yelling like cowboys, a platoon from the 2nd of the 12th arrived in a deuce and a half to take over our position. Bearded and wild, they left a lasting impression. Their clothes were in the final stages of rotting off their backs and some of them were wearing only tattered, cut-off fatigue pants and web gear. They spilled from the truck in front of Mama San's and went no further.

I showed the platoon leader around the bridge while he yacked away in an uninterrupted manic stream. They had been in contact with the NVA nearly every day for a month. His platoon was down to 23 men. Twice in the space of 15 minutes he took off his helmet and pointed out a deep, angular dent where a shell fragment had hit. "Look at that," he kept saying. "Holy Christ! Knocked me fucking cold."

Delta Company was trucked through the village of Hia Lang to the staging area for the assault. Only the girls in front of the local whorehouse took any notice of the little convoy. The staging area, a grassy field, presented only casual organization. Everyone was standing around awkwardly, a little hinged over at the waist under the weight of a heavy pack. My shoulders ached and a bag of 40 grenade rounds banged into my thigh at every step. The men in the mortar platoon

57

were burdened like pack animals. I didn't see how they could move, much less board a helicopter.

It was Aguirre's responsibility to break the platoon down into lifts and he went off to confer with the first sergeant. I trotted awkwardly over to Bannerman who was already talking to the other platoon leaders. He pointed out the location of our landing zone ("probable location" he said) and said that it would be a one bird LZ. Then he eyed the grenade launcher I was carrying.

"That thing is as useless as tits on a boar where we're going."

I was nervous. This was the first assault I had ever been on and in fact it would be only the second time I had ever ridden in a huey. While I was at Fort Benning, many of the available hueys, already in scarce supply, had been devoted to the filming of the Green Berets. As the choppers came into sight I reflected briefly on the army's priorities; at least if I had been an extra in the movie I would have had some practical experience in what was about to happen.

In principle, a combat assault is very simple. You get into the helicopter, it flies to a designated point on the map (the "insertion grid"), lands, and you get out. Doing that with large numbers of infantry over hostile and difficult terrain without getting a lot of people killed is a very complicated business, however.

A troop-carrying huey (a slick) has a four-man crew—pilot, copilot, and two door gunners, one of whom is the crew chief. Depending on the altitude and the temperature, four to eight fully loaded infantrymen can be carried. The slicks land in flights of four or five, are boarded and take off. Two gunships provide protection. The term combat assault is something of a misnomer since it implies that you are being deliberately landed on top of a hostile force. This happened, of course, all too often, but was seldom deliberate (in 1968) unless another unit was already heavily engaged.

Just before the slicks land, the LZ is hit with artillery, typically 12 to 18 rounds, the last of which is a smoke round which is the cue for the gunships to take over. They continue to hit the LZ with rockets, machine guns, and grenade rounds until just a few seconds, a very few seconds, before the slicks land. All this looks impressive, but if there are any enemy forces dug in around the LZ it merely serves to keep their heads down until after the infantry is on the ground, which, to those riding in slicks is a great deal. The chubby, slow moving hueys are completely vulnerable to ground fire as they come in to land.

58

The slicks land or just hover a few feet off the ground. The infantry climbs out, or jumps out (no one charges out of a helicopter with 60 pounds on his back), scuttles from under the aircraft's big sweeps and begins to form a perimeter. The platoon leader noses around for a few minutes and basically determines whether or not someone is shooting at him. If no one is shooting at him, or more to the point, since he will have been moving around in the open, if he has not been shot, he reports the landing zone safe (green). If it is not, the LZ is hot (red) and the gunships which will have kept half their ammunition in reserve immediately go back to work. It was Arizona Six's decision that once an assault started it would not be halted, no matter what. "I believe that we should continue to insert people even if we are presented with difficult conditions on the ground," was the way he put it. When I was in the lead slick, I thought that a very wise policy.

Sometimes the process was magnified to the point that all eight maneuver battalions within the division, plus supporting artillery, were on the move at once, as was the case during the raid into the A Shau Valley. Enormous assaults were made in the face of radar directed anti-aircraft fire. The cost was high. Operation Pegasus saw repeated flights of a hundred or more helicopters lifting a battalion at a time. Batteries of artillery were inserted on the top of a hill and the passage of less than an hour found them firing in support of another assault miles away. The lead slicks had yellow smoke grenades tied to their skids. "The Cav came in streaming yellow smoke," several men had mentioned with noticeable pride. Dead NVA were everywhere and the Air Force had been so often overhead that Captain Wright had been hard pressed to designate likely targets.

At the time I was only dimly aware of any of this and was not comforted by the advice given to me by the first sergeant: "You just have to play it by ear." I could have used a few specifics; but it was good advice. The assault was already well underway when, with three other men, I boarded a slick. The ship immediately took off, climbed to altitude, and then promptly turned around. One of the pilots looked back over his seat, pointed to the instrument panel and bellowed something about pressure. Too much or too little pressure in what? He didn't seem very concerned. I was back on the staging area within minutes trying to catch up with my platoon.

I jumped the line and got on the next lift out. As the huey bumped along, climbing steadily toward the mountains, scattered

59

hamlets and dry paddies gave way to a carpet of scrubby trees and bushes. I could look directly down and see an infinity of dry stream beds braiding out of the foothills. Over the mountains the forest canopy was deep and impenetrable, nothing could be seen beneath it.

The landing zone turned out to be an enormous bomb crater (you could put a house in it) which opened enough of the forest canopy at the top of a high ridge to accommodate a single huey. Our slick descended partly into the crater, near one side, so that the rotor blades were flashing a few feet over the rim, and came to a hover five or six feet above the churned up ground beneath us. Already stand- ing on the skids, we jumped and went spilling down the steep sides of the crater in a tangle of arms, legs and equipment. The medic tumbled all the way to the bottom and was gasping for air and holding his side. While the other two men hoisted him painfully to his feet, I paddled through loose dirt clods and up the side of the crater. Peeking over the rim, I saw nothing; nothing but tall trees and scorched underbrush. There wasn't a man in sight. Fleeting thought: "They've landed us in the wrong place; we're the only ones here!" Another slick was dropping fast, evidently trying to land on my head. I scrambled out of the crater and into the trees to get out from under the huey's big sweeps.

Okay, now what? I moved a little further into the dense forest, neck turtled forward, eyes swinging from side to side, the way you do when you find a neighbor's house unlocked and then discover that no one is home: "Hello, hello, anybody here?" like that. As soon as the next slick pulled away, I could hear American voices. I looked and could just make out Bannerman, Ogletree and Hardoy (third platoon leader) through the underbrush. When I got there, Bannerman's RTO was on the radio reading off the serial number of an AK-47. Ogletree waved expansively to his left. "Found the little rascal [the AK-47's previous owner] over there, just off the ridge. Red Leg [artillery] got him a few days ago."

Bannerman was emphatic: "I want three man foxholes with overhead cover . . . fucking tree bursts are going to murder us up here. Any movement—you know it's not some old lady taking a shit—I want M-26s [fragmentation grenades] in there right away. . . . And you might want to blow one of your claymores early; I don't want some gook with a lot of hair sneaking up and turning those things around on us. Stand to at 0500."

"Stand to" is a ritual and an old one—"stand to arms"—that ensures that everyone is awake, in position and looking down their weapon at a time when an attack is anticipated. Some units, but I would guess not many in the First Cavalry, did that every dawn. Dawn from our point of view brought gunships, or could within minutes, and it was alleged that our brigade commander had long since worn the knees out of his starched fatigues praying that the NVA would attempt a mass attack during the daylight hours. It was not hard to imagine the brigade commander doing that and some weeks later, when the company was guarding the perimeter of a fire base, Lang from the Second Platoon, gave us his impression of the general at prayer. Standing stark naked on a rock he bellowed at the sky. "Oh God, protector of the Big PX, provide me, Oh Lord, with an Asian horde. Thou knowest I deserve a second star." It was explained to me that Lang was from Southern California.

By the time Bannerman had finished giving us our orders the perimeter had taken shape. Constrained by the narrow ridge, it stretched around in an elongated C that closed on the bomb crater which had dished out one side of the ridge providing a view of the valley below. At no other point could you see more than 75 yards beyond the perimeter.

The mortarmen, absorbed in the tasks required by the weapon they served, a single 81mm mortar, were encamped like gypsies next to the bomb crater and underneath the only opening in the canopy through which they could shoot. The heavy tube was set on its bipod and the base plate seated firmly in the ground by firing a couple of rounds. There was no need to be worried about where they would land; there wasn't anyone within miles of us, unless they were NVA. Aiming stakes went out and a few rounds, which come packaged rather like tennis balls in a large cardboard cylinder, made ready. As a rule, the mortar platoon would fire a few H and I rounds (for harass and interdict) during the night; any trails leading into the perimeter, or a ravine, or any likely looking avenue of attack, would have at odd moments a mortar round slamming into it.

First Platoon was already partly dug in when I arrived at our section of the perimeter. Besides the issue entrenching tool, which everyone carries, each squad also carries a large D handled shovel and can move a lot of dirt very fast. In front of the fighting positions a few men were whacking at the underbrush with machetes. Inside the perimeter, hooches were beginning to sprout.

I didn't at first see Aguirre. Then I saw his feet. He had scrunched his half inflated air mattress between the flaring buttress roots of a large tree and was reclined in Nabob contentment spooning down some sort of canned pastry his wife had sent from Puerto Rico. I did not feel the least bit content and dug in like an aardvark.

Aguirre later shared some of his treat which he said was made from fried bananas. It was very very good. C-rations had by then become an abiding preoccupation. Everyone knows the various meals intimately and the taste, texture and smell of anything—carrot sticks, powdered eggs, the army's generic cake; just about anything edible, that breaks this numbing routine becomes a permanently accessible recollection. The usual method of heating your Cs is to take a small piece of plastic explosive (C-4), about the size of a walnut, pinch one end of it thin and light it. It burns intensely and will heat a cup of coffee in 20 seconds. You do not, I was warned, stamp on a piece of burning C-4 to put it out. If you do that, it explodes. Actually, some of the C-ration meals were pretty good, it's just that you had to eat them all the time. But some were bad. Worst of all, I believe, was the infamous B-3 unit which contained as its entree a sort of compost of finely chopped ham and eggs. It was universally dreaded. B-3 units, or more accurately the desire to eat something besides a B-3 unit, occasionally provoked fights.

About the only practical way to carry C-rations was to break the individual meals apart and stuff the cans into a long GI sock which was then tied to your web gear. Three days rations required several socks, unless you threw a few items away. Most people did. Once we were issued a week's rations and for the first two days Delta Company on the move resembled a column of helmeted mops.

There were three items of creature comfort that we relied on: a poncho, an air mattress and insect repellant. The poncho, apart from being a poncho, could be used as a shelter half. Two ponchos were snapped together and a sapling inserted in the hoods to stretch it taut. This arrangement is called a hooch. The air mattress basically served as a ground cloth. Except for tires, few things in the army designed to hold air ever did for very long. Air mattresses never. On an abnormally good evening you set up your hooch, inflated your air mattress and laid down. As the air slowly leaked out, you went to sleep. In the morning there was usually just enough air left in the mattress to keep the edges off the ground and you didn't wake up covered with leeches. The issue insect repellant worked very well on mosquitoes and tended to discourage leeches. It was so strong that when the rains came we used it to keep warm. Soaked to the skin and shivering with cold we would strip to the waist, splash on a half a bottle of "bug juice" and for a few minutes would feel like we were under a sun lamp. Then we were cold again.

Throughout the late afternoon machetes bite into saplings, shivering leaves, shovels and entrenching tools grate into sandy soil, ponchos are shaken out and snapped together, hooch poles are banged into the ground with helmets. It would become a familiar constellation of sounds, with, always, the same coda. In the evening the underbrush beyond the perimeter rustles softly as deliberate, watchful men set trip flares and claymores.

Suddenly, it is very dark and very quiet. The first hourly call for sit reps circles the perimeter. Around midnight, two mortar rounds are fired in rapid succession. What? Then I remember: H and I. Strangely enough it took little time to get used to this and in a twilight sleep the hollow sound of a mortar round thumping out on low charge was comforting, like the town clock striking the hour.

Dawn saw us glaring down a gun barrel for 20 minutes. Within an hour the company was ponderously on the move. In the mountains, all of the mortar platoon's burdensome paraphernalia—aiming stakes, bipod, tube, base plate, rounds—must be carried. The tube alone weighs 50 pounds and the base plate, even more cumbersome, nearly as much. Each mortar round in its canister weighs about 15 pounds and normally 15 to 20 rounds are packed by the mortarmen. Any more than that and riflemen must also "hump" (that's the word for it) a mortar round. I soon learned that the typical rifleman would rather carry a dead wart hog than a mortar round. If you distributed 30 rounds throughout the company in the morning you would be lucky after a hard march to have 20 by nightfall. The remainder will have disappeared into streams and ravines.

The company also carried a 90mm recoilless rifle which had both beehive and high explosive rounds. It was heavy, unbelievably loud, and had a vicious backblast. Nearly everyone hated the damn thing, especially the man who had to carry it, but it was a potent weapon which had been used to ghastly effect at Dong Ha. Lugging its ammunition was no more popular than carrying mortar rounds and I can remember the bleak look on Ogletree's face when he discovered that his men had been carrying the 90mm for several days (they avoided saying just how long) *without* any ammunition.

"Jesus, why didn't you tell me you didn't have any rounds for that thing? I would have gotten you some rounds." An afterthought: "What happened to the rounds you had?" . . . silence.

Web belt and broad web suspenders were fairly standard; *everyone* wears a helmet. Beyond that there was wild variation. Magazines were stuffed in shirt pockets, looped over shoulders in bandoliers, or just carried in a sand bag. A few men actually used the standard ammunition pouches but these held less than half a basic load. Hand grenades hung from suspenders or ammunition pouch, or, in fact, from anything. Ponchos were rolled up and tucked behind pack straps, or crammed into the pack, or tied to the web belt. Machetes—two or three to a squad—were slipped under a pack strap, minus sheath, which had long since been thrown away. Attached to the web belt very often was a large bowie knife (handy for cutting hooch poles) and some men carried a bayonet since they make excellent tent pegs or can be pounded into a tree to suspend your pack. Only two or three times can I remember seeing a bayonet attached to the end of an M-16. In close cover a bayonet only made the weapon cumbersome. Fixed bayonets were *not* allowed during Charlie Alphas and, after my first gazelle-like leap from a chopper, it wasn't hard to figure out why.

Without exception, M-16s were rigged with a GP strap. One end was attached to the stock, the other to the muzzle. The strap was looped over your shoulder so that the rifle hung about waist high and parallel to the ground and whichever way you turned the muzzle of the weapon was in front of you. A round was always chambered.

Pack, poncho, water, ammunition, M-16—however arranged, it still added up to more than 45 pounds. Machine gunners, radio men, and grenadiers carried more. But, of course, that was for openers. Add to this trip flares, smoke grenades, frags, claymores, blocks of C-4, shovels, gas masks, belts of M-60 ammo, rounds for the recoilless rifle, and C-rations, and you end up with a rock bottom minimum of 55 pounds per man. Sixty pounds would be a better guess, with some men humping 80 or 90 pounds. Three to four tons of munitions, food, water and equipment distributed among 120 men: a rifle company in the mountains was essentially a very well-armed pack train.

Ogletree, the most experienced platoon leader, had the point platoon and it was his job to see that the company was not ambushed. Navigation was another responsibility. Most of the route that Ogletree followed was over a trail that burrowed through triple canopy forest. The straight line distance to the point on the map that Bannerman had indicated as our new base was less than a mile away but included what seemed to be an endless series of hills and ridges.

The mountains weren't much as mountains go, the highest I can remember on our maps just topped the 1,000 meter contour line, but they were rugged, steep, strewn with boulders, and fissured with ravines that seldom showed on the map. Our maps revealed the world as seen from above the forest canopy but that world we traveled beneath.

The company strung out along the trail for 400 to 500 yards and most of the time it just sat while Ogletree sniffed out the route ahead. Periodically as was standard, Ogletree stopped and executed a "clover leaf" in which three squads circle out clockwise — *always* clockwise — to a distance of 100 to 200 yards.

Navigating in the jungle is like piloting a ship in the fog. You can't see where you're going and mistakes are all but impossible to recant. Tactically it was much the same. If you heard something (by the time you saw something it would be too late) the standard practice was to simply come on line rather like battleships crossing the T, a dangerously clumsy thing to do. But get fancy and send a squad around the flank and there was every chance that one part of the platoon would start hunting the other. Go counter-clockwise on a clover leaf and you run smack into the other squad. Try to link up with a friendly unit without warning them and you are virtually guaranteed casualties. Every man had to be warned: "Check fire, check fire, that's so and so coming in." Just leaving a column was dangerous. A platoon 30 yards off the line of march became invisible and transformed itself into suspicious movement.

When the company is on the move, most of the burden falls on the point platoon. It is acutely nerve-racking work. For everyone else, usually, it is just miserably hard work. All are oppressed by heat, bugs and leeches. Pack straps cut into shoulders which soon develop sores that do not heal. When the column stops, men flop down, resting on their packs, drink and pop salt tablets. Canteens are rapidly drained.

Around mid-day two NVA bodies, bloated and discolored, were

discovered and dutifully reported. Probably they were wounded during the air strike on the LZ and, unable to go any further, crawled a few feet off the trail to die. Maybe their friends just got tired of carrying them and dumped them. That explanation was more popular.

Late afternoon the company labored up a steep hill and when I arrived at the summit, I could see that company was already circling into its night perimeter. By nightfall Delta Company sat on the hill top, like a crown of thorns, dug in, claymores and trip flares out. We remained on that hill for three days, fussed over it, and made it home.

Holes: our lives now revolved around holes. Sandy soil lifted our spirits; rocks and roots and heavy clay, "bad digging," produced gloom and resentment. When there was time, as there was on this hill, men manicured holes, fussed over them, the way they used to wax cars. A good three man hole, deep, square, and camouflaged, is a thing of beauty. I took a picture of "a good position" and sent it to my wife. In a following letter she asked me why I was sending her pictures of holes. It is hard to explain.

That night an 18-year-old rifleman who had recently returned, much matured, from R and R in Bangkok came down with all the B movie symptoms of malaria—soaring fever, chills, delirium—and the medic sweated out the night with him, periodically shaking him out of his nightmares for fear he would give away our position. We requested medevac but the mission was refused; it was impossible we were told to get anyone out of our location at night. Medevac pulled him out at dawn. He returned several days later; the doctors said he had a kidney infection. One wonders.

I took a small patrol out the following morning, poked around for the better part of a day and found nothing but a few oddments of modern warfare, 20mm shell casings, the tail fin of a mortar round (one of ours) and no sign of the NVA.

All the same, we were virgin pure innocents in the jungle and that made for an eventful day. About two hours into the patrol we came upon an area of disturbed, rooted up soil. From about 100 yards away in scrubby undergrowth came a lot of rustling and scraping. I was instantly on the radio telling Bannerman that we had movement and giving him our location. To say that I was excited would be an understatement and Bannerman had to remind me to depress the push-to-talk button on the radio *before* I started to transmit because I was cutting off the first two or three words.

66

"Okay," soothed Bannerman, "we have your location, just check it out."

I did that but in dangerously complicated fashion, stationing people here, there, and everywhere as security and then sending one squad around the flank. It was a foolish thing to do but, in this instance, highly successful. After a tense five minutes, I heard a series of startled snorts followed by the clattering flight of hard little hooves. "Pigs!" bellowed Aguirre, "fucking pigs." Much better pigs than NVA but the resulting report to Bannerman was deflating.

After the pig episode, we worked our way cautiously down the side of the hill and onto the sandy valley floor. There we took a break only to be chased by leeches, dropping onto us from the trees and diligently inching toward us over the ground were dozens more. "Buggy whips," Aguirre called them because they would stretch themselves thin, twice their normal length, as they obscenely probed the air.

We were covered with them. We quickly retraced our steps, stopped, stripped and, puffing cigarettes, burned the little carnivorous worms off our necks, backs, arms, legs and genitals. The ancient Asian forest had imposed an inescapable atavism; we were as dependent on mutual grooming as a troop of monkeys.

Leeches: we hated them. You had to burn them off because if you pulled them—it's like pulling on a rubber band—the head stayed underneath the skin and caused a festering sore. For this reason the practice of splatting the bloated leeches on a man's back with the flat of your hand (true, they make a satisfying pop) soon grew tiresome. And, even if you burned them off, the anticoagulant secreted by the leech meant that the little puncture where the animal had inserted its head would continue to ooze blood for several minutes. Often you didn't feel them; they just gorged and dropped off leaving behind a trickle of blood. Nostrils, genitals and rectums they loved and we learned, after our medic received an urgent call from Apache's medic, that they sometimes wriggled up a man's urinary tract.

"Apache Two Six has a leech up his dick. He's in intense pain; anything I can do?"

"Can't he take a whiz?...over."

"Negative. We tried that; he can't stand it. I'm gonna medevac him. Can't you think of something?"

"Negative."

We kept our trousers bloused and squirted bug juice on our boots and around our waists. But when we took our boots off, on those nights when we could do that, a viscous clump of blood-swollen leeches would often fall to the ground.

Our company perimeter was totally covered by trees, some of them enormous, perhaps 100 feet high with huge flaring buttress roots. Beneath the trees the hill was relatively cool, especially in the evening, and mosquitoes were not much of a problem. But supplies could not be landed (although if need be C-rations and ammo could be tumbled through the canopy, and sick or injured men winched up to a hovering helicopter), and beneath the trees the mortar was useless. Or so we thought. That first night the mortar platoon set up in the center of the perimeter, gazing periodically up at the canopy which shut out the stars. Their annoyance grew all the next morning and finally, out of frustration, or perhaps for the hell of it, they fired a round right through the canopy. Bannerman's usual cigar-chewing serenity lapsed and he yelled at them in astonishment. "Hey! Christ, no more of that."

"No problem, sir," came the cheerful response. "It's on fuse delay."

Had it not been on that setting it would have exploded about 50 feet over our heads. The mortar platoon to a man was confident that there was no danger in this practice, in fact they had staked their lives on it, but no one else agreed with them.

A single huey, the first aircraft we had heard for two days, thumped in the distance gradually working its way toward our position. A smoke grenade was thrown, followed by a short wait while the smoke filtered up through the canopy. "I have red smoke," announced the pilot. We confirmed the color, a routine precaution. The helicopter hovered just outside the perimeter. A rope was tossed out and two engineers repelled down. The second man became inverted and then fell about ten feet into scrub bamboo. He was unhurt. A chainsaw, a can of gas, and several cases of TNT followed.

For the next few hours we were chased from one side of the perimeter to the other as huge trees came crashing down, pulling with them a frigate's rigging of vines and branches. The largest trees had to be blown down. The engineers would notch a great buttressed tree with their chainsaws, pack in TNT, insert a blasting cap attached to about 30 seconds of fuse, yell "Fire in the hole," and scamper to safety. Hands pressed to ears, mouth open, we would wait for the explosion.

68

One giant, more than five feet in diameter, required 45 pounds of TNT to bring down. After each explosion more light streamed in and bits of bark and leaves danced and glittered in the sun.

By the end of the second day the company perimeter had been transformed into a hot, dusty confusion. Equipment was lost, hooches flattened, fields of fire masked by fallen trees, and you couldn't walk ten feet without having to crawl over or under something. Splintered stumps oozed sap, sometimes dark red, and attracted swarms of insects. I wish we could have left that hill alone.

Two portholes had been opened to the sky, one more or less in the center of the perimeter allowing the mortar platoon to lob shells in all directions and one slightly outside the perimeter for resupply. Our hill was so steep that a log platform that jutted out from the hillside was built as a sort of helipad. It reminded me of those forlorn constructions that cargo cultists sometimes erect. Nor in our case did it serve any purpose much beyond the symbolic because the pilots do not trust it. (Another day of work with axe and machete was required to expand the LZ to a more agreeable size.)

Supplies were soon overhead. Smoke was popped and identified, followed by a demonstration of what the division considered routine flying. The pilot hovered briefly over the hole in the forest and then in a tornado of leaves dropped down through the canopy. He inched forward until the tip of one skid rested lightly on the platform and the huey's big sweeps were spinning beneath overhanging branches. A day's worth of C-rations was tossed to the ground, the ship gently rising and falling like a moored dingy, while the engineers, their work completed, gingerly mounted the platform to board the ship. They had to approach the huey from the rear because up slope the rotor blades were nipping the underbrush. With the door gunners craning their necks to see that the tail rotor was clear, the huey backed away from the platform and levitated to freedom. Nose slightly down, it picked up speed, banked, heeling over like a galleon, and swooped down the side of the hill. For a couple of minutes the characteristic "whop whop" of a huey's 50 foot rotors dominated the forest and then everything was quiet.

Hueys: there was very little in the First Cavalry that was not periodically suspended from the rotor blades of a huey and ultimately from the "Jesus nut" which holds those blades in place. Heavy cargos were lifted by other helicopters; the twin bladed chinook and the gigantic, mantis-like "flying crane" which can lift a 155 howitzer and its ammunition. For the infantry in the field this dependence was complete. Hueys brought you into danger and rescued you from it. Hueys brought food, clothes, ammunition, water, priests, mail, beer. Dead or alive the first part of your journey home would be aboard a huey.

The second day on that hill shells passed over our position just clearing the trees. A large shell even when well overhead makes an impressive noise; these sounded like box cars and had us scurrying around like mice. Fired on a flat trajectory (on the deck), the shells roared past us, just above the trees, but landed so far away we could not hear them explode. After about five minutes they stopped shooting, whoever they were, and Bannerman got on the radio to battalion. Battalion, after frantic inquiries, located the culprit, a South Vietnamese 155 battery, and notified them of our location. "It won't happen again."

The next day, at roughly the same time, the box cars came screeching over again. Livid, Bannerman was on the radio in an instant. "They're doing it again," he shrieked. "Stop them. The dumb fucks are doing it again." Again, after a few minutes, the shells stopped. "Not us," said the South Vietnamese the second time around and, in fact, we never found out for sure who it was.

First and Second platoons joined forces to patrol well away from the perimeter. Ogletree had point. The canopy shut out so much sunlight that even off trails we covered ground swiftly. It began as a relaxed and easy patrol during which we made a pleasant discovery. There are squirrels in Vietnam, big orangy squirrels that race through the underbrush like cats and disappear into the canopy. We also, for the first time, encountered a bamboo viper. After a shout and some furious slashing with a machete, the mangled corpse of a little emerald green serpent was held up for display. Bamboo vipers are very toxic and were unofficially defined as "two step snakes," meaning two steps and you're dead. (Immediate action? "Lean up against a tree and light up your last one.") And you usually did see them in clumps of bamboo...at eye level, but not until they moved. That no one was ever bitten was a surprise to us all. Sometimes after we killed a viper, a man would claim the corpse and skin it to make a helmet band. This became the height of fashion at company headquarters.

Ogletree called frequent breaks, to rest, and to listen, and seemed

70

to alter course on a whim, which made sense. It's hard to ambush someone who behaves as though he doesn't know where he's going. In other words, this was a routine "snoop and poop patrol," so called, I suppose, because there was ample time for both activities. Bannerman had merely told Ogletree to "head out about a click and check around."

So why Ogletree led us into a narrow little canyon was a mystery. And why I followed him is another. Aguirre took one look at it and radioed that he was going to take two squads along the rim for security, which, from where I was, looking up at sheer rock walls 50 feet high, seemed like a terrific idea. At least one of us was thinking.

A couple of months later a river must have roared through that little canyon but then the sandy canyon floor contained only a trickle of water linking waist deep pools. We were putting ourselves in jeopardy to investigate an NVA swimming hole. I kept thinking that Ogletree would give it up and turn around but we just kept strolling along, Aguirre fortunately keeping pace above us. "How far does this thing go?" In stunned exasperation, Two Six Mike dropped a very broad hint.

"Navaho Two Six, this is Two Six Mike . . . Didn't the Lone Ranger get his butt kicked in a place like this? Over."

"Affirmative."

After a hundred yards or so, Ogletree came to a break in the canyon walls and angled the patrol up and out of danger. It would be interesting to know Aguirre's thoughts as he stalked the rim above us. A central feature of his view of the world was that God had placed infantry lieutenants on earth as a special punishment.

The following day, a patrol into the same area saw a single NVA soldier (it's unlikely, of course, that he was alone) and after some disagreement as to who was going to get use of the M-14 sniper rifle, had managed to wing off a couple of shots before he disappeared. A few 105 rounds were dropped into the jungle but no one imagines that they could have had any effect beyond elevating NVA blood pressure.

Why those few rounds—or a few dozen rounds—would have had little effect became even more obvious as the company Charlie Alphaed out the following morning. Thumping along at 3,000 feet there was an uninterrupted jungle canopy beneath us. It was as though the Annamese Cordillera was the sea and we were divers. For vast stretches there was nowhere that even the smallest scout helicopter could land

and the First Cavalry's recon teams only gained entrance to the deep sea world beneath the canopy by ropes or wire ladders suspended from a hovering helicopter.

After only a few minutes, we were on the ground again. The platoon ahead of us had already pushed out a ragged perimeter but this was not to be our night position. Bannerman gave the order of march and the company moved out through heavy forest on a compass heading toward what showed on the map as a rugged, elongated hill some 700 meters high. After about three hours we broke into a small clearing—probably an old Montagnard field—perhaps 400 yards long and 200 yards wide. Looming over us was a high dragon tail ridge.

The clearing was splashed with the remains of a chinook; broken rotor blades, rumpled chunks of fuselage, a big dish-shaped aluminum object, and a wire ladder. How many on this disastrous mission survived? They all didn't. The forward part of the ship had broken off and lay in a ravine just outside of our perimeter: Four men, now just jumbled skeletons, were still in it. Nearby was a downed medevac ship. A flight helmet still attached to the radio lead was found inside. "Musta been a fast exit," someone said; but it was not funny. We took the helmet back with us. On it was the name Foster.

A huey landed bringing two engineers to deal with the 2.75 inch rockets attached to what was left of the chinook, and two men from graves registration. As we were digging in for the night the men from graves registration rooted through the cockpit and, after about a half an hour returned, bantering back and forth quite happily as they walked across the perimeter, with several sand bags full of bones (no more than a representative sample) and four sets of dog tags. They acted as though they didn't expect anyone to talk to them and no one did. The engineers, a dour, business-like pair, quickly rigged explosives to destroy the rockets, retreated to the clearing and without preliminaries blew the charge. Debris and black smoke leaped out of the ravine. "Ah Christ, shit" (several voices here); the explosion had released the smells of decomposition.

Another huey arrived with the all purpose U.S. Army restorative: hot food—powdered eggs, milk, coffee, carrot sticks and some sort of pudding. A chow line, a row of insulated food containers called mermite cans backed by GI servers, was set up and men began to file through. Everyone was wearing a helmet and had a rifle (not necessarily their own) slung on their shoulders, a ritual that First Sergeant Honeywell absolutely insisted upon. No one carried a mess kit. Incongruously, we ate off paper plates with plastic cutlery and there were even "Wash-n-Dry" napkins to clean our hands and faces. Someone, who had evidently run afoul of Sergeant Honeywell, worked on a trash pit.

Halfway through the meal movement was spotted high on the ridge above us. Men pointed, the mortar tube was swung around and a white phosphorous round fired. It landed short and slightly off line, but it was a very good first shot considering that the target was 800 or 1,000 yards away and high above us. Bannerman, who was going through the chow line, had also seen the movement and began to call out the adjustments to the mortar crew 75 feet away.

"Right 100; add 200."

And then to the server in front of him, "Eggs please."

The round lands.

"Right five zero; drop 100."

Bannerman held out his plate for carrot sticks and put a carton of milk in his pocket. The round landed.

"Repeat three rounds hotel echo" (high explosive).

To the last server — "What is that stuff?"

"Pudding, sir."

"O.K."

Thump, thump, thump — the rounds were quickly on the way and Bannerman eyed the results while spooning down his meal. The mortar crew looked over expectantly, one of them dangling an HE round by the tail fin. Bannerman, mouth full, shook his head. End of mission. We might need that round tonight.

It took Bannerman all of five minutes to finish his meal. He dumped his paper plate and plastic utensils into the trash pit, pulled a foil packet from his pocket, opened it and wiped his hands and face with the treated napkin. I walked over to the trash pit and Bannerman examined what I was about to throw away. "Don't you want your 'Wash-n-Dry'?" he asked.

"No," I said, "it's bad for my complexion." Bannerman pondered this possibility in silence and then turned to stare up at the ridge.

A huey landed to retrieve the mermite cans and then quickly flitted away into the dusk. Domesticity increased. Gear was stashed by positions and men took a few minutes to enjoy the pleasure of not having 60 pounds on their backs. Unlikely headgear materialized; a black beret with a Cav patch on it, a tan pork pie hat. Here and there men padded around in Ho Chi Minh's. Air mattresses were optimistically inflated and chunks of C-4 were fired up to brew a last cup of coffee. I settled in behind one of the chinook's rotor hubs. Night fell; it did not rain and I slept.

The following day I fouled up what should have been an easy patrol by getting us lost. It was Bannerman's patrol but I was navigating. After several hours of snooping around (we avoided the ridge that day) Bannerman said to head home. I should have just circled back on a course that would have cut our old trail and then paralleled it back to the perimeter (retracing your path is a good way to get ambushed). But I didn't. I thought I knew exactly where the perimeter was and headed for it on a bee line. We crashed through an old brittle fence constructed of twigs about as big around as the base of a man's thumb and into a dense thicket that had overgrown a Montagnard field. By the time we had cut our way through—it took us over an hour to go 200 yards—everyone was striped with leech bites and exhausted. Another hour passed before we got to where I thought the perimeter was and another hour before I realized that I wasn't even close to it. I set another course back towards the ridge figuring I couldn't miss that and finally, as it was beginning to grow dark, we hit the trail we had made early that morning as we left the perimeter; but from the opposite side. I had spiraled completely around the perimeter like a moth. Bannerman found the whole episode amusing and kept saying that I had been "temporarily disoriented." Everyone else said I was "fucking lost."

In the mountains, beneath the canopy, being uncertain of your position, or "temporarily disoriented," or "fucking lost," was routine. The established procedure if you were "temporarily disoriented" was to call in an artillery round (usually white phosphorous) on a set of map coordinates and then shoot a compass heading to the explosion. Estimate the range to the marking round and you had a direction and a distance from a fixed point on the map. Most of the time you asked for the round to be set to burst in the air so that there was a better chance of seeing it in heavy cover. But even if you could only hear the round it usually allowed you to get some idea of where you were. Bang! Get the direction, estimate the distance, check the map: "We gotta be right about fucking here." Sometimes, however, your calculations showed you to be halfway up the side of a hill when, in fact, you were

74

really down in the bottom of some rock strewn valley. Then you were "good and fucking lost."

Bannerman's successor had the disconcerting habit of calling marking rounds right on top of our estimated position on the assumption, I suppose, that given the terrain and the maps we couldn't possibly be exactly where we thought we were. But sometimes we were where we thought we were and, Bang!, a WP round would crack off two or three hundred yards over our heads.

Some weeks later, when the company was toiling up the side of an open grassy valley we got word that we were getting a special treat — ice cream. We couldn't tell Arizona Six to shove his 15 gallons of melted ice cream and so for longer than we could afford the company sat and spooned down lukewarm ice cream from little styrofoam bowls. The CO decided that he would use this time to confirm our position and called for a high streamer smoke round. We were standing in a little expectant huddle when the round came screeching up the valley at about eye level. The smoke canisters popped out in front of our noses, skimmed over a low rise and bounded along like cannonballs.

"Those artillery assholes always shoot things on the deck," scowled the CO, "but I think we're about where we thought we were."

Bannerman took out another large patrol the following morning, both the First and Second platoons combined, and again I had the lead platoon. Under high, cloudless sky, we moved quickly into the tree line and then turned toward the ridge. It was very hot and several point men were exhausted as the column hacked and shoved through tangled, bug-ridden vegetation. Wait-a-bit vines, nature's answer to the number 12 fishhook, ripped our clothing, leaving legs bare and deeply scratched. From time to time, Bannerman would cluck encouragingly over the radio: "We're not in a race, just keep them moving. . . Roger this heading, continue to march."

In front of the ridge, down by the very tip of the dragon's tail, was a shallow ravine. To me it could have been the Rhine River. I fussed around, putting out an M-60 for security and looked for a better place to cross; but, in the end we just slid down into the ravine on our butts and clawed up the other side.

The ridge was another world, topped by enormous trees that seemed to allow only a sparse almost lacy undergrowth. It was cooler.

A well-traveled trail ran along the top of the ridge and the men in front of me automatically crouched, spread out and stalked forward.

We were inside the bunker complex before we realized it. Constructed low to the ground and carefully masked by vegetation, we could, at first, barely make the bunkers out from a distance of ten feet. Without a word from me, two men slipped up to the nearest bunkers and tossed in grenades. Each time there was a muffled boom and dust flew from the top of the bunker. Even though everyone knew that had the complex been occupied we would never have made it across the ravine, the precaution of fragging bunkers was repeated six or seven times. I joined into this business and was politely warned that sometimes NVA bunkers had loop holes out of which grenade fragments flew. A few men dealt with this hazard by tossing a frag into the bunker and then immediately jumping on the roof, which seemed a little adventurous. "It's okay," I was told, "as long as it ain't an old bunker." These bunkers looked new.

The rest of the patrol joined us on the ridge and the task of checking out each bunker proceeded; but without the use of grenades. We couldn't spare that many. "There must be thirty bunkers up here," whistled Bannerman. I would have guessed more but oddly enough I don't recall that anyone got around to actually counting them. Perhaps we didn't think of that because we thought in terms of units; this had to be at least a battalion-sized base camp and it wasn't very old.

The bunkers straddled the ridge in a very elongated oval perhaps 300 yards long. In the center was a large command bunker that was fronted by a square pit about four feet deep and ten feet on a side. This was covered by a thatched roof. It looked, and was, cool, dry and comfortable. Each bunker, usual size about eight by ten feet, was very solidly constructed of logs covered with a foot or more of packed earth. Only a direct hit from a 105 or 155 would have done any damage and a direct hit was a virtual impossibility. Most of the trees were between two and three feet in diameter and layered canopy above us soared to over 100 feet. Dominating everything was a stupendous strangler fig almost 15 feet in diameter which had been used as a lookout. Notches and hand holds had been cut into its trunk. Still, enough light peeked in to support smaller trees. A web of paths connected the bunkers together and along each path from a height of six feet down to the ground the vegetation had been carefully trimmed back. No other vegetation had been touched — none; and all of the hundreds of logs used to construct the bunkers had been cut and carried in from some distance off the ridge. The complex was absolutely invisible from the air.

It was all but invisible from the ground. I walked back down the path leading into the bunker complex; once outside I turned and looked. From 50 feet away, even when I knew it was there, it was hard to see. From 50 yards away the forest had totally closed in; I stared but could not make out a single bunker. In front of the formidable perimeter bunkers the NVA had not so much as cleared fields of fire as landscaped them, clipping a few branches low to the ground, bending saplings, or just picking off a few leaves; it was nature subtly altered, like a Taoist garden. This whole crafted enterprise was augmented by foxholes dug between the buttress roots of the larger trees. A foot above each foxhole a small loop hole, just barely big enough to sight and shoot through, penetrated the flaring root. Any unit trying to fight its way onto the ridge would have been met by a storm of ankle high grazing fire. The NVA liked to do that I had been told. "The shit comes at you four inches off the ground; there's no place to hide."

Arizona Six was advised of what we had found and dispatched more supplies for the engineers. While we were waiting, Bannerman sent out a small patrol to search further up the ridge and we continued our inspection of the bunker complex. The most amazing thing about it, perhaps, was the most obvious. It was clean: no paper, no food remains, no discarded equipment—nothing. The only thing we found was a small iron pot that had been jammed in the crotch of a tree a little outside the perimeter. At one point, I came upon a low bunker that had a small hole in the roof; something new and sinister. Without giving it much thought I ordered it fragged and fell under Sabalch's perplexed gaze.

"Excuse me, sir, but that's where they go number two."

After about an hour, a squad leader from the Second Platoon, the man who had taken the patrol up the ridge, reported to Bannerman ostentatiously fanning himself with a palm frond fan that he had picked up along the trail. We examined it. Still green and supple, it had just been made.

A huey whopped into earshot (the doppler effect of the craft's big sweeps betraying changes in course) and had to be coached to a point where the pilot could see our smoke drifting above the trees. The craft hovered overhead at tree top height, chasing yellow smoke back down through the canopy, and 22 cases of TNT and several rolls of det-cord came crashing through the branches.

The engineers quickly set about blasting their way down the ridge. First all that TNT and det-cord was collected and carried to a central stash in the middle of the complex and then some of it moved further up the ridge. The easiest way of carrying the cumbersome cases of TNT was balanced on one shoulder with the strange effect that the bunker complex soon began to resemble a gigantic colony of leaf cutter ants. It took 20 to 25 pounds of TNT to destroy each bunker. Charges would be rigged in several bunkers, linked by det-cord and then blown simultaneously. I had assumed that such a large amount of explosive would have blown those bunkers sky high but they were so well constructed that it only served to cave in the roof.

A grave was discovered, or at least what looked like a grave. At one end of a low mound of earth was a flattened metal sheet, part of an ammunition container probably, with nail holes outlining what we thought were two names. Battalion was notified of this and we were ordered to "make sure."

Who was to make sure? Naturally it was the new platoon leader. Judging from Bannerman's reaction, which was amusement, I must have started wide-eyed at this news.

"Look," said Bannerman around his cigar, "this is standard stuff. Battalion wants to know if there's really a dead gook in there and they wanna know what killed him. If he's missing parts, it's artillery; that's what we usually say."

I gave the order to one of the squad leaders and then tried to find something else that required my attention. But after a few minutes I joined the men at the grave (any doubts about that had been fleeting) and took a turn scraping at the loose lateritic soil. The pick end of the entrenching tool I was using caught in something; I wrenched it free and pulled up some scraps of thin dark plastic, a "gook poncho." For 20 minutes we prowled around the grave like crows at a road kill, darting in one at a time to dig for as long as we could hold our breath. The stench crept over the ridge. Beneath the plastic we found a corpse, the consistency of cold stew, encased in a rotting green cotton uniform. Grey, greasy rib bones protruded from where I had gotten the entrenching tool caught. The man was wearing a brown plastic belt with a starred buckle. "Gook NCO," someone said. Everyone gathered around to look.

"All right, fill it in, cover him up."

I retreated a little down the ridge to where we had been taking turns vomiting and then reported to Bannerman. "There's a guy in there with a star on his buckle. He's got two arms, two legs, and a head." I didn't have to tell him that the body was half decomposed. Bannerman nodded and told his RTO to call battalion. "By the way," cooed Bannerman, "you're looking a tad peaked," and beaming like an evangelist, he handed me a little blue and white packet—a "Wash-n-Dry."

"I smell gooks," bellowed Aguirre, but he wasn't referring to the man in the grave. He had decided that there was something further down the ridge and wanted permission to investigate. Taking about ten men with us we followed the trail, Aguirre in the lead, nose high and sniffing. As with most men in the field, Aguirre smoked three packs of cigarettes a day and probably couldn't have smelled a circus. But his field instincts were uncanny; that was what he was trying to tell me with this performance. Then, again, maybe he could smell gooks because after only a few minutes we came upon a cache of 24 82mm mortar rounds.

The mortar rounds, still in their wooden cases, were stashed in a pit, and protected by a thatched roof. A platform about a foot off the bottom of the pit kept the rounds dry. After checking for booby traps, a case was tossed out and opened. The rounds, painted brown, were unusually long and resembled a two quart thermos with a tail fin; an odd type. We were told that battalion wanted a few specimens for examination. One of the engineers arrived, two men in tow, each with a case of TNT over his shoulder. Both cases were placed directly on top of the cache and wired for detonation. Throughout this entire process, leeches dripped steadily from the trees.

Along with the engineer I crouched behind a stream bank while the charge was blown with a tremendous reverberating crash. The engineer didn't even bother to inspect the results and headed back to the ridge. Curious, I stayed behind. The pit looked as though it had been scrubbed clean by a German housefrau. The thatch roof, frame and all, had, of course, disappeared and the trees were stripped of leaves and leeches for a radius of 50 feet. And, drifting everywhere were bits of charred paper, burned black and all of about the same size. I kept this mystery to myself.

It was solved a few weeks later; the mortar rounds, or at any rate,

79

some of them, had contained propaganda leaflets aimed at black soldiers. They all had a picture of a black infantryman crawling through rice paddy crud. "Why fight for a country that exploits you?" was the message. Good question. I was told that the intelligence types believe that the leaflets were the result of a visit by black activists to North Vietnam. Their reason for believing this? The message on the leaflets is written in perfect English. Obviously, no North Vietnamese could do that.

After some hesitation, which was unforgivable, I handed out all the samples I had been given to the platoon. So the leaflets were delivered, but not by the route that the NVA had anticipated, and if they had any impact on morale I saw no sign of it. The leaflets may have made a positive contribution since our supply of C-ration "shit paper" fell very short of demand. It struck me at the time that the manufacture of propaganda leaflets of a size and texture suitable for use as toilet tissue was psychologically unsound. Our propaganda leaflets were identical to theirs, except that they were printed in several colors, and we all assumed that they served an identical purpose.

I could not understand why all this effort was lavished on the destruction of bunkers that would in very little time rot and become untenable. And, if we were trying to find the NVA, why discourage their return to a location that we had pinpointed? It was better to blow the trees and open the bunker complex to the sky, and anyone occupying it to observation. Such reasoning, and my timidity, brought that about.

Late that afternoon it was decided that one platoon would return to our perimeter and the other would remain behind just outside the bunker complex as security while the engineers completed their work. I was to stay behind with the engineers. But in the natural military order of events, one platoon simply followed the other all the way back to base. I was left on the bunker complex with my RTO, two unhappy engineers, armed only with .45s, and, I counted them, 12 cases of TNT. I ordered most of the TNT stacked between the enormous buttresses of the lookout tree. The remaining TNT went into nearby bunkers and everything was rigged to go at once. I stood guard with my RTO while the engineers, working like demons, constructed the cat's cradle of det-cord required to link the charges. They were just as fearful as I of being pinned down by a sniper next to a large pile of explosives.

The job was completed in an hour, maybe less, but it was already getting dark as we pulled down off the ridge playing out the last spool of det-cord behind us. When we had reached the end of the det-cord (I think there is 1,000 feet on a spool) one of the engineers attached a blasting cap and a short fuse. Then, before I could report to Bannerman, he applied his Zippo. We sprinted another 100 feet further up the trail before an enormous black cloud of HE smoke gouted above the ridge in the single most stupendous explosion I have ever experienced. The concussion clouded the air around us, our ears rang and we stared goggle-eyed at the huge column of smoke, burned leaves, and tumbling branches rising above us.

Bannerman was on the radio within seconds demanding to know why I didn't advise him before I blew "the whole goddamn ridge. What the hell is going on?" His voice sounded tinny and distant, as though he had been inhaling helium. I wanted to check the ridge, but there wasn't time if we were going to get back to the perimeter before it was completely dark. Bannerman was still in a stew when we returned, and I suspect he thought we had gone up in the explosion. "Jesus," he said, "we could feel that thing go from here."

CHAPTER 5

"To all Navajo stations: welcome to the Giant sump."
— *Tex, July 1, 1968*

I don't know whether Aguirre's nose for NVA munitions would have produced more discoveries because the following day the company was lifted to a position near a small firebase called LZ Mooney. We were told that tomorrow was Ho Chi Minh's birthday and that Mooney, by way of celebration, would be attacked.

LZ Mooney was one of several small firebases that the division had established in the mountains and it was distinguished only by the persistent rumor that it was constructed on a ridge that did not appear on any of our maps.

The company landed in an open field about two miles from Mooney and set up a night perimeter. I was ordered to take First Platoon onto a ridge just across from Mooney and set up for the night. Bannerman indicated on the funny papers just where he wanted us to be. "There's an old perimeter there," he said, "you can't miss it."

It was true, you couldn't miss it, unless you fell down the side of the ridge. High and narrow and jutted with rock outcroppings, the ridge stretched out from the hill on which the company perimeter was located and after an hour or so of pushing through brown, half defoliated forest, we broke into a small open area that must have had a hundred foxholes dug into it. Repeated occupations, first by the NVA and then by us, had left a confused pattern of defensive positions to which we added. No one, of course, would use an old foxhole. I examined an NVA spider hole that had been dug between two root buttresses. It was about 15 inches in diameter, 5 feet deep, and the walls were carefully shaved as though by an archaeologist. "I don't know how they

83

do that," mused the man beside me, "a gook entrenching tool is bullshit." The contrast with the hastily dug American three-man positions was stark.

Across a cratered valley was a shantytown of bunkers that stretched along a high, humpbacked ridge. This was LZ Mooney. Roughly in the middle, on the flattest part of the ridge, a battery of 105s was banging out fire missions. Around Mooney's outer edge, barbed wire had captured windblown trash and it looked from a distance like the firebase was surrounded by an untidy clothesline. That afternoon, a thunderstorm swept over the ridge and I watched two men pick their way down to the clothesline to disconnect the fuses on the perimeter claymores. Since they were electrically detonated, lightning sometimes set them off. The men walked from mine to mine pulling fuses like gardeners pulling weeds. As they approached one mine, a bolt of lightning flickered out and exploded it. The black HE smoke rapidly blew away revealing one man lying facedown and the other sitting. Other men ran frantically to their aid and carried them up the hill.

I had been advised ("be advised") that if we were about to be overrun our position provided an "opportunity" to use direct fire from Mooney's artillery. "*If you have to,*" counseled Bannerman, "call it in right on top of your perimeter. They can just bore sight. You know how those Red Leg fuckers love that." I shared this information with the platoon and everyone dug in very deeply.

Evidently Arizona Six was convinced that there would be an attack somewhere around Mooney because late that afternoon battalion called us directly wanting to know if there was anything that we needed. "Claymores," said Aguirre, "we need claymores." About an hour later, a huey hopped over from Mooney and dropped off two cases of claymore mines which were received with undisguised joy. You learn something every day. Before I realized what was going on, the squad leaders had pounced on this windfall and scavenged the one pound blocks of C-4 from several claymores. I soon put a stop to that, but I've always suspected that a few of our claymores were set out empty. Even so, by nightfall we had so many wires running out of our little perimeter that some of the guard positions could have used a switchboard. And, for the first and last time, I set out booby traps—hand grenades rigged to trip wires. This was a practice that the division frowned on (it often backfires) but which the battalion, nevertheless, sometimes employed. A week before, C Company had set a similar

84

"dirty trick device" and had been rewarded with an AK-47, a pack, and a blood trail.

We waited out a tense night within our explosive little fortress but Ho Chi Minh's birthday went uncelebrated, at least locally. We rejoined the company in the morning and breakfasted on C-rations. A sandbag command bunker built the evening before now served as a trash container and was burning, the green plastic sandbags giving off ropy coils of black smoke. Under the glare of the first sergeant, all unopened cans of C-rations were punctured before they went into the fire because the NVA would frequently root through our trash for food. A good sign we thought; if they were down to eating B-3 units, which made up a large portion of what we threw away, they must really be hurting. The other reason for puncturing the cans was deeply personal. Over the course of many years of field soldiering, the first sergeant had come to seriously regard an unopened can of C-rations as a form of submunitions; especially the little flat can of peanut butter which, if tossed unopened into a fire, would explode with a loud pop and splatter everyone within ten feet with blistering hot peanut butter. He called them peanut butter grenades: "M-26 Ps, grenade, fragmentation, peanut butter." They symbolized to the first sergeant an undisciplined world, and then he would have a "case of the ass."

The trail to Mooney was very steep and passed through an all but impenetrable second growth of bamboo and hardwood. As we approached Mooney, which was just beyond the highest point of the ridge, the trail crossed a field of command detonated mines: clusters of 105 shells still in their shipping containers, claymores by the dozen, and a 55 gallon drum of jellied gasoline to which phosphorous grenades had been lashed with det-cord. Three rows of concertina sprawled across this very dangerous junk yard.

A tangle of wires connected the mines to a listening post (LP) located no more than 50 yards from the napalm. "Crispy critters," said the man behind me as we passed by this set up. Other wires, including the wire attached to the barrel of napalm, led directly to the LZ command post on the assumption that the men manning the LP would not themselves choose suicide if there was an attack. I tried to imagine, and later learned, what a night on that position would be like during an electrical storm.

The engineers had scalped the ridge on which Mooney was situated and done a thorough job of surrounding the perimeter with concertina, tangle foot (strands of barbed wire set about ankle high), and trip flares. But Mooney's defensive positions were short-term rentals and looked it. Each of the four rifle companies in the battalion would spend a few days on perimeter defense and then return to the field. Preceding companies had little reason and no motivation to maintain, still less to improve, the bunkers and we complained mightily about the crap they had left behind. Midway through our first stint at Mooney, I ordered the bunker I was in deepened only to discover that we had been treading on a hand grenade and an M-72 rocket launcher for days.

Half of Mooney's inhabitants were field soldiers, used to moving every day, or every second or third day, and leaving their litter behind them. Put them in one place for a week at the very tip of a 10,000 mile long supply line and the remarkable amount of trash that the US Army can produce accumulated in heaps. Mostly it consisted of containers, the real stuff of industrial society; containers of paper, wood, plastic or metal which ended up in Mooney's smoldering trash pile. The artillery battery had its own dump, one that catered to the specialized junk that a battery of big guns will produce — ammo crates, plastic, the elaborate metal boxes that fuses are shipped in, and so forth. Daily, hundreds of excess powder bags were burned in ferocious fires that left everything covered with a chalky grey residue and manufactured the illusion that a slag heap was spilling out from Mooney's perimeter.

I think it was Tex, the company commander's steadfast RTO, who first dubbed Mooney the "Giant Sump." The name stuck. Field soldiers meant field sanitation. More to the point it meant the "green latrine." In the field that meant that you moved a little outside the perimeter, dug a "cat hole," and relieved yourself. Usually, the cat hole was dispensed with. At Mooney it was often the same except that you couldn't leave the perimeter.

There was one Victorian concession to hygiene in the form of the "E. Hemingway Grace under Pressure Memorial Latrine" (as proclaimed by its most memorable grafitto) which was an elaborate two-holer with a screen door that served to trap flies. To me, since it was in my sector of the perimeter, it was a constant headache. Infantrymen I soon learned, and could have guessed on my own, do not feel that they should be required by the army to risk their lives and also burn shit. I got tired of ordering that the barrels of shit be burned, "definitely, this fucking afternoon," and then discovering that they had not; so I

86

scavenged an armload of unused powder bags from the artillery and trailed by several curious men approached the latrine. The barrels were pulled out, a powder bag placed in each barrel and ignited. As one bag burned down we tossed in more; then a lot more. A plume of grey smoke rose to the sky, the barrels glowed red, and the shit was consumed in short order; also part of the latrine, before we could put it out. I considered the problem solved but Mooney's more permanent residents were angered. I had severed a link with civilization.

Campaigns against litter and garbage were frequent and largely futile. The biggest problem was that everything not staked down was scattered by incoming helicopters and those men living along the flight path soon gave up on their hooches. Rats prowled around at night and from time to time woke us up by running over us. But despite these intrusions we coexisted: we didn't shoot at the rats and they did not bite us, or at least I never heard of anyone being bitten.

The thing that produced the greatest misery at Mooney was the guns. We grew to hate them. The 105s, especially on a light powder charge, were not bad. There would be a sharp bang and then the soft duck pinion whistle of an outgoing round which was no more disturbing to us than a police siren to a resident of Manhattan. But the 155s were different. These arrived majestically one day by "flying crane," a huge helicopter with a hurricane rotor wash that sucked letters, maps, T-shirts and poncho liners out of our bunkers and turned hooches into flapping rags.

To the infantry living in front of the artillery battery, the report of a 155 on heavy charge (charge four—four bags of powder) was genuinely punishing. The concussion was like a blow and seemed to bounce you right off the ground; the noise unbelievable. We would wait within our bunkers, hunched down, mouth open, hands to ears for the fire mission to end. After several days of this, men began to display a characteristic reflex. At the sound of an unexpected outgoing round, necks would cord and jaws snap shut with tooth-cracking violence. By the end of our second stay at Mooney this reaction was nearly universal and would punctuate our attempts at conversation. You would be standing in a group talking; Ka-Blam! out would go a fire mission and the next thing you knew everyone was snapping away like crocodiles.

The division lived within the protective embrace of its artillery. Each firebase was supported by other firebases—often several firebases—and each base was ringed by defensive targets. Response to any unidentified movement was all but immediate and very impressive. The second night at Mooney one of my squad leaders urgently reported movement; he was obviously convinced that there was somebody out there. I was far from convinced but since it was one of the areas where Mooney might plausibly be attacked I reported it to the company commander. I did not request a fire mission but got one anyway. Minutes after and without warning, four 155 rounds came roaring down to impact in shattering fireballs about 50 yards outside the wire. I was stunned.

"How was that?" came Tex's call over the radio. I can't believe my response was very useful. Four more rounds probed into the darkness and the mission ended. There was no more movement that night.

In the mountains away from any friendly population, the division destroyed anyone out of position and everyone knew that a patrol or ambush jesuitically reporting its location was committing a dangerous folly. If detected out of position, you would very likely be killed before you could identify yourself.

The battalion regarded passwords as a useless affectation. We never used them. If you wandered out of the perimeter at night, you would be engaged without the slightest hesitation by the first guard position that heard you. "Those guys'll whiz a frag past your ear in a second," was the way it was put to me. The most reliably dangerous part of any patrol night or day, but especially at night, came when you entered the perimeter. At night you *had* to come in at the point where you left the perimeter and you *had* to establish radio contact first.

There was always the danger that someone on guard would fall asleep. I do not know that this happened at Mooney but in the field, as I learned that first night at the bridge, it did sometimes happen. One of the dangers associated with this—the principle danger is obvious—was that the dozing guard would be startled by the man relieving him and open fire. Only an idiot would deliberately try to catch a guard sleeping. One night the perimeter was awakened by a series of unearthly howls followed by desperate, pleading shouts.

"Don't fire! Check fire! Oh please Jesus!"

When I got to the position, Palovick, second squad leader, was still curled in a ball ten feet in front of the muzzle of an M-60. Half asleep the gunner had somehow faced his weapon *in* toward the perimeter and it was then that his squad leader had tried to relieve him. For fully ten seconds the guard had yelled in terror and jerked spasmodically on the bolt of his M-60 while Sergeant Palovick begged for his life.

It was during our first stay at Mooney that Ogletree was reassigned to the rear. He was overdue and for several weeks had been suffering from jungle rot which he showed to me by way of explanation. He evidently felt badly about leaving the field. All up and down his back were brown raisin-like growths of fungus.

The company had an assortment of skin problems most of which were called jungle rot. By far the most common problem came from sores that refused to heal; a lot of men had those especially where their pack straps had cut into their shoulders. About the only thing that was not called jungle rot was ringworm which the division did not regard as much of a problem because the men who had it could still function.

Mild forms of dysentery, as nearly as I could tell, were officially defined as a recreational activity and malaria was kept under control by the pills that were issued by the medic, who made sure that everyone, myself included, swallowed what he had given you, especially the big yellow pill. It was like taking communion. Anyone going on R and R was admonished to "take their pills" and usually did. In the evenings there would be a call for "malaria control" and we would roll down and button up our sleeves to cut down on mosquito bites. Still, now and again men ran very high fevers, due to malaria we supposed.

Taken together, medevacs for illness, broken bones and wounds probably did not make up a third of those required for heat exhaustion which on really hot days was accepted as a matter of ordinary operational routine. One blazing hot morning—we never knew, of course, what the temperature was and were probably better off not knowing—someone asked Hardoy who was going to take point that day.

"Medevac," said Hardoy, "fucking medevac."

He was right. Three times that day, the Dust Off chopper hovered over the column and winched kitten-weak, puking men up through the canopy on a gadget identified with what may have been Freudian insight as a "jungle penetrator." A jungle penetrator is nothing more than a collapsible seat folded up inside a canvas case, but it has undoubtedly saved many lives. Sometimes when you unzipped the case, comic books, girlie magazines, and paperback novels (called "fuck books" in the army) would spill out, a note would say, courtesy of this or that medevac unit.

After Ogletree left, I took over the Second Platoon— reluctantly.

First Platoon was home. Goodbyes were perfunctory because platoon leaders come and go. Walking over to Second Platoon I was struck by how narrow my perspective had become. Most of the men in the Second Platoon I had never met. I didn't even know who my squad leaders were. My perspective had become platoon and company and extended no further. Contact with the other companies of the battalion was minimal and, except for the 2nd of the 12th, all other battalions as far as I was concerned existed only in the realm of myth. I knew nothing whatsoever of what the rest of the division was doing and had not seen a newspaper in over a month.

I dropped my pack at what looked like platoon headquarters and announced that I was taking Ogletree's place. If this generated any surprise or interest it was not visible to me. I met with my platoon sergeant, a buck sergeant in his late twenties, and the three squad leaders, none of whom had been in the army for more than two years. On the other hand, they had all been in the field for several months and that was by far the most important statistic. Everyone looked very tired.

The section of Mooney's perimeter guarded by the Second Platoon was next to the artillery dump, which was a defensive liability, and just under the flight path of most incoming helicopters. Men were continually restoring flattened hooches and chasing down items of equipment. Worst of all, it was very close to Mooney's guns.

Platoon headquarters, located next to the slag heap, was a large box constructed of dirt-filled ammo crates. It masqueraded as a bunker but in fact you could see light through the walls. Second Platoon tied in vaguely with Echo Company, the battalion recon unit, on our left flank and that too was no source of comfort. When Echo Company was in the field, as it usually was, their sector was thinly held by men who rarely left their bunkers—day or night—and if they maintained any guard positions at night as far as I could tell they were largely fictional. Hourly requests for sit reps were, I suspected, answered from inside their bunkers. In short, I came to realize that all the sins of LZ Mooney had been visited upon Second Platoon. No wonder they looked tired.

But it must be admitted that LZ Mooney offered a number of diversions and minor delights. First on the list was a change of clothes. Each platoon received two duffel bags of clean jungle fatigues which everyone searched through for something approximating their size. Our old field clothes were stuffed into those same duffel bags to be taken back to Juliet to be washed. I would guess that a new pair of jungle fatigues went through no more than two or three such cycles before they became too ripped or rotted to be usable.

"You don't take no baths in the field." We did of course; but rarely, and only after putting out security. Even then it was a bad practice. The only safe method of bathing was to wait for a heavy downpour—never a long wait—strip and lather up. Mooney was ideally suited for this; we called it the "rain dance." It wasn't as much fun as gamboling around in a stream but far safer. Both sides regarded likely swimming holes as prime ambush sites.

Beer was delivered every few days, as always in duffel bags, and paid for by money collected by the platoon sergeant. The beer ration was never more than two cans apiece, although this was subject to increment through negotiation, and never in any other form than Ballentine Ale. The beer was warm but still contributed to pleasant nights of bunker-top conversation beneath incredibly bright skies. Often these conversations would last well into the second or third watch before people drifted back to their positions and to bed. I cannot remember what we talked about.

Sometimes at night the sky would begin to emit incandescent flashes far off to the west toward Laos. Then would come the dull, distant thud of bombs. In the field, beneath the canopy, we would only hear the bombs but on Mooney it would seem that the entire horizon was flickering as strings of bombs marched across the forest. It was a powerful, unnatural thing to see as though part of a dire, unexplained medieval sky.

Father Grayson, a pleasant, dark-haired man in his early thirties, held mass at Mooney on a couple of occasions. I did not attend these services but once overheard Father Grayson state that it was okay to kill the enemy, "but not with hatred in your heart." He did not explain how that worked in practice. When he could, he also visited Delta Company in the field where he would amble around the perimeter, handing out toothbrushes, shaving cream and stationery. Father (and Captain) Grayson's indifference to military rank bordered on the absolute. On one memorable visit, he was approached a little too obsequiously by Home, a product of the Detroit ghetto and a man who made no effort to dispel the rumor that he had done some hard time. "You've got some act," said the good Father, fixing Home with a shining smile, "but you can blow that jive smoke right out your ass." I believe that Home was impressed.

LZ Mooney had an air show but it was not spectacular. Well to our north was a high hill that had long before been blasted bald and brown. Every so often (there seemed to be no pattern or urgency to this) two phantom jets would show up and methodically bomb it. One phantom would orbit down, drop a bomb, and curve back into the sky. The other phantom would do the same. When they were out of bombs, they would swoop down one last time in a shallow dive with their 20mm cannons growling. Then the phantoms would go home. No one from the captain on down had any idea why that hill was being gradually reduced to a pile of sand and, since it was out of our area of operations, no one cared.

Perimeter duty offered an occasional chance to get back to Evans or to visit friends or relatives elsewhere within the division. Steve Jerome, my RTO, celebrated his eighteenth birthday by visiting his uncle who was on a neighboring LZ. Steve had already been in the field for four months and bore no malice towards the imbecile who had talked him into volunteering for Vietnam (he need not have gone until he was 18. Steve was from Oklahoma and talked of tractor pulls and his mother. His father he never mentioned. I gather he had enlisted on his seventeenth birthday. He seldom received any mail.

Most of the men in my platoon were not much older than Steve and there were times when I was the oldest (I was 24) and had been in the army the longest — a little over two years. Instant officers, instant NCOs, instant riflemen: whole units within the First Cavalry were monuments to on-the-job-training.

It was during this interval that I was sent to Camp Evans along with Hardoy to attend a lecture on NVA sapper tactics given by two young ARVN officers from the First ARVN Division. The lecture was held *outside* the greenline in the division training area and was largely incomprehensible because the lecturer spoke almost no English. One phrase was repeated again and again and I came to understand it as (I can't reproduce the accent): "Firepower of the First ARVN Division." There would be an anecdote, I gathered, followed by "firepower of the First ARVN Division;" something, something, something, "firepower of the First ARVN Division." It went on like that, in the blazing sun, for what seemed like a very long time. Eventually, the lecturer's assistant wrote something in English on the blackboard: "Blooming Flower." And the lecture continued except that a pitched, clipped-sounding word kept appearing, something like "tictics." Then followed

a diagram which rendered the lecture partially comprehensible. "Tictics?" . . . tactics, of course, "Blooming Flower Tactics." NVA sappers
would penetrate the perimeter at several points, move to a prearranged
part of the LZ, drop back and begin to expand several footholds within
the perimeter causing, in an especially Asian metaphor, the petals of
the flower to bloom. Defense? Don't let NVA sappers inside your
perimeter. Hardoy complained of a headache.

It took little imagination to appreciate the chaos and carnage that
took place when an LZ was overrun. Associated tales were gruesome;
it was said that when LZ Carrol, a base to the north of us, was overrun a satchel charge changed hands several times before it finally
exploded—inside the bunker. This prospect terrified me, and I would
not sleep in a deep bunker. I had no intention of waiting in the dark
pit for the arrival of a 15-pound charge of TNT.

Although the visit to Evans had taught us nothing it was worth
it. We enjoyed an enormous hot lunch of chili and rice, and I suspect
that was Bannerman's reason for sending us. Retaining our lunch proved
difficult on the flight back to Mooney. Twice on the return flight the
huey we were riding in was vectored to a lower altitude to avoid artillery
strikes and each time the procedure was the same. Without warning,
the pilot would flatten out the pitch allowing the ship to drop like a
safe. Then, after finally leveling off, the pilot swiveled his head around
and gave us a warm smile.

Mooney was in a dither when we returned; a general was arriving
in two days. A thorough police was ordered and the trash heap began
to burn, occasionally cooking off rounds. We gave it a wide berth
because some weeks before "a fat artillery sergeant" had been severely
wounded when an M-79 shell had exploded. A certain amount of what
passes for landscaping in the military was accomplished. Shell casings
were scavenged from the artillery battery and pounded into the ground
to outline walkways that no one used. Sergeant Honeywell pronounced
it, "outfuckingstanding." The first sergeant also provided stern advice
on how to talk to the general who had expressed his desire to mingle
with the hoi polloi and learn of their problems. "Stand at attention,"
said Honeywell (some of the men had been in the field so long they
might have forgotten to do that), "and tell the truth. But I don't want
to hear minor bullshit complaints. . . like maybe your carrot sticks ain't
crisp."

I used C-ration cardboard to set up range cards for each bunker diagramming in Fort Benning style how each weapon was to be used. Just in case the general should ask someone about the cards I went over the symbols with each squad leader. They listened to me patiently with glazed eyes. Each man knew his sector better than I did and would no sooner have relied on such cryptics than the Egyptian Book of the Dead.

"What's that?" said Bannerman when he walked through our area to see how things were shaping up. I explained that it was a range card. "I know *that*," said Bannerman, "but what's it *for*? Awright, never mind, maybe he'll buy it. And for God's sake, don't forget to call attention when the general comes through."

The general and his entourage arrived the next day around noon, never left the vicinity of TOC, dined on steak (we did not), never talked to anyone below the rank of captain and departed an hour later.

Delta Company's Chieu Hoi, Van, whom I got to know while at Mooney, was a shy unassuming boy who spoke enough English to give the impression that he sometimes understood what you were saying. He claimed to have been kidnapped by the VC and forced to serve as a medic. I believe that to be true. Chieu Hois, men who came in under the government's "open arms" program, were routinely assigned to American units as scouts and interpreters. In the villages, Van had walked point because he knew them as well as the VC—he had been VC. Van hated the mountains but he would take point if Ogletree, or later, Hardoy asked him, which wasn't often. Gradually Van slipped into the role of company mascot. We liked having him around.

Now and again Van would go back to his village to visit his mother and, we all supposed, his girlfriend. When he returned, he would be teased.

"You look tired, Van—no sleep? How's your girl? You see Baby San?" and so forth.

Van got the drift of this and would be acutely embarrassed.

At Mooney, Van had a small bunker to himself which was enough to rouse the CO's suspicions. He accused him of private wickedness.

"Van keeps to himself a lot. Ever notice that? I think he jacks off."

Hardoy broke the uncertain pause that followed. "Sir, does that mean you don't want him to walk point anymore?"

Payday procedures: I was selected as payroll officer, a loathsome chore that normally would fall to the executive officer but with only three officers in the company there was no longer anyone available for that slot. Even though nearly everyone sends the bulk of his pay home, the army regards payday as a moral factor and on or about the last day of the month men in the field are paid even if the payroll officer has to crawl to their foxhole in order to pass them their MPC (military pay script). Sergeant Honeywell asked that I get as many small bills as possible. Payday means gambling: the smaller the bills, the lower the stakes, the fewer the fights was his reasoning. Honeywell also asked that I stop off at Camp Evans and pay Sergeant Le Joy ("He is a good man") who was attending the division school for new squad leaders.

And so the itinerary for a two day junket was established: first to Juliet to sign for the money, then to Evans to find and pay Le Joy, and finally back to Mooney to pay the company.

At Juliet the money was counted, about $5,000, and clipped to individual pay forms on which I had to get each man's "payroll signature." By some bureaucratic alchemy these forms would eventually find their way into each man's 201 file (personnel file) which was maintained at Khe San. For officers, the form would include deductions for meals; an officer pays for his food even if it is C-rations. The deduction wasn't much, only a couple of dollars a day, but I sometimes thought about it as I probed into the delights of a B-3 unit.

By long tradition Delta Company provided the payroll officer with a battered blue gym bag to transport the company pay. I stowed this beneath my cot. At Juliet there was always the luxury of a roomy GP tent and a comfortable cot. After weeks of sleeping on the ground or on a platform of ammo boxes I found that hard to resist even though I noticed that the PX had acquired some new perforations.

Apart from counting money, there was ample time for a cold, trickling shower, a warm beer, and a hot meal. In the fading afternoon I lingered over coffee beneath a softly billowing parachute and idly watched a series of savage dog fights. LZ Juliet was well supplied with stray dogs, always called "soup bones" because of their probable fate in a Vietnamese village, and, naturally, the battalion mess tent was a dog battleground. My companion was a burly ranger officer who was due to go home in a few days. He was, he said, looking forward to "running around Fort Benning," by which he meant that he was assigned to teach at the Ranger school. He struck me as a very tough man, but I suspect we both had the same ironical thoughts as the dogs tore and slashed at each other.

Many rifle companies had one or two soup bone mascots. For a time Delta Company had a small, brown, affectionate dog that never barked at night, unless, it was said, VC were outside the perimeter. I never saw this undesirable talent demonstrated. In the mountains the terrain was too rough for the dog to keep up and so he had to be carried. A sweating grunt would pick the animal up, carry it, and then put it down; it would trot along happily for a time and then beg to be carried, would be, and then after a little while returned to the jungle floor. In this way the animal traveled steadily toward the rear of the column. At night Soupbone would plunk down exhausted by someone's position and sleep the sleep of a good dog. One day he fell behind the column and was lost.

That evening I went off to pay Captain Wright who was still carried on the company payroll even though he had been reassigned to brigade staff. I announced myself to the guard and was ushered past several barbed wire barricades—at night brigade HQ spun itself a cocoon of concertina—and into a warren of deep bunkers. Captain Wright, about whom I was curious, proved to be a thin, soft spoken man in his mid-twenties; nothing as I had imagined the architect of the ambush at Dong Ha to be nor the man who had stood shaking his finger and bellowing at a gunner from Apache who had started firing a heavy machine gun right over Navajo's positions. "It looked like those big fucking tracers was going right through him," I was told.

Wright wanted to know how Bannerman was doing and how things were going in the mountains. "Fine, okay," I said on both counts, "but so far I haven't seen anything but wildflowers." Wright smiled and then shrugged, implying that you have to take the bad with the good. He brightened. "We expect to find those people for you pretty soon." I managed to look pleased.

I went to bed early and was soon deeply asleep only to be awakened hours later by a horrifying nightmare, perhaps a legacy of the ARVN lieutenant's lecture which had left so much to the imagination. Mooney was being overrun and I was trapped in a bunker. Then I remembered that I was at Juliet and, in a tent 50 feet from the perimeter, went blissfully back to sleep. Actually another dream would have been more appropriate or at least more immediate: I am sitting in front of a poncho that has stacks and stacks of MPC piled on it; out of nowhere comes a huey and, whoosh, thousands of dollars of MPC go swirling into the forest. I finish my tour burning shit at Camp Evans. That theme was on my mind for all the next day. I did not want to end up owing the army $5,000 in real money.

It was mid-morning before I caught a chopper to Camp Evans and had set about, gym bag under my arm, the task of locating Le Joy. Evans was big, with fields of tents, enormous sprawling stretches of supplies and open areas of red clay dominated by rows of helicopters in revetments; hueys, chinooks with tired drooping rotor blades and cobra gunships that looked from a distance like resting wasps. It struck me as drab and lonely, like an industrial park. A dusty hour was required to find the training center. After a few queries I was directed to a tent and located Le Joy in the middle of the most outlandish celebration I have ever seen. Fifteen men, an ethnic rainbow, and none, I think, older than 21, alive, drunk, and reasonably certain of minimal comfort and survival for an entire week, were singing and capering about among cots, rifles, and packs to an enthusiastic guitar. I had crashed a fundamentally exclusive party: members only — men who had survived over six months in the field with the First Cavalry Division. I didn't belong. But Honeywell was right; Le Joy was both surprised and pleased to see me (D 2/5 takes care of its own was the message) and the arrival of a first lieutenant with his pay in hand did no injury to his status. I was introduced around and a beer was thrust in my hand. Le Joy pointed to an empty cot onto which I tossed the gym bag.

Whoever was responsible for the squad leader's course deserved a medal, for it honed the division's most basic resource: its amazingly tough, canny, fieldwise survivors. Le Joy I suspect was typical. He had been in the field for almost eight months and seemed to thrive on it. When the company was attacked in its night perimeter near Khe San, Le Joy had blown the head off an NVA soldier with a grenade round. The man had tripped a flare and for some reason kept peeking up to try and see the company positions. Le Joy knelt on one knee holding the bobbing head in his sights, fired and hit the man directly in the face. The NVA were laughing and giggling when they formed up for the attack, my RTO insisted they were high on something, but, he said, "That laughing stopped when Le Joy took that gook's face off." Then they had blown the claymores.

The celebration continued as though I was not there; a joint materialized (the *only* time I saw Americans using marijuana in Vietnam) which I ignored. Their sense of humor was robust. Towards afternoon there was a loud crack followed by dead silence. "That's it," someone said and in an instant everyone had spilled into the slit trench in front of the tent. The very expensive gym bag lay abandoned on my cot. Incoming mortar round? No—one of the division's future squad leaders had taken the fuse out of a fragmentation grenade and tossed it behind the tent. I decided that I would try to get back to Mooney that day.

At the time, Camp Evans was probably one of the world's busiest small airports, so catching a hop to LZ Juliet was no problem. But LZ Mooney was Podunk with only a few flights a day carrying ammo and rations. I rode back to Mooney perched miserably atop an unsteady pile of mermite cans. Neither gunner seemed very concerned that an air-pocket might bounce Apache's hot chow out of the chopper's open doors but I felt that there was a lot riding on it and pictured myself plummeting to my death through a cloud of scrambled eggs and carrot sticks. At Mooney I learned that Navajo was in the field and that nothing would be going out to them until morning.

In the morning I connected with Navajo's outbound C-rations, which are far more comfortable to sit on than mermite cans, and made it back to the company. Then, finally, sitting cross-legged on a poncho, a .45 acting as a paperweight, I paid everyone and came up only $20 short.

Navajo was dug in on the knob of a high, pinnacle hill (a mountain really, 465 meters by the map) that provided a Tibetan view of a broad, open valley a half mile to the north and a thousand feet below. An ancient trail (if it was on our map, it was ancient) ran through the valley. Probing down toward the valley the day before, First Platoon had a brush with a unit of undetermined size. They killed one NVA and took no casualties. Artillery was called in and then an air strike. Evidently, or, anyway, this is what I was told with appropriate hand gestures, the Air Force jets, F100s, came in very low and swung out over the A Shau Valley after they released their bombs. It only took once for the NVA gunners to get the range. After the second run, one of the jets came screaming by the company perimeter on fire. Commanche about a mile north of us called to report that they had seen the pilot eject near our location and that his chute had opened. Third Platoon had been sent out to try and find him which was an all but hopeless task because they could have passed within ten feet of the man and not seen him.

They searched until well after darkness. The rest of the night was spent crawling up the side of the mountain to get back to the perimeter. Sometimes they could move only by the light of flares. Hardoy would call in an illumination round and they would pick their way over rocks and tangled roots for perhaps a hundred yards and then it would be pitch black again. It was dawn before they got back to the perimeter. A scout helicopter found the pilot that same morning; he was dead.

I spent much of the day blowing down trees to enlarge the LZ which was very tight. My prior training in demolitions consisted of once inserting an electrical blasting cap into a quarter pound block of TNT, retiring to a bunker, and listening to a loud bang. But the engineers made it look easy: pack one side of a tree with explosive, stick in a blasting cap, and blow the charge. The tree snaps off against the force of the explosion leaving a stump that looks like a frayed toothbrush. It isn't as easy as all that.

That afternoon and on two or three other occasions my assistant was a young, freckle-faced mortarman who looked upon working with explosives as a pleasant change of routine. We used what we had: TNT and primer cord. The primer cord, after being crammed into someone's pack like so much clothesline, tended to go out and then one of us would have to sprint to the charge and pull the fuse. This was exhilarating but probably not very dangerous. At a high cost in interrupted naps and displaced card games, we eventually managed to drop a dozen trees without killing ourselves or anyone else. Bannerman was, therefore, pleased and said that the "training" would come in handy which was true.

Late that night, Third Platoon saw "a string of lights" in the distant valley. I did not hear Hardoy report this and, in fact, only awoke when the FO began to slam 105 rounds into the valley. The fire mission ended after only a few minutes and Hardoy stated that he had "negative further lights." On the hour, I heard Third Platoon answer in turn, "sit reps negative" but the guard's voice carried little conviction. Shortly after that the lights appeared again. In my stocking feet I tenderfooted across the perimeter to Third Platoon's sector in time to see a line of dim, yellowish pinpricks of light that bobbed and jiggled in a curious sort of Brownian motion. It was a column of men, every third or fourth man carrying a hooded lantern. This time the FO responded with firecracker rounds that exploded in a rippling series of loud cracks and bright flashes as though a giant was popping some stupendous brand of luminous popcorn in a black kettle. The lights went out and stayed out.

Early the following afternoon, Commanche excitedly reported springing an ambush and killing five NVA with frags and claymores. The location they gave was a little to the north of us well down toward the valley below. We had not heard a sound; the forest sometimes swallows everything. We remained on that hilltop for another day cautiously patrolling down its ankle-busting scree. My amazement that Hardoy had been able to navigate at night in this jumbled landscape, even by the light of flares, grew with each patrol.

Amid rumors that someone at brigade had finally decided we were too close to the A Shau Valley, we were lifted out and, after a short flight, dumped into a field of elephant grass that draped over a broad ridge. The chopper pilots would not, or could not, hover down into the head-high grass so we all thudded onto the LZ from a height of six feet or more, losing in the process our FO to a broken wrist.

Bannerman went with Third Platoon for a look around the area while the rest of the company stayed back to clear the night perimeter. That left me in charge. An hour of slashing and trampling the tough resistant grass revealed that the location I had chosen was neatly bisected by a deep, overgrown ditch. It was not a natural feature and I can only suppose that we had landed on the site of an ancient Montagnard village. At the time, though, it only meant to me that I had to shift the perimeter. A lot of grumbling, made anonymous by the high grass, followed that decision, but the ditch was an NVA sapper's dream.

Bannerman's patrol returned that afternoon having found nothing. But in the early evening a guard peered into the grass and scrub beyond the ditch, which now marked one side of the perimeter, and saw several men from the waist down wearing green utility pants and Ho Chi Minhs. A few seconds later the "gook feet," as the guard described them, ran away. Bannerman was irritated at the lost opportunity but with many in the company padding around in racing slicks he understood why the guard did not fire.

The following day Second Platoon explored down into the valley to the west of our perimeter. We skirted around the area where the "gook feet" had been observed, headed north through open, oddly stunted forest, and then turned toward the valley. It was very hot and after perhaps an hour I called a long break. I stretched out and studied

100

the funny papers while the men with me pulled on their canteens and admired a foot long green centipede that was making its way along a branch just over our heads.

My map showed the valley to be shaped like a soup tureen with steep sides or (better analogy) an elongated chamber pot. The floor of the valley — the bottom of the pot — was presented as broad and rather flat. The west side of the company perimeter, facing a grassy swale that stretched far down to a woodline six or seven hundred feet below, was midway along the valley rim. We were at the far end of the valley, up where one of the chamber pot's handles would have been.

Rested and fairly certain of my position, I gave the order to move out. As we headed down into the valley, the forest turned by gradients from green to brown and by the time we arrived at the bottom everything was utterly desiccated, brittle, and noisy. The valley smelled like New Jersey, the part that has all the oil refineries. Defoliant hung acridly in the air, constricting our throats and burning our eyes and at first I thought we had been sent into an area that had been dusted with C-S gas. The broad valley floor was only a French cartographer's fantasy; beneath the trees the valley was a deep, V-shaped notch through which, all out of place in that dry, killed environment, a small, pleasant stream chased.

We filled our canteens, crossed the stream and moved along the far side of the valley. Then we recrossed the stream. And so on. I had all day to search the valley and this allowed frequent breaks. Before and after each break, I would order a clover leaf. One of these produced an interesting discovery.

"Navajo Two Six, this is Two Six Mike. . . We got a . . . tunnel and a foxhole with cement rim. Over."

"Say again."

"We got a tunnel and some kinda cement thing."

"What? Never mind, okay, I'm coming up."

The "tunnel" penetrated an incredibly dense thicket of scrub bamboo and at the end of it, some 30 yards in, there was . . . something. Two men crept up beside me and peeked uncertainly into the thicket.

"What is that?" I asked.

"Looks like a foxhole with a fucking cement rim."

I had to admit that it did but had no intention of reporting any such vision to Bannerman. It was part of company lore that our former executive officer had requested that a gunship investigate six elephants that could be plainly seen lumbering in the distance across Dong Ha's heat-distorted landscape. Other people had seen them, too, including Sergeant Honeywell, who told me the story. The pilot, said Honeywell, had wanted to know what color the elephants were. Pink? They were trucks.

I borrowed a .45 and wriggled into the thicket. The tunnel ended in a little open area, more like a tiny room, about five feet in diameter. There was no foxhole and the cement rim was only the grey ashes of a fire which had been built there because the mat of bamboo overhead would dissipate the smoke. The fire was probably several days old. I crawled back out, sputtering curses and alive with leeches. In the same area we also found several raised sleeping platforms and a hooch.

An hour later Six called, faintly — radio reception was poor at the bottom of the valley — to say that an air strike was coming and that battalion wanted to confirm our position. Where was I? The map contours were next to useless and it was difficult to judge how much ground we had covered in our drunk's walk down the valley. I guessed; calling in our coordinates in the clear, as ordered. Battalion obviously wanted no mistakes.

We waited by the stream, some of the men ladling helmets full of water over their heads. Ten minutes, twenty, a half an hour — nothing: not a hint of a forward air controller's prop plane overhead. I concluded that the air strike had been cancelled or had gone in so far away that we couldn't even hear it. The roar of jets dismissed those thoughts and almost immediately there was an earth shaking, booming explosion that turned the valley into a kettle drum. In fact the bomb had landed somewhere far back along the route we had taken into the valley. The second bomb was closer and we stared at each other, bug-eyed, as debris pattered down through the dry canopy.

"Six, Two Six, do those fast movers [jets] know where we are? Do they have our correct location?"

I could make out only part of Bannerman's reply, but the gist of it was clear.

"How the hell should I know?"

We crashed noisily down the valley. Only two more bombs landed but each, in our imagination, nearer than the one before.

Apparently we weren't the only ones who thought the bombs were a little close because shortly after the bombs stopped we picked up movement, a lot of it, two or three hundred yards off to our left and moving on a parallel course. If it was an animal that we were hearing, it was a very big animal and also a very long animal—about as long as a squad of men. No one believed that it was an animal.

A ponderous, heavy-footed dance followed. We stopped; the noise stopped. We moved and the noise kept pace. Normally in such dense cover two columns could have passed within 50 yards of each other without either one being the wiser but now it was like maneuvering in a forest of dried flowers. We doubled back, keeping close to the stream which I thought might mask our movement, and then worked up the side of the valley hoping to get above them. We set up and waited. Were they gone or were they waiting for us? After an hour, we slipped away as quietly as we could and headed back to the company.

Hours spent in the valley's petroleum atmosphere and the long uphill climb had us all wheezing like asthmatics by the time we arrived at the perimeter. Bannerman notified battalion of the cooking fire and sleeping positions we had found but made no mention of the "pretty good movement" I reported. There was no point in crying wolf, I supposed. And privately, very privately, I was beginning to doubt that there were any NVA in that valley. Maybe I had just maneuvered around a couple of deer. Why not? I had already flanked a herd of pigs. The reason for the air strike I never learned.

In the cool early evening, after shaking off a buzzing headache left over from the patrol, I answered a pointless call to the CP. "Somebody at battalion wants to know if we have any artists," said Bannerman wearily. "You got any?" Then I checked the platoon perimeter. This was a daily chore that intruded into the private universe of each squad but pleasant enough, especially when there was a canteen cup brimful of hot coffee at each position. A few sips would be offered with some tiny formality and gratefully, carefully accepted. Coffee, or what we called coffee, was valuable and usually made by pouring every obtainable packet of sugar, instant coffee, dried cream and chocolate into the same communal cup. The resulting beverage had the specific gravity of mercury and would just about float a plastic spoon.

Only two positions covered the open side of the perimeter because it overlooked an area that was very steep and completely exposed. Bannerman would have paid the NVA a large sum of money to mount an attack up that slope. I sat there until darkness watching the treeline far below turn from grey-green to deep purple to black. Finally I could see

103

nothing but an endless succession of shadowy ridges and I was for a time inexpressibly homesick.

It proved to be a jittery night because Third Platoon kept tossing frags into the grass and scrub beyond the old ditch which 50, 100 or 500 years before had probably protected a Montagnard village. "Just a few hungry gooks checking to see if we're still here," sniffed Aguirre in the morning and I realized that what he had told me some time before was true; in the field men will often sleep through the crashing noise of a frag unless it is thrown in their sector. A shot, on the other hand, wakes everyone up, instantly.

We pulled out that morning, heading for a very high ridge over a mile away. I ran a nervous point. For some reason it had settled into my mind that we would be ambushed that day and I reconned-by-fire the entire morning, shooting up bushes, fallen logs, the trail ahead, and the entrance to a large rodent burrow, until Bannerman told me to cut it out because I was using up so much ammunition.

Around midday we passed a Montagnard field that was covered with cut brush. The brush was tinder dry and had probably been there for a very long time; some tribesman's work wasted by the war. That night the mortar platoon dropped a WP round on it so that we could watch it burn.

The Montagnards had cleared much of the valley ahead of us and in the process had created spectacular scenery. Contrasting with the darker forest, bright green fields reached halfway up the mountain sides and the floor of the valley was broad, open meadow, knee deep in grass. A single squad was given the lonely task of securing the far side and then Navajo crossed the valley in an easy weaving road march. We waded a cold, clear stream — full of fat trout, someone claimed — and passed by the spare framework of a house. Grass grew high through the collapsed floor and nearby a hollowed out section of tree trunk bred mosquitoes. I have sometimes wondered about the Montagnards who lived out their lives in this valley. At the time we were in danger of doing the same and Bannerman hurried the column into the forest.

For two hours we plodded up the side of a high ridge which just kept getting higher and steeper. Near the top the forest thinned and in places was dominated by scrub and bamboo. Exhausted, I crawled the last few yards to the summit and I wasn't the only one who arrived that way. A few men shed their packs and began to search out the ridge top; the rest of us lay flopped on the ground, panting like dogs, while the medic handed out salt tablets.

Toward evening Bannerman confided with some satisfaction that battalion had *not* expected us to make our assigned position and was impressed that we had done so. "Just where the fuck they did expect us to set up, I don't know," he added. The valley that we had crossed in the afternoon, now some 700 or 800 feet below us according to the map, was already filling with fog and would not have been so pleasant after dark.

We had not finished digging in as darkness approached. In the grey light I watched as two men suddenly jumped out of their foxhole — just, sprong! three feet straight up to straddle the side of the hole they were digging. The bottom of their hole was covered to a depth of three or four inches with flying ants, thousands of them that suddenly began to take wing. They rose in a column as dense as oil smoke, up and out through the broken canopy above us. A dozen kite-like birds appeared overhead to twist and dive among the flying ants.

Two Six Bandaid, who was a premed student until captured by the draft, said that it was nuptial flight and that the ants mated on the wing. I don't know if that's really true but the happy possibility that it was absorbed us for a while. Within 20 minutes the ants were gone; the two men dropped back into their hole, and went back to work.

In the morning, to everyone's surprise, since we had been out for only a week, the company was lifted back to Mooney. In a grey chilly rain I talked briefly with one of the Charlie Company platoon leaders. His platoon sergeant stood beside us glowering at his men on the bunkers below us. "They're just fucking animals," exploded the sergeant. "Fucking animals."

Neither the lieutenant nor the sergeant gave any hint as to what provoked that outburst. It was a not a matter to be shared with outsiders. "Cold," said the sergeant. "We're gonna be suckin cold cold titty up in those choppers." The lieutenant nodded. Then he leaned forward, closed one nostril with his thumb, and expertly blew a plug of snot into the mud. Without a word, both men heaved on their packs and trudged heavily up to the helipad. Their platoon followed.

CHAPTER 6

search and evade   v. 1: to provide dissembling
information about the position, status and aggressive
intent of an ambush or patrol (see simulate)   2: the use
of tactics allowing a small unit to engage only under
the most favorable circumstances if you know what's
motherfucking good for you.   3: to stay off trails.
—Anonymous

Under our new battalion commander, a stocky, rather formal man, the pace of patrols and ambushes picked up and we spent a lot of time sniffing around outside the perimeter. Bannerman would sometimes just say, "Look around over there," and wave in the direction of "over there." Given that kind of mission statement, a patrol could move slowly, with frequent breaks, and stay off trails. If you did those elementary things, the chance of being ambushed was small even assuming (and I always did) that there were any NVA around willing to risk being spotted by the 1st of the 9th's scoutships which were as aggressive as magpies. I nearly always returned from these very modest adventures feeling better than when I left because they provided escape from Mooney's dust and noise.

Here and there in the half dead forest around Mooney you found bodies. One afternoon we came across a young man dressed in dark green NVA fatigues, dead perhaps a week. On his chest was a Cav patch. In the same area we found some communication wire for which, I supposed, there could only be two explanations: either it was to be used by an FO to direct mortar fire onto Mooney or they planned to run the wire right up to Mooney so that sappers could follow it at night into the perimeter. Cutting back and forth across the wire we tried to discover its source. After several hundred yards the wire led us to a rectangular wooden contraption, the standard "gook spool," I was told, and it still had a hundred yards or so of wire on it. We found nothing else on that hill; just a lot of commo-wire, a gook spool, and a dead man. The wire we took back to Mooney for our own use.

After we returned to Mooney, I took some of the captured wire (or, more accurately, recaptured wire — it was American) to TOC. The intelligence officer was busy so a sergeant emerged, looked at what I had in my hand as though it was a worm and said, "Guess they're trying to ring this place with wire," turned and left.

The dead man, I later learned, had been the work of one of Commanche's night ambushes. In the dark they had not noticed the wire which, anyhow, is nothing new. Apache has found a strand of wire running to within 50 yards of the perimeter.

A new first sergeant arrived during this second stint at Mooney. Honeywell was stung by having to give up his job (his rank was sergeant first class, E7 — not first sergeant) but after meeting his replacement felt better. A tall, lanky Appalachian, Sergeant William Chisholm had been in the army since 1939, seen combat in World War II and Korea and, as was fairly common among senior NCOs of the time, was a product of the CCC camps. He was genuinely comfortable in the field and in defiance of all risk wore an enormous set of yellow diamonds on each sleeve of what was by some sergeant's magic always a clean fatigue shirt. I never heard him raise his voice but he had a look that froze lieutenants and NCOs. That look conveyed no threat; it meant only that you had disappointed him but you feared doing that. He would not refer to an infantryman as a "grunt" or a "crunchie"; always it was GI, which to us sounded almost archaic. Chisholm's fundamental contribution to the company stemmed from the fact that everything about him implied that he thought the life we were leading was *normal*. I'm sure to Chisholm it was normal. At some point, in France, or Korea, or during his first tour in Vietnam, the tumblers of reality had shifted within the brain of this gentle, dignified man and warfare became the way things really are. Perhaps he was right.

At Mooney, rats and fire missions conspired against sleep and I often monitored the company radio net far into the night. There was a lot of traffic. Guard positions called each other to pass the night, and to keep awake, and company headquarters called hourly for sit reps. As time passed, radio procedure became more and more informal.

"Good evening fun seekers. This is RED-Y NAV-A-JO. How do you report. Over?"

"This is One Six; sit-reps negative. Over."

"This is Three Six; sit-reps negative. Over."

"Navajo Two Six, Navajo Two Six, report. Over."..."Wake up shit for brains!"

"This is Two Six; sit-reps negative...dickhead. Over."

Such shenanigans tapered off when word got around that Arizona Six's bunker was furnished with only a cot and four PRC 25s. "He goes to sleep with the motherfuckers on," said his radio operator. "I don't think he ever turns them off."

Early one morning an excited voice came over the radio: "Gooks ...think we got a KIA," followed by a long burst from an M-16. About a mile distant, the First Platoon had sprung an ambush and the radio message had outstripped the sound of the firing. The disjunction was eerie. Immediately there were several more bursts, also from an M-16. Then silence.

The ambush made it back to the perimeter within less than an hour. I could hear their calls to the LP for clearance to come through the wire. They had been moving to their ambush site when they saw four men about 30 yards away heading in their direction. The first NVA in line was shot dead and the others had gotten away. There was no return fire. The dead man was carrying a brand new AK-47 with a full magazine. Had he been more alert... There has been a lapse of tradition, in that no one remembered to leave a Cav patch at the ambush site, but one member of the ambush did have the presence of mind to strip the NVA belt from the body. Now he wears the belt.

"We seem to operate as effectively at night as they do," pronounced a satisfied Arizona Six the following morning. It was my impression that he had been listening when the ambush took place and I wondered how many men in Vietnam half-slept the night long in mountaintop bunkers waiting for such reports.

Bannerman, his time in the field finally over, departed for a staff assignment. As the company was being lifted out of Mooney, he stood on the pick-up zone and shook hands with each man as lift after lift boarded and took off. Our new commander was a tall rather chunky ROTC captain—Bannerman's long awaited "Double Banana"—named Speare. A tough man and a good officer, he learned field soldiering as fast as he lost weight which was very fast. Curiously, he took me for an old hand. Under Speare's captaincy, Navajo progressed by a relentless schedule of Charlie Alphas, night perimeters, patrols and ambushes into the monsoon. LZ Mooney, when we saw it, usually lay in mud under grey clouds and rain.

As a rule we had little advance knowledge of our landing zones. A location was selected by Arizona Six or a staff officer and the hueys took you there. Sometimes they took you somewhere else and then there would be a lot of head scratching before we could figure out our position. I can remember seeing only one LZ before a scheduled assault and on that occasion we flew high, straight and not very close to the designated site, a small brown patch on the top of a ridge line. I barely caught a glimpse of it but there was never a second pass over a prospective landing zone.

The following morning (shortly after Speare joined the company) we Charlie Alphaed onto the ridge. I was on the lead ship for this assault, an honor conferred by strict rotation because, as Honeywell, who had a way of getting to the core of things, said, "People get killed doing that." After the usual ten minutes of bumping along in a slick, black puffs of smoke began blossoming over the LZ as we approached it. This lasted for perhaps two or three minutes. The final artillery round was a "high streamer smoke" that left three gently curved trails of white smoke extending all the way to the ground. Anticipating this, the two gunships had left their protective position at our side and were rocketing the LZ before the tall smoke columns had started to break up. They expended half their ammunition and held the rest in reserve. Our slick broke down toward the LZ before the gunships had finished their work, one flashing just beneath us to cover the LZ with grenade rounds. I sat with Steve Jerome, our legs dangling over the side of the ship, and watched these vicious little rounds explode a few hundred feet below. Smoke now partially obscured the LZ. The last few seconds were covered by the door gunners who sprayed the bushes with their M-60s. Then we were out, jumping from the skids, the weight of our packs driving us to our knees, running hand to helmet for the nearest cover.

Our slick soared away to join the other ships circling above. A fire licked away at some nearby bamboo which began to explode with sharp pistol-shot reports while the four of us, Steve, myself, and two men manning an M-60, scuttled here and there checking for enemy positions. If the NVA were well dug in they would wait until more of us were on the ground before opening up. We found nothing.

110

I called on battalion frequency and cleared the LZ.

"Prescott Arizona, Prescott Arizona, this is Navajo Two Six: Lima Zulu Green; I say again, Lima Zulu Green."

I realized after I clicked off that I had been repeating that transmission like an incantation as the slick descended.

The remaining slicks came in and one by one little groups of burdened men scrambled to positions I indicated. Within less than 45 minutes, the rest of the company had been shuttled from Mooney and the perimeter established. . .another routine day at the office.

Speare called together the huddle that preceded moving out and gave us our orders. On information that the NVA were moving through this area in large groups, First and Second platoons were to set up ambushes roughly at either end of the ridge and maintain them for a couple of days. Third Platoon would remain with Speare on the LZ, midway between the two ambushes, as a reaction force.

Within ten minutes we were filing along the ridge. But, after only a few hundred yards I received a call to stop "immediately," and hold position. "Do not move out until we give you the word. There may be a Lurp Team in your area. Don't move!"

A long range reconnaissance patrol (LRRP—hence "Lurp") was a team of four or five men who were inserted into an area to search out the NVA. They operated for days at a time in complete isolation and even though their mission was to avoid contact they had a well earned reputation for shooting anything that moved. In the remote possibility that my point man had detected the Lurp Team first we would have done the same.

We sat quietly (very quietly) for over an hour, sweated, smoked and burned off leeches. Finally we received a message that they were not in our area but were on the other side of the "little blue" (little blue for stream; a blue line on our maps). "Do not go into that area."

We moved out again along the trail that topped the ridge and after a few hundred yards came to what I judged to be a good night position. On the assurance that we would be in that position for at least two nights we dug in elaborately only to be informed that we had to "be in close proximity to the little blue." We dug in again, on the point of the ridge just where the trail headed steeply down to the stream. Speare called to check our position. "Can you see the little blue?" "Affirmative," I responded which was a half truth but I had no intention of putting the platoon at the base of that ridge where radio contact, at best, would be sporadic. Nor did I feel like asking my platoon to pack up, move and dig in for the third time in six hours simply because battalion kept changing its mind.

The trail leading up the ridge was almost three feet wide and packed hard; there were no fresh prints but the bark had been recently scuffed off the roots that protruded from the trail. At some time not long before it had carried heavy traffic. A new innovation (to me) materialized. The squad responsible for covering the trail leading up the ridge hung fragmentation grenades about six feet off the ground along the side of the trail. The fuse had been replaced with the electrical blasting cap from a claymore. They had been carrying the extra claymore fuses all along.

In a secure position, enjoying good weather, we passed all the next day in gourmet C-ration cooking...and sleep. Rested, a double guard manned the tangle of wires leading to the command detonated frags that festooned the trail. That short time, those two nights and the soft, intervening day, was among the few happy periods I spent in Vietnam. And to this happiness the NVA contributed. Alerted by the Charlie Alpha, which no one within five miles could have failed to notice, they avoided the area.

Our self-imposed reliance upon helicopters meant that, however rapid, our movements were reliably known to the NVA and the several obvious elements of tactical sneakiness we commonly used, such as taking an indirect route to an LZ and fake insertions, probably confused the NVA very little. Furthermore, battalion sometimes seemed bent on providing us with things which we did not need or want. Warm ice cream was something that we did not need and seldom wanted; but we got it anyway and at inconvenient times. The idiocy of bringing an operation to a grinding halt so that 120 men could stand in the rain and drink warm ice cream should have been obvious.

It was the following day, or maybe the day after, that battalion's tendency to cram helicopters bearing unwanted cargoes down our throats, rose to new heights. After digging into our night position close to a trail that ran beside a stream, Speare was advised that there was a helicopter enroute with a blivet of water which he refused, saying that our canteens were full and that the delivery would give away our position. Battalion radioed that the blivet *would* be delivered and that we were not under any circumstances to use the "local water supply,"

112

meaning streams, which was exactly what we had been doing out of necessity for days. Speare's voice became progressively higher pitched as he tried to get the chopper turned around. As we all listened, Speare, who was by then in a strangling rage, was forced to apologize for identifying qualities in the man who had insisted on the water delivery. This man unfortunately outranked Speare.

When it was growing dark a huey arrived and lowered a blivet of water through the canopy. A few men strolled over to top off their canteens but most of the water we simply dumped. It was over an hour later before a chopper returned to retrieve the blivet, by the light of a trip flare. Then, since our position had been hopelessly compromised, we had to move. Battalion ordered us to a location over half a mile away. Radios turned down, foxfire smudged on the back of our helmets, the company crept beneath black canopy, each man following the ghostly marked form in front of him. Hours went by. The column would stall and then break. Someone would have to be sent back along our trail to regain contact. Finally Speare guessed (it could only have been a guess) that we had made our assigned position and, after a head count revealed that by some miracle we had not lost a man, the company circled into a tight perimeter. Very tired men tried to concentrate as they set out trip flares and claymores. Then, everyone dropped. We lay with our heads facing out, packs pushed in front of us, and I suspect that within an hour everyone but Speare, who still seethed, was asleep.

Speare had us up before dawn for stand to and we pulled out very early for our next position, too tired to eat. Sergeant Chisholm was philosophical about the whole episode. "It's a damn lucky thing," he said, "they don't have any encyclopedia salesmen back at battalion, or they'd be shoving a set of those up our asses."

The longer the battalion remained in the mountains, the more it came to resemble its enemy. This resemblance was only superficial but it was there nevertheless. For a time, captured anti-aircraft guns dotted Mooney. A cache of several large bundles of NVA uniforms was uncovered and a few of our smaller men wore these deep green cotton fatigues because they were warmer than the light, rip-stop American clothing. No one wore them in the field, of course; that would have been suicidal, but on Mooney you could see small men in NVA field clothes, starred buckle, and Ho Chi Minhs. It took a little getting used to. All who could get them, padded around the night perimeter in racing slicks. We took care, as we should have been doing all along, to camouflage our positions and it became natural to leave the vegetation alone as much as possible. We no longer hacked out fields of fire that resembled fire breaks; we cut away only just enough to see and then only a few feet above the forest floor. It became dangerously easy to walk out of the perimeter at night without realizing it.

More and more we began to sleep in hammocks made of poncho liners or, if there was time to construct them, on low sleeping platforms. At first glance, until you noticed the litter of C-rations and the big three-man American foxholes, our night positions looked NVA.

Toward late summer, our New Model Arizona Six severed our umbilical connection with the helicopter. Issued several days' rations, the company slipped beneath an unbroken canopy to successive night perimeters which were essentially company sized ambushes. All air traffic was vectored away from where we were operating and for days helicopters were neither seen nor heard. On such missions we ate less or perhaps just more erratically. It was often feast or famine: everyone ate a lot the first day or two — less to carry — and then the company was down to one meal a day. Our preoccupation with food increased. We were often issued freeze-dried rations (Lurp rations, we called them) which were very good and consisted of meals like spaghetti or chili and rice or stew. It was a lot like packing around an instant diner (just open the foil pouch and pour in water) and I soon acquired a taste for cold crunchy chili. The Lurp rations reinforced a tendency that was already there. We spent more of our time in the valleys never far from water — like the NVA.

For much of this period we were often only a few miles from the Laotian border. Never logged or defoliated this was wild, untouched forest with vast stretches of deep, unbroken canopy. Huge epiphytic plants hung in the trees above us, gibbons, which we once or twice saw, boomed and hooted at our intrusion, and a squad I sent out on security came across the pug marks of a tiger beside a stream.

If the Montagnards had ever lived here we saw no trace of them. "Where are the yards?" To the extent that we had fallen under the spell of Sergeant Chisholm's worldview, we all believed that God had placed Montagnards on earth because their old fields made good LZs.

Every day we moved along the half-lit trails that tunneled through this Miocene wilderness; some were wide enough for Jeep traffic. Along some stretches, when the trail led up a steep ridge, stair steps had been

114

cut into the hard soil and thick vines tied to trees as a handrail. Barked trees every so often bore signs; hash marks, arrows, dots, we didn't know what they meant. Commanche reported finding a rest camp equipped with a shower made with bamboo pipe. They have also found a communal grave containing seven decomposed bodies. Apache came across a land line and followed it to a complex of six large huts. Underneath the huts were huge "split level" bunkers. Working in the same area we also encountered Apache's land line or maybe it was another. Strung about ten feet high through the trees there were four strands of bright, quarter inch copper wire which seemed to lead generally toward the A Shau Valley. We guessed that it was an old fashioned telegraph system, but how the NVA could have manhandled miles and miles of heavy wire through this kind of country was beyond our understanding. We just cut the wire and used it to tie up our hammocks.

Every few days we would have to clear an LZ. In triple canopy forest the tangled thatch of vines and branches overhead can actually support a tree blown off at the base, so it made sense to blow several trees at once. Repeat that process three or four times and the result is a jackstraws-pile of tree trunks at the bottom of an overhung shaft 75 or 100 feet deep. At twilight, hueys with food, ammunition, and water dropped down this sinkhole shaft to hover just over the chaos of jagged stumps and fallen trees around which Delta Company had dug its holes.

The NVA, for reasons of their own, seemed content to give up the caches of equipment (heavy machine guns, several new 82mm mortars, a stash of hundreds of mortar rounds, case upon case of AK-47 ammunition) that the battalion found and allowed us to roam this ancient forest at will. Contact with the NVA was ephemeral. On a moonless night a clipped voice woke me up. "Movement." I scrambled down to the perimeter and into a foxhole behind an M-60 that covered the trail leading into our night position. The man beside me whispered in my ear. "Flashlight, somebody shined a flashlight...close." He pointed down the trail with his chin; his hand was on the claymore detonator. He would blow it the instant a trip flare popped. We waited out the night. Nothing. Several times we had contact like that; a light just outside the perimeter. Someone would peg a frag and the light would go out. Once or twice frags came back in to land short of the perimeter, injuring no one. The FO would call in a fire mission and a few rounds would land with heavy forest-muffled booms well outside our positions or back along our trail. I would guess that the majority of the company slept right through these affairs and only learned of them in the morning.

Delta Company returned to Mooney in late August. Mooney oozed mud and the bunkers filled with water. It grew cold.

In a chow line ankle deep in mud, Sergeant Honeywell eyed my rainsoaked scrambled eggs and announced, "FTA Sir." I was surprised; FTA stands for Fuck the Army. In 1968 FTA was scratched on the walls of every latrine on every army base in the world. In bright paint it materialized briefly on water towers and the walls of NCO and officer clubs. It decorated bus stations. FTA. Honeywell beamed: "Fun, Travel and Adventure . . . for three months and twenty-three days and then I'm going home to Mrs. Honeywell and the five little Honeywells." He did.

More often what passed for humor among us had been disemboweled of everything but cruelty. The story of the "sniper with a knife" made the rounds. Commanche, so the story went, had been clearing a bunker complex and found it empty except for a young NVA soldier. Armed only with a knife, he was sitting in a tree about 20 feet off the ground and whether he was just hiding or intended to jump someone was impossible to say. When the men from C Company saw him they roared with laughter and according to the version I heard it was some time before they recovered from their hysterics enough to shoot the unfortunate man who was frozen in terror. We thought it humorous.

Men fought over food; things were stolen. We seldom wrote home. A night ambush brought misery. I drew such an assignment and it stank. There was no moon and a driving rain that showed no sign of letting up so the radio was certain to be wet and unreliable. But worse, much worse, we were told not to go out until midnight which meant that the NVA might already be set up and waiting.

I talked to Speare and requested to go out earlier. "No, this comes from Arizona Six. He wants your people to set up along that trail." Speare motioned toward the upper end of the LZ indicating the trail that led past the LP. We would have to pick our way through the three rolls of concertina protecting the LP before we could get into the trees. The area, by design, was difficult to cross and very exposed, about the only available cover was a barrel of jellied gasoline.

Around 11:00 that night, Second Squad, resigned to a cold, wet, sleepless night, collected in front of my bunker. I took a count, ten men plus myself; it's easy to lose someone on a rainy night. I had already informed the mortar section of where we would be so that they would not mistakenly drop an H and I round on us, something that had nearly happened to a squad from First Platoon the night before. It was mandatory that anyone moving around the LZ after dark wear a helmet; otherwise you might be mistaken for a sapper. That night, however, I had no fear of being mistaken for anything: visibility was nil. We plodded through greasy mud to the company CP where I reported to Speare. On the way up to the LP I called to announce our arrival; it would have been very foolish to startle the men on that position.

At the LP, I found Peterson, who I had been told "was good in a fight," peering over the top of the bunker, a grenade in his hand. He had heard something. A quiet, withdrawn man, Peterson had long insisted that his feet bothered him (probably they did) and so he had removed the laces from his boots. That gesture came before I joined the company and it occurred to me that he had probably shuffled his way across half of I Corps. So far it had come to a draw: the army wouldn't let Peterson out of the field and Peterson would not lace his boots.

I called Six and reported that the LP had movement, hoping not to have to go out. Six called back a few minutes later and said to wait. An hour passed during which some of the squad wrapped up in their ponchos and went to sleep, as water puddled around them.

How Peterson could have seen or heard anything in such a rainstorm was a mystery to me but I walked a few mortar rounds up the trail just in case. The last round, hissing in the wet air just before it hit, fell much too close to the mines in front of us. I ended the mission and complained: "Are you letting those charges get wet?" The response from the mortar platoon was a sharp "Negative." (Translation: "You called in a short round, you dumb fuck.") I chalked up their surliness to the fact that they had been put to work on a rotten night and reflected irritably on their elegant lifestyle, which was exceeded only by the artillery.

It was by then nearly 2:00 and anything seemed preferable to standing hour after hour in that cold driving rain. I told the squad leader that I was going to "poke around out there" and that under no circumstances was either he or Peterson to leave off watch until I got

117

back. Without a radio for clearance, a new man, tired and frightened, would probably kill me on the way back into the LP.

It took a long time to get past the wire and into the trees. And once into the trees I had to feel my way along the trail for the trip wires that activated the flares beside the trail. I found them easily, and so it would have been for the NVA. Under the canopy the rain drummed and there was almost no light. I could have neither seen nor heard a man at a distance greater than ten feet and I was glad that I had thought to borrow an M-14. It simply felt better, more solid. But I had already decided that if I detected anything that might be larger than a rat I would run; scuttle a grenade down the trail and run. The advantage to going out alone, I realized, was that there was no one behind me to impede my getaway. I worked my way slowly down the trail, stopping at each bend to listen; 10 yards, stop, listen, 30 yards, stop, listen and so forth. It did not take many repetitions of that before I decided that I had gone far enough.

There were no NVA on the trail that night, or at least not on the upper part of it, and probably there never had been. The trip back took little time, and I came out of the trees "whistling Dixie" — identifying myself.

"Peterson, this is Two Six; check fire, check fire."

All the way up the trail, I had been thinking of Peterson poised, ready to uncork an M-26, and the thing I dreaded was to hear the "ting" of a fragmentation grenade as the spoon flies off. It didn't come. Peterson was wide awake and a little concerned. "Okay Two Six, come in."

"Anything out there?" Peterson asked, although he knew the answer. "Naw," I said, trying to sound casual, "the gooks are simulating tonight." And probably they were; deep inside some dry bunker, rocking in their hammocks to opium dreams.

Everyone had a sense of the agenda to follow. We waited for half an hour and then I walked down to the CP and gave Speare a creative report, saying that the trail had been searched to the base of the ridge (I had not gone that far) and leaving the impression that the entire squad had gone out. Speare would not have been impressed in the slightest that I had gone out alone; he would have thought that sheer stupidity. Speare looked at me intently, his antennae out for "search and evade." Finally he said, "That's good enough." Anyhow, it was nearly dawn.

Bunker politics: One afternoon a solemn delegation of platoon elders gathers in drizzly rain in front of my bunker. They have come on a grave matter and something that I should have prevented: the two RTOs have been ransacking the cases of C-rations for the best meals. The men on the bunkers get what's left. After some huffing and puffing at the RTOs, I state that the unopened cases of Cs *will* go directly to the bunkers. For a week, platoon headquarters goes on a very public chopped ham and eggs diet. The RTOs sulk.

And there was another matter. Gagne, eight months in the field, digs holes all the time. He starts to dig in on a ten minute break which is something that I eventually notice. Two Six Bandaid has been waiting for that. "I think you should get Gagne out of the field," he tells me.

"Why?"

"He hardly talks to anyone...digs holes all the time. Right sir? Big Man won't put him on anything but last guard. He'd kill his relief—that's what Big Man thinks."

"I can't get a man out of the field because he digs holes. It's not gonna happen."

All the same, I talked to Captain Speare about it and he said that mortars was short a few men and that I could send Gagne to mortars.

I called the squad leaders over and made a little ceremony out of telling Gagne that he was going to mortars, saying that after so long in the field he deserved it and so on. Big Man, who has been in the field far longer than Gagne, shifts on his feet uneasily and nods his assent. Gagne showed no emotion. There was a thick, deliberative quality about him; he moved like a man covered in dried mud.

It was during this stay at Mooney that Second Platoon was designated the "Quick Reaction Force" to support Echo Company, the battalion's recon platoon, in case they stirred something up or got into trouble. They stirred something up.

Around 10:00 one morning Tex called: "Get yer Quebec Romeo Foxtrot up to the log pad."

"Say again,"...the message sank in; "Oh shit, Roger."

"No packs," I told the squad leaders, "just a basic load and water. I want you up at the log pad in ten minutes." We *had* to be there before the slicks arrived. I put on my web gear, made sure the RTO had an extra battery and the long whip, and then realizing that I had been shouting and hopping around like a cheerleader, forced myself to walk (not run) over to the CP. I reported to Speare and learned that the situation was not nearly as bad as I had imagined it (Tex had sounded very urgent over the radio). In fact, it was quite routine. We were to set up a blocking position to intercept an estimated squad of NVA that had bumped into Echo Company. Only a few shots were fired before the NVA broke contact, shedding their packs in the process. A scout dog team had been called. Speare showed me roughly where the contact had occurred but added that there was no way of knowing, except very generally, where we would be inserted. That decision would be made in the air by the commander of the recon helicopters.

The platoon, minus two or three men from each squad to man the bunkers (those men graced with sprained ankles, fevers, or bad cases of jungle rot) arrived at the log pad on time. As the slicks thumped into earshot I explained the mission and within minutes we were in the air, jinking around at one or two thousand feet with two gunships sticking close. In the distance a small scoutship of the type known as "the pregnant guppy" was darting around at low altitude looking for a place to insert us. The guppy nosed down, poked into a bomb crater and then dodged away. A column of red smoke drifted from the crater; the guppy had dropped a smoke grenade. Shifting around, the door gunner roared in my ear, "Hot!" Too hot for us to land and the slicks changed course while the guppy warily circled the bomb crater. The gunships stayed with us.

Our flight picked up a stream and followed it into a deep V-shaped valley, on either side green, vine-hung ridges loomed above us. Quickly another possible LZ came into view, a little spit of scrub covered land ending in a sand bar. The stream curled around this. Halfway up the spit of land was a huge bomb crater. The gunner pointed at the bomb crater and nodded vigorously. He needn't have because the gunships were already arrowing rockets into the ridge just above the stream. They made only a couple of passes with rockets and then dusted off the scrub around the bomb crater with grenade rounds. One by one, in rapid succession the slicks hovered over the crater and we tumbled out. We took no fire; the LZ was green.

We all hunched down below the rim of the bomb crater as the gunships dumped the rest of their munitions around, and very close, to our position. Then they climbed out of the valley and disappeared. Silence. Dust and smoke drifted over our bomb crater.

A blocking position is not a picket fence and we held tight around the crater, maintaining security in all directions. The valley was very narrow. If the NVA continued along the stream it would be difficult for them to get by but if they were moving high up along the ridge, as was my guess, they would escape.

The recon platoon leader (Cheyenne 6) called on our frequency and it soon became all too clear that neither one of us had any idea of how far apart we were from each other. Cheyenne had not seen the helicopters bring us in and I had not risked my map to a huey's 80 knot slipstream. They popped smoke which was futile, but at least I knew they were not immediately in front of us. After a few minutes Cheyenne Six called again and announced that they were going to "toss a good ole Michael Two Six." They did. We could hear nothing.

Snapping and popping came from the tangle of scrub bamboo just across the stream. First Squad, closest to the thicket, was convinced that someone was in there and, in a sort of rippling motion, each man momentarily looked back at me, eyes wide, and then returned his attention to the ridge. More popping and rustling, this time a little higher up the ridge, prompted another backward glance. I nodded to the squad leader. Immediately, five men, maybe six, removed a grenade from their web gear, pulled the pin, and in unison pitched the little bombs toward the ridge. The spoons flew off in a sort of tinny musical bar as the grenades arched heavily into the thicket to explode within a second of each other while we crouched below the rim of the bomb crater to avoid the fragments sheeting overhead. Then everyone on that side of the crater cut loose; M-60s and M-16s raked the thicket while grenade rounds cracked higher on the ridge. It took over a minute to shut down all that wild firing. Finally it was quiet. More moving bushes; I shook my head. If there had been anybody on that part of the ridge, the issue was settled. First Squad stared fixedly ahead, still intent on the ridge.

Canfield, my RTO that day, and until three weeks before a machine gunner, asked for his old job back. I said okay and motioned Steve over to take his place. Canfield sprinted to Second Squad all the while yelling at his former assistant gunner, "Kerlinger, get away from my gun!" Kerlinger slid over without complaint and Canfield settled in behind his weapon as eager as a spaniel.

Minutes passed slowly while I tried to get Echo Company to give me some indication of their position. "Shoot off some rounds, you may be getting close, over."

"Negative, Navajo, wait one and I'll pop smoke again."

More long minutes.

"Cheyenne Six, this is Navajo, have you popped smoke? I have to know where you are."

No response.

"I have to know where..."

There was movement to our front, a lot of it; someone, either NVA or American was heading directly into our position. To my everlasting gratitude, our fire discipline held and seconds later a welted, sweat-sheathed grunt emerged from the scrub not 20 feet from the Second Squad. I watched as Canfield softly let the bolt of his M-60 slide forward, taking it off cock. He was obviously disappointed.

As the recon platoon filed into our position, their platoon sergeant stood on the lip of the bomb crater and summed up the day to no one in particular.

"I've got 13 years in this motherfucker [the army] but if I ever leave this place [Vietnam], I'm never coming back."

The scout dog, which I had expected to be a slavering, wolf-eyed German shepherd, turned out to be a big amiable labrador retriever. According to the handler, the scent trail his animal had been following led just outside our position, along the side of the ridge, so perhaps there had been some NVA in that thicket after all. Fearing a search for bodies in leech infested scrub, I kept my suspicions to myself.

I walked over to the platoon leader. "You slammed right into my position; didn't you hear us shooting?"

"It didn't sound that close."

Maybe so. And I knew that it wasn't his fault. At the very least there should have been a scout helicopter overhead to coordinate movement on the ground.

The contact Echo Company had made was pretty much as described to me by Captain Speare. Their point man had rounded a bend in the trail and confronted an NVA soldier about five feet away. Instantly both men turned and fled. "That's what usually happens," chuckled Cheyenne Six. "We got off a few rounds, but they dumped their packs and a radio and di di maued." He guessed that there were only about ten men in the NVA party. Echo Company still had their Russian-made radio, an M-16 round had gone right through it. How the man carrying it on his back had been able to get away was a mystery we didn't trouble ourselves with.

Bad news: Arizona Six has decided that we should join forces with Echo Company for a few days. Hueys soon arrived with C-rations, our packs, a mortar crew (where they came from I don't know) and, despite the fact that we were 50 yards from a stream, a blivet of water. From the final huey a stiff and remarkably clean first lieutenant from brigade staff emerged. He was to be the commander of our ersatz unit; a senior NCO to act as first sergeant would have been far more welcome.

We moved into the trees and established a perimeter while the mortar crew sat up on the sand spit. A round was dropped to settle the base plate, but produced only a dull, disappointing thunk. Misfire. Then came the ticklish process of sliding the round out of the tube and catching it. Another round was dropped; same result. The mortar tube evidently had no firing pin. This was reported and produced apoplexy back at battalion. A brand new tube arrived within an hour.

We remained on that position for two days; the two platoons longing for separate existences. Frequent patrols and ambushes produced only sparse sign of the NVA and no contact. A minor puzzle was solved when I learned that Sergeant Malone, who had uniquely volunteered for a night ambush, was an avid fisherman. I took a small patrol a mile or so along the ridge that First Squad had fired on and for hours we crouched a hundred feet above a beautiful crystalline pool waiting for NVA to risk a bath. None did and we all suspected that there was a duplicate NVA ambush on the other side of the valley waiting for us to make the same mistake.

On the third morning the Siamese platoons, joined at the hip by an aloof, scrubbed staff officer, crabbed their way downstream to another night perimeter. No one had remembered to load the empty water blivet onto the last supply helicopter and, instead of admitting the error and calling in another chopper, the decision was to carry it. Our unexpended mortar rounds, 25 of them, perhaps more, must also be carried. And so we moved out, our speed dictated by two men staggering under the 100 pounds of water blivet slung from a 10 foot pole. For hours we plowed glacially downstream as quiet and maneuverable as a Mogul army complete with elephants and concubines in palanquins. My platoon was at the rear of the column. At one point I set out security and for a half hour we frolicked in the stream. In that time the column had moved only 50 yards because there had been a problem getting the water blivet around an obstacle. What Echo Company's Chieu Hoi scout thought of all this can only be surmised, but the opinion of my men was clear and universal: "Charlie see this shit he gonna rupture hisself laughing." Altogether we covered a little over a half mile that day.

We dug in that evening on an old LZ situated on a low knoll. The saplings and brush that once covered it had been cut and tossed into a bomb crater some weeks before. The mortar rounds—those few that arrived—were fired uselessly into the forest and a new supply brought in by helicopter. We finally got rid of the water blivet. The day had a fitting climax; a man from Echo Company accidentally fired a burst of three rounds right across the perimeter. Miraculously, no one was hit. Stunned, he stared at the weapon while the man beside him, whom he had nearly killed, screamed at him, "You're really fucking stupid, you know that? Fucking stupid."

The only consolation to be derived from the past several days came from the fact that my new platoon sergeant, Staff Sergeant Taliferro, was proving to be an asset. His predecessor, who had come and gone in less than a month, had been marginal at best. Capable of getting lost in places where you shouldn't get lost and unable to get along with his squad leaders, he boarded a helicopter and disappeared forever into some bottomless rear echelon region several days after he coolly informed Captain Speare that he (the sergeant) had been shooting at a squirrel.

Sergeant Taliferro was an earnest, 20-year-old Mississippian with a wife and small baby. An instant NCO, he had been in the army for only a little over a year. He was the only man in the platoon who was openly patriotic (I believe that he had volunteered for Vietnam) and on the one occasion when I was asked, "Why are we here?"—actually it was more like, "How the fuck come we're in these fucking hills killing gooks?"—I left the explanation to Sergeant Taliferro. Taliferro told the man of the International Communist Conspiracy and said that if we didn't stop it here we would have to do it somewhere else, closer to home. Taliferro believed that and was convincing. I myself no longer knew why we were in Vietnam; nor did I care.

That night's ambush (our third in as many nights—Echo Company had pulled none) I assigned to Sergeant Taliferro and by the following morning he had established his right to be platoon sergeant which is not an easy task for a man just out of his teens.

The ambush returned in the morning, hollow-eyed and empty-handed. "Nothin'," said Taliferro, "nothin' movin' along that crick. One of the fellas was a little squirmy but he calmed down OK. I had to talk to him." Taliferro's report, I later learned, left out certain details. They had set up along the trail that led into our perimeter and, as ordered, very close to the stream. The area was full of leeches and, unable to light cigarettes the ambush had had to endure them for 12 hours. One man, tormented and miserable, as they all were, kept muttering and shifting position. After an hour of this, Taliferro crept up to him like a cat and laying the cold muzzle of his rifle against the man's neck for emphasis whispered an ultimatum: "Sit still or get out of my ambush." Taliferro meant that and the prospect of sitting out the night alone in the forest had turned the man to stone.

With open relief we were lifted out that morning after going through the ritual of a fake extraction. This consisted of having the men in the last lift return to the pick up zone laying flat on the decks of the slicks. When the slicks lift off again, the men sit up. The idea was that from a distance it would look like more men were being lifted out than really were. In this case two platoons instead of one. The recon platoon, as happy to be out of our shotgun marriage as we were, remained behind and set up an ambush in the hopes that the NVA would be caught poking around our old perimeter.

From the air, our section of Mooney's perimeter looked abandoned until the men we left behind, who had been pulling double guard assignments, stood on their bunkers and waved as we came in. They resembled the survivors of some strange muddy shipwreck. Everyone was, I believe, genuinely overjoyed to get back to Delta Company. I personally felt as though I had escaped from an asylum.

CHAPTER 7

"Go fucking swimming."
—Orders

A treat: we are given a chance to go swimming. Each morning for three days running a chinook picked up a group of about 25 funseekers and deposited them on Wunder Beach, a half moon perimeter that opened onto a mile or so of the South China Sea. The Southern Californians among us spoke highly of the surf.

My turn came on a slate-grey day so unpromising that a few men had to be ordered to "go fucking swimming" to ensure that the chopper was at least half full. The beach was empty except for rusted machinery and a few enormous amphibious vehicles off loading supplies from a small freighter. A cold stiff rain was falling and no one had any interest in swimming, which was just as well because the surf looked very dangerous. A few men asked permission to visit friends on a nearby LZ and the rest of us took in the only other area of interest: the PX. There, as at Juliet, you could buy cigarettes, cigarette lighters, and several varieties of canned food. I bought some chili and looked for other ways to kill time; there weren't any.

Bearing petty thefts and purchases, we drifted back to the open stretch of sand just behind the beach where the chinook had dropped us off three hours before. At the PZ a group of men from another company were already waiting, also with all manner of scrounged goods including a large section of plastic roofing. A chinook arrived, picked them up and departed in a swirl of water. An hour passed; the rain increased. We waited, huddling against a sand dune as the rain drove diagonally past us. When I could reach them, battalion kept insisting that the chinook would return.

127

A couple of men among us had volunteered for Vietnam in order to get out of the stockade, a decision they said they regretted, and the conversation turned to the advantages of being in the stockade as opposed to being in the field: (1) "you fucking keep *all* your fingers and toes" and (2) "three hots and a cot." But I didn't take it seriously because stockade time is "bad time," you still have to finish your tour; and, both the army stockade at Long Binh and the marine brig at Da Nang are by reputation *very* bad places.

We talked about food. Todd, who was possibly 18 but looked younger, was reminded of the time he got his fill of carrot sticks, the army's all purpose vegetable. The company had been without a change of clothes for two weeks and had not had a hot meal for nearly as long. With one pant leg gone and crotch open from zotz to belt, Todd was serving in the chow line behind the carrot sticks which everyone avoided. "I know why you guys didn't take no carrot sticks," said Todd. "Kuz my dick was hangin' out." "More for me," he concluded.

It was nearly dark before I finally agreed that "you can't fly in this shit" and we left the PZ looking for a place to spend the night. Keeping the sound of the surf on our right, the only way I could be sure that we weren't heading out of the perimeter, we approached the grey rectangular form which soon transformed itself into a frame building; absolutely the only structure or sign of life we could see in that cold, opaque storm. The building was empty except for a raincoat, which I claimed, and a machete, which someone else claimed. Wet sand was thrown on the floor and a fire kindled from panelling ripped from the wall. Cans of beer emerged from pockets and we settled in for the night. All thoughts of battalion slipped from my mind. (I later learned that my behavior had taxed Arizona Six's vascular system. "That officer wants to stay at the beach.")

About an hour later a sopping wet major appeared in the doorway. His eyes widening as he looked around, he asked what we were doing in "his" building. (It had not occurred to me that it was anybody's building.) I explained, as the men with me, who were paying no more attention to the major than if he were a beetle, scuffed among cans and equipment, dozed, or squatted by the fire which was beginning to eat through the floor. "Okay, fine," said the Major. "You kin stay. I just happened to see your...fire and, ah...wondered. No problem." He backed out the door and into the storm as though he had stumbled onto a witch's sabbath.

Shortly after the major fled, a deuce and a half pulled up and two squads of drenched infantry dismounted and ran to our building. A chaplain and a lieutenant followed. The chaplain, Father Grayson, warmed himself briefly by our fire and told us that they had come to hold a memorial service. I recognized the platoon leader from Division training. Fat and cocky, he had avoided the first two days of training, choosing instead to play cards until an astonished captain chased him out of his tent and into the sunlight. He had lost weight. His company was operating out of Wunder Beach. Every day, he said, they would go out and just about every day they would take casualties until finally, one of the platoons—not his he was careful to say—had refused to leave the perimeter. He was down to 18 men. What I had taken to be two squads was his entire platoon.

Father Grayson invited us to stay for the unknown man's service but his death was none of our business. We filed outside, hugged the lee of the building and sipped beer. After Father Grayson's eulogy, the lieutenant described very simply the circumstances of the man's death. He had been shot in the stomach and groin. At night, the platoon pinned down, he could not be medevacked. He died before morning. Unreliable and a loner, the man had no friends and it was plain that he would not be missed. He had wanted to know, said the lieutenant, that he "really wasn't a fuck-up." Nothing more was mentioned of what had happened that night. The lieutenant soon waved his men onto the truck and they headed back to the perimeter.

For a time the wind threatened to peel off the roof. Then, abruptly it died beneath a clear sky and a moon bright enough to write by. A few of us stepped outside to admire the towering, sand-churning surf. An hour later the wind and rain returned.

Late that night a call came from an armored battalion that was headquartered nearby. I was given their frequency ("from Jack Benny") and told to report there in the morning "at 0700, *exactly*."

By morning the surf had moved well up the beach and the rain had slackened to an ordinary cloudburst. Even the prospect of breakfast failed to generate enthusiasm and it was hard to get people moving. Finally, in frustration, I stepped purposefully into the rain ("Are you people coming or not, dammit?") and immediately sank to above my knees in the water-saturated sand. Everyone congregated in the doorway to take in this spectacle. After I was pulled free, we tried the other door which opened onto more solid footing.

I located the armored unit without difficulty. A straggle of disabled vehicles, some of them under repair, led us to a cluster of command tracks parked under a copse of trees. The area was already half under water. We were met by a staff officer, taken to an empty GP tent, which I gathered from the officer's attitude was the battalion leprosarium, and told to stay there. After a few minutes I was conducted into the presence of the battalion commander who said we would be pulling perimeter duty until "I can get you out of here." He made it clear that getting rid of us was a high priority. "And make damn sure you police up that tent your people are in." I puzzled over how to do that since the tent was ankle deep in water, but did not ask the colonel for advice. After I returned to the tent, we made a show of splashing cigarette butts into the rising tide and sloshed to the mess tent. Going through the chow line (powdered eggs and carrot sticks) required balancing on floating duck boards.

The portion of the perimeter we were to help man began at the surf, which had already engulfed one bunker, and extended for several hundred yards along a curving path marked by a six-foot high berm of sand. The bunkers were dug into the berm. It was guarded by a platoon of five APCs (armored personnel carriers), big boxy, gas powered, vehicles known for their tendency to become crematoria when hit by rockets. For that reason you were often better off riding on top of an APC than in it. In Vietnam an APC was essentially a platform for three crew served weapons—two M-60s and a .50 calibre—and much of what had been originally designed as crew space was taken up by layer upon layer of ammo cans.

Evidently the crews normally slept in shelters of canvas and plastic constructed on a light wooden frame. These had been shredded by the storm and were surrounded by a sad, boggy confusion of web gear, blankets, C-ration cans, and limp cardboard. Scattered throughout were dozens of one-pound blocks of C-4 which to us was treasure. "Help yourself, we kin always get more." Amazing.

We spent part of the day bouncing around in an APC. I got a chance to drive, which was fun—no trick at all. I was beginning to welcome the possibility of joining our hosts on a mission until, in a curiously singsong voice, one of the crew told us that a week before the track he had been driving had been hit by an RPG, and that by a fluke, the rocket hit in such a way that the engine block had absorbed much of its force. He had been blown clear out of the track but got only a

130

few scratches. So—back to the field. Every vehicle in that platoon was gouged and starred by small arms fire.

All day long the radio, when it worked, provided news of vehicles awash or marooned by high water. A tank was stuck, somewhere.

Nervous tracers began to fly as soon as night fell and we crept into our bunker. After several hours of crouching in water up to our knees, we gave it up and sat outside a little less miserably in the rain. It was cold, visibility was next to nothing and the radio no longer worked. In the end, those in my group spent the night crammed inside the crew compartment of a track. A third of that space was taken up by hundreds of ammo cans stacked on the floor. One man, draped in a poncho, stood in the open hatch and kept watch while the rest of us curled fetally against the armor plate. The crew kept warm by igniting a lump of C-4 in a helmet that sat directly on all that ammunition (they said they had done this before) and for part of the night we either roasted or froze until I decided that we were better off just being cold.

I can remember being struck by the fact that this unit used passwords—sign and countersign. In fact the whole setup seemed strange. The APCs were stationed at wide intervals and relied on the use of Starlight Scopes to see at night. These worked poorly in the rain. At unexplained intervals one of the APCs would crank up, race around, and then fall silent again. At other times, instead of simply just driving over, someone would be sent dangerously on foot from one track to another with what struck me as a pointless message. I was afraid that one of the men from Navajo, accustomed to shooting at anything that moved, would kill a messenger.

In the morning, things were no better. An APC, stuck the day before, was now under water, more vehicles were down, and one unit, isolated by high water, could not be raised on the radio. The battalion commander, dressed in a rain suit and looking like a Baptist preacher on a fishing vacation, ministered over this chaos with perfect calm. I seemed to be his only source of stress. Finally news came that we were to be lifted out by chinook and with that the colonel's mood brightened perceptibly. "Tell your commander," he said, "from now on to keep his people together." That, of course, I did *not* tell him.

We were picked up, taken to a small firebase and installed under an awning with another group of refugees. I feared yet another night of perimeter duty among peculiar people but an hour later we were lifted into the rain and returned to Mooney.

Mooney was a sodden mess. There had been no resupply for two days and just about everything down to the dregs of the most undesirable C-ration meals had been eaten. Some of the companies in the field had been without food for 24 hours and had little prospect of receiving any for another 24. It was cold, colder than at Wunder Beach, and the only way of keeping warm was to burn gasoline in a sandfilled ammo can. Many hooches had gaping holes because the roof had caught fire. Rain soaked bunkers had collapsed, injuring a couple of men, and the mud was ankle deep everywhere. The artillery, short of ammunition, could be used only sparingly and the situation at those firebases supporting us was reported to be the same.

That night Echo Company's frequency bled into ours, and I listened as Cheyenne Six browbeat one of his squad leaders into shifting the position of his ambush. The squad leader didn't want to move, not along a trail, not on a black, rain-driven night, and he wanted to get off the radio because it was giving away his position. His radio cut in and out and he was stammering with fear and cold-soaked misery. I have never heard a voice so bleak. Threatened with a court martial, he moved.

For three days we huddled cold and wet, surrounded by a sea of milk glass fog. The day after that beamed bright and clear and to our amazement all of Vietnam from the foothills to the coast appeared to be under water.

On that sunny day, one of our patrols returned with a conical peasant's hat which they found just outside the wire and close to the artillery dump. Finding that kind of headgear in the mountains made only a little more sense to us than finding a top hat and kid gloves, but it was clear that someone had gotten a look at our perimeter the night before. And worse, they had been able to do it without being detected.

The two nights that followed the discovery of the "gook hat" came and went without incident but the third night brought an urgent report of movement from Second Squad's bunker which was the bunker closest to the artillery dump. When I got down to that position it was obvious that everyone was taking the movement very seriously. There had been some bumping and crashing around in the dry scrub just outside the wire. It wasn't the wind; an animal? "Must be an animal," I said, "too much noise for a gook."

"We got gooks out there."

132

Heads cocked and necks stretched out like geese at every little sound. Suddenly there was a flurry of shooting which the other two bunkers immediately took up. Red tracers spewed everywhere as the men on all three bunkers hosed down the area to their front for fear that someone had already gotten inside the wire. In the repeated, rapid muzzle flashes we all seemed to be moving by instantaneous jerks as though reality did not have enough frames per second. The firing slackened, and then in the hissing light of a trip flare started up again. After the flare died everything went black.

I called Four Six and ordered up some flares so that we could get a good look at the wire. The mortar tube banged a couple of times and after a wait of 20 seconds or so there were two soft pops high up and well beyond the perimeter. The flares drifted lazily down towards the wire and revealed nothing.

Sergeant Taliferro who was an enthusiast for these occasions joined me on the bunker. I was annoyed at all the shooting, and told everyone to stick to frags, "and only if you really have something." Big Man Cordova who hailed from the Philadelphia ghetto and who was the best field soldier I have ever known seconded this. "A frag is better than a whole magazine a sixteen," he counseled. "You salvo some frags on Charles and he gonna look at his funny papers and di di mau."

We sat tight for a while.

Movement. Several frags went bounding out to crash in the wire. Silence. More noise; more frags. One of the men on the bunker, called Ti Ti because he was short, let out a yelp and grabbed his stomach. Big Man at his side was more worried than Ti Ti who was gingerly inspecting his anatomy. Only a welt; it was a spent fragment. Close friends, both men were longterm survivors. They always worked together on point, surgically probing, one covering the other, slipping into a high gaited crouch when they expected trouble. They were deadly.

More firing from all three bunkers. At what? Hand clamped to one ear, handset to the other, and shouting over the radio, I tried to get more illumination rounds. Six cut in and said no: "They've already seen too much of the perimeter." I still doubted that there was anyone outside the wire and wanted the flares to calm everybody down...myself included.

Sergeant Honeywell tumbled into our position. Captain Speare had probably sent him to find out what was really going on but, whatever the reason, I was glad to see him. With Honeywell, helmet strapped on tight, bayonet fixed, and looking like a time traveler from the Second World War, was Two Niner Mike India. Big Man who was sitting on a case of fragmentation grenades regarded this apparition with astonishment and then returned his attention to the wire.

Honeywell's car carbine kept jamming. He would try to loose off a burst and it would quit after two rounds. Honeywell would curse, clear the weapon, fire again and it would jam. "Damn short gun." Sergeant Taliferro knelt in a marksman's position, as intent as a leopard, trying to catch something in his peripheral vision. When he did he snapped off a few quick shots; then everyone else would open up again. And so it went for perhaps half an hour during which I saw nothing—no shapes in the wire, no return fire.

I was convinced that there was nothing out there. This was not the first time the platoon had spent half the night throwing frags at noises. On one occasion the mortar platoon had taken advantage of our exuberance by giving us all their old frags, those with twisted and bent spoons—dangerous things, two helmets full. Sergeant Taliferro, with whom I shared a position that night, gathered about ten of these evil gadgets together and whenever he heard the slightest noise would peg one into the darkness. I woke up the next morning with my arm thrown over a little turd-like pile of grenades and leaped up as though I had seen a viper. Sergeant Taliferro had straightened all the pins! News of my sleeping arrangements soon reached Aguirre who howled with glee. "I hear something really snapped you out of your shit this morning, Lieutenant." And, then to everyone: "Two Six wants pitchers. We got too many pitchers; you all want to be pitchers." Aguirre was sure that there had never been anything out there that night.

The last thing I wanted was another night of "trigger-happy bullshit" and I said so, heatedly, to everyone on the bunker. My timing could have been better. A few minutes later green tracers swept diagonally across the front of our bunker and into Echo Company's sector. "Sir, I believe we are taking incoming rounds," intoned Honeywell. I could not see his face but I knew he was enjoying the moment.

The commander of Echo Company immediately called to complain about our careless shooting. "Be advised," he said prissily, "we have rounds going right over our position." It was a pleasure to tell him that someone was doing that deliberately.

I called in one of the defensive targets and walked a half dozen rounds across the front of our perimeter. For a while everything fell silent, only to start up again. I called for illumination and was again refused. By then the NVA had probably gone. If their mission had been reconnaissance (the only realistic guess), they had only partially succeeded. I suspect that the reason they stuck around for as long as they did, or even bothered to shoot back, was to determine the location of our M-60s. None of our gunners had opened up.

After a couple of hours without movement, tracers, trip flares or frags, Six called to tell me to leave two guards on each position and let everyone else get some sleep. I left only one guard. On this, Hardoy and I thought alike. "You put two guys on a guard position, all they do is talk."

New moon dark, the night continued in silence. We had a patrol in the morning, a long one, and it soon occupied my thoughts. I claimed a flat area just behind the bunker and lay down, the radio propped up beside me. A little further up the slope, Stanhope, a small tough man who sometimes walked point, was already sleeping. I dozed lightly, cozily aware of the routine chatter on the radio and then awoke to fret about what the day would bring. We were to search a valley several miles away (over five kilometers on the map) which meant that we would have to move rapidly and by trail. I detested such assignments — feared them — and considered them to be nothing more than ambush drill for the NVA. But Arizona Six expected you to complete such patrols or show evidence of busting your ass in the attempt. Other platoons, I knew, had done as much and more. I remembered listening in astonishment to a platoon leader from Alpha Company, Ranger trained and proud of it, brag about his coup. "Arizona Six didn't think we could make it," he puffed. "Six fucking klicks to that ridge. We were fucking double-timing." I thought him a fool. But now, I thought, in the morning, on a couple of hours sleep...shit. I could see the guard on the bunker shifting back and forth; peering ahead, then to one side. Nervous.

It happened in the twinkling of an eye but to me so slowly that I could count the shots. The guard wheeled: "Sir, I got movement!" and opened fire on full automatic. One, two, three, four rounds gone; it was the last round, I think, that hit Stanhope in the thigh as he lay on the ground, traveled up his leg and into his abdomen. The guard had just shot his best friend.

"He shot me," said Stanhope softly. Then louder, the intensity growing, "Ow, my God, ow, it hurts, Jesus, it hurts!"

"Medic! . . . Medic!"

Several men crouched beside Stanhope who was moaning. The guard sat dazed on the bunker, his rifle beside him. Two Six Bandaid emerged from the darkness at a dead run and checked the wound for a few seconds.

"Let's get him to the aid station. Put him on a poncho."

Awkwardly, one man on each corner of the poncho, half running, sometimes stumbling, we carried Stanhope across the darkened LZ to the aid station. Stanhope was in agony the entire distance and kept begging us to put him down. I watched as the medics cut off Stanhope's clothes and put in an IV. A small hole in the front of his thigh oozed dark blood. I could not see an exit wound but at that range there must have been one.

Medevac arrived within 15 minutes thumping urgently up the valley to land in front of TOC. Shadowy figures, one holding a plasma bag, placed Stanhope aboard. I waited until the chopper disappeared into darkness and then walked over to the company CP.

Captain Speare's bunker was large, unfurnished except for two radios and a couple of air mattresses, and absolutely dark. He was awake. After telling Speare what had happened and that Stanhope would probably be all right, which was what I had been told, Speare lit a cigarette. Only then could I see his eyes. "Dumb, bullshit mistake," said Speare. "He [the guard] should have known there was no one inside the wire. Those damn flares of yours lit us up like Saturday night." But I knew I should have kept two men on that position. Speare didn't dwell on this and the topic shifted abruptly.

"I don't think Arizona Six likes us," said Speare. His eyes darted around the bunker. "Navajo gets shit assignments. He doesn't like us." Speare lapsed into uncomfortable silence as though he had been caught picking at a scab in public.

"I think we do all right," I said, a lame and useless statement.

"All right doesn't fucking get it," he snapped.

Bunker politics: Navajo had not been producing like the other companies in the battalion. What the battalion produced was NVA bodies; bodies that were added up, graphed out, and apportioned into "good" kill ratios that meant good efficiency reports and sometimes even whiskey and cigars. A company, battalion, brigade, or division that did not leave behind enough moldering corpses also left in its wake stunted careers. The spores of ambition and duty drifted from

136

every dank command bunker in the division and sometimes you could see that cloud of spores, mustard brown, settling on everything.

Not long after first light, we were told to check the perimeter for bodies and, as I expected, found none; only the recent prints of four or five men wearing NVA canvas boots. An hour later the patrol robotically assembled itself. We left by the wire in front of our sector and followed a trail that passed through a grey, skeletal forest and then dropped steeply down for several hundred feet into a field of brown elephant grass higher than our heads. As soon as we entered the grass, Ti Ti, who had point, selected a blade of grass, trimmed it to a length of three feet and began to wave it back and forth at ground level to check for trip wires. He moved quickly but his eyes never left the ground. Big Man, a foot taller and just behind Ti Ti, scanned ahead.

"What's in this grass?" I called for a cloverleaf and sat on the trail swatting flies while one squad circled out from the front and another from the rear. It took them about 20 minutes to labor back to me. Nothing. A couple of hundred yards further down the trail I called for another cloverleaf. This time First Squad came back with the news that "there are some fucking rockets over there." The rockets were ours, 2.75 inch rockets, eight of them, stacked neatly in a pile. Two of them were evidently duds; the rocket motors had burned but the warheads had not exploded. The others were live, both warhead and rocket, and I concluded that they had been taken from a downed gunship. After shooing away all the sightseers, I reported the rockets and was told to wait for engineers to come and destroy them.

We sat on the trail in silence until finally three engineers toiled down off the ridge above us. We stood up, waving our rifles so that they could see us. The engineers arrived and I guided them through the grass to the rockets. "How did you find them suckers in all this fucking grass?" asked the Spec 5 in charge. What he meant was, why did I bother to report them? As far as the engineers were concerned those rockets would have rusted in that grass for eons if I hadn't bumbled across them and ruined what had promised to be a pleasant morning of sunbathing.

After checking for booby traps, they set to work, one of the engineers explaining that the charges had to be placed at the juncture of the warhead and the rocket motor. "You wanna set 'em both off at the same time. Rockets are tricky, you'll see." The warheads all went up but the rocket motors just burned. Giving off a ferocious hiss they snaked and pinwheeled through the grass while we lay glued to the ground. "See," said the engineer, after all the snakes had finally died, "tricky."

Coming on the heels of a stretch of cold rain, the afternoon seemed doubly hot. We pushed our way out of the grass onto a dry bony ridge and soon picked up a broad trail that took us beyond the defoliation around Mooney. With Ti Ti and Big Man still on point, we crossed an open, grassy saddle, dotted with clusters of startlingly blue flowers. In an ordinary world these would have been ordinary flowers but one of the consequences of defoliation was that you didn't often see certain colors. The sky was blue of course, sometimes, as it was that day, but usually it was brown land under grey cloud. The brightest things on Mooney were the green plastic sandbags and those soon faded to the same ashy-green as our washed out fatigues. That is why I remember those flowers.

As soon as the forest resumed, the man in front of me fished a main-meal C-ration can from his pocket, ratcheted open the top with the little issue can opener (a "P-38," two come in each case of C-rations) and after flipping off the covering layer of congealed grease began to spoon down beans and motherfuckers. He finished in less than two minutes and never broke stride.

I guessed that the trail we were following passed close to the valley we were to search; anyhow, I saw little choice but to stay on it because off trail we would never make our objective. My greatest fear, probably everyone's, was running into a Chicom claymore. A Chicom claymore is as big around as a metal garbage can lid, weighs over 25 pounds and only one of them could have blown half the platoon to rags. I kept imagining one of these things just ahead of us, well camouflaged, sitting on its curious wire stand like a funeral wreath. The funeral director just sits along the trail, the detonator in his hand, and blows you away.

Around mid-afternoon our foot race ended. Ti Ti suddenly spun around to his right and sank to his knees. Big Man, just behind him, sprang off the trail. I could hear both men breathing from 50 feet away. There was a spider hole dug down between the buttress roots of a tree that grew beside the trail. The position was absolutely undetectable to anyone coming up the trail and, had it been occupied, Ti Ti would have taken a round into the side, just below his flack vest, and up through his rib cage. None of us doubted, least of all Ti Ti, that the NVA had soldiers who would hold to such a position for the satisfaction of killing us in so personal a manner. From then on we moved slowly and carefully, and stayed off the trail.

A little further on we came across another spider hole which was covered by a curved mat of tightly woven bamboo. It looked rather cozy and we decided that it was the position of a trail watcher who had wickedly given in to creature comfort. "Slack motherfucker," pronounced Ti Ti, who had spotted the matting immediately. The position had not been used since the last rain. Perhaps a hundred yards further up the ridge was a big storage pit. This scared the hell out of me when I first glimpsed the thatch roof that covered it because I thought I had walked the platoon into another base camp. Then I saw that most of the thatch had been burned. The storage pit, about 35 feet by 15 feet, was empty and there was nothing to indicate what it had once contained except that nearby someone found the barrel and receiver of an SKS carbine. The Hansel and Gretel trail of cigarette butts, gum wrappers and C-ration cans that grunts leave behind was not in evidence around the storage pit (or anywhere else on that ridge) so it must have been spotted from the air by the 1st of the 9th. A lingering acrid smell suggested that one of their daredevil scoutship crews had hovered down over it and dropped a white phosphorous grenade. They did such things routinely.

I never found the valley. Somehow in the Crab Nebula of ridges around Mooney the valley wasn't where it was supposed to be. In other words I was fucking lost again. But we did find water and that enabled us to get back to Mooney without hailing medevac. We returned by the same route and came to the elephant grass at twilight. Bats swooped and twisted after the insects we scared up as we wove through the grass toward Mooney's high ridge.

The climb to Mooney was punishing. Dehydrated, we puked our way up the last steep several hundred yards and entered the perimeter with thick, caked tongues and beehive headaches. Speare, predictably, was not pleased about having to inform Arizona Six that I had failed to reach the valley. Later, in the cool evening, I realized that I had not eaten for nearly 24 hours. It was too late to fire up a chunk of C-4, so I had cold Cs for dinner.

The following day, Sergeant Honeywell went to see Stanhope in the hospital at Quang Tri. The round had left a maggot's burrow through Stanhope's intestines which the doctors claim to have patched. "He's got a fucking colostomy bag," said Honeywell, "but he's gonna make it to the World. He'll be back in the World in a few weeks." It was easy to see that the hospital had left Honeywell unsettled; he repeatedly mentioned seeing a big pile of cut-up boots and bloody fatigues waiting to be burned.

A blatant case of simulation came to light. First Squad sent on a night ambush at dusk was discovered six hours later playing cards at the LP. Captain Speare was livid and Sergeant Palovick was instantly broken to private. Palovick mothered his squad — he would sometimes sneak up to Mooney's supply depot and steal an extra case of C-rations for his men — and now he had allowed himself to be talked into a stunt that was certain to be detected. I blamed his squad and told them so, striking a nerve. Palovick moped. He was not regular army but was stung by the demotion all the same. That evening he ripped off his stripes.

The LP was so removed from the perimeter that it invited mischief. Bochek received, ominously, a "care package" from his ex-wife, an immensely valuable bottle of Jack Daniels which he shared with two other men on the LP. They killed much of the bottle within an hour and then went...NUTS! Sobbing and shrieking, they threw down their weapons (fortunately) and ran in all directions. One man had to be retrieved from a roll of concertina. Another ran the length of the LZ and then darted back and forth in response to unseen horrors. No one could calm him down. Finally after two hours all three men dropped from exhaustion. Evidently, or so I was told, the bourbon had been laced with LSD. Speare, dumbfounded and dubious, hinted darkly that I had better take control of my platoon.

CHAPTER 8

"If I die in a combat zone
box me up and ship me home."
—Cadence call: basic training—
Few take it seriously.

As we were being lifted out of Mooney a pudgy lieutenant carrying a clipboard walked up to me. I had never seen him before and he seemed out of place because his fatigues were clean and unfaded.

"I need some information on your man who died. This man who was shot the other night." He glanced at his clipboard, ". . . this man Stanhope."

"How? They said he was doing okay."

"You know what a sixteen does to people." The lieutenant made an abrupt expanding motion with his hands indicating an explosion. He had a look of distaste on his face. Grunts were always shooting each other by mistake and now he was stuck with this chore.

"What was he doing when he was shot?"

"They said he was doing okay."

"Just put something in here." He handed me a pencil and pointed to a space on a form, an accident form.

I could not write.

"Where were you when this man was shot?"

I told him.

"That's fine; that's all I need. Just sign it. I'll fill it in . . . we gotta have something in there."

I sprinted to catch the choppers.

Mead had learned of his friend's death in the same manner. After that he withdrew and seldom spoke to anyone. Several weeks later, as

141

Navajo pushed along a ridge to make its night perimeter, he informed me that his legs didn't work.

"I can't make 'em work," he bleated, genuinely scared. "They won't fucking move."

He had to be medevacked. I think that he believed that it was somehow due to heat exhaustion. And so did I at the time.

Our LZ that morning was a bomb crater that had taken a melon bite out of a high narrow ridge. There were two possible LZs on that ridge; we happened to land on the one that was not booby-trapped, a fact which deeply impressed Hardoy who was in the lead chopper. We came upon the second LZ as we worked our way up the ridge. Several foxholes had pressure release devices in them and 81mm mortar rounds, rigged to go off in the rotor wash of a helicopter, hung in the trees. Speare took no chances and called for engineers to deal with them. It took an hour to clear this area before we could move through it. Everyone not involved either dozed or spooned down Lurp rations.

A cold rain began that afternoon and continued into the next day. Our night position, further up the ridge, was a dreary parrot's perch that looked down on open valleys nearly a thousand feet below. The ridge was so narrow that Navajo simply stopped and dug foxholes on either side of the trail. The only possible avenue of attack was along the top of the ridge, but that was little consolation when I discovered the men who were supposedly guarding the trail under a poncho playing cards. They were either convinced that there was no possibility of an attack during the day or they were too wet and miserable to give a damn.

A call of nature meant hanging over the side of the ridge and, since most of the company was dysenteric to some degree, few of us could avoid that adventure. At night, the issue was more problematic than usual and men chose to shit beside their position. By morning the ridge would drone with flies.

The rain had the rest of us glum and shivering but seemed to make no inroads on Sergeant Chisholm's contentment. He stood for a long while, meditating on the spectacularly green valley far below us and, I'm sure, on his nearly 30 years of field soldiering. "It's times like this that you remember about being in the field," he said, "you're not going to forget that valley or being on this ridge." Chisholm was right, as he usually was, but I also remember the shit, flies and cold rain.

The day after we had to move to a line of knobby hills that ran roughly parallel to the ridge — a straight line distance of two miles but the actual distance, down the boulder-strewn ridge, across a broad valley and then to the top of a 1,500 foot hill was much greater. Speare requested that the first part of our line of march be salted with 155 rounds and our relentlessly cheerful FO proceeded to give us a lecture on artillery spotting. As we waited for the first round, he chattered on about atmospherics, gun target line (the line between the gun and its target; if you were on the gun target line, a short or long round could kill you) and the need for high angle fire in the mountains which, he said with a sneer, meant turning your artillery piece into a mortar. The first round (I suspect deliberately) fell far below us into the valley, exploding in a small black blotch against a sea of green. The FO reported its location and I could hear the fire control officer reply, "I thought we needed more oomph on that one." The next round landed well up on the side of the ridge and the one after that at the top. At 50 meter intervals — "drop five zero, repeat Hotel Echo" — the FO walked the rounds toward us. The last round cracked off about 150 yards away and provoked howls of indignation as a few fragments whined over our heads. The FO shrugged. "You have to expect that with big stuff."

We moved briefly along the trail, cautiously, fearful of booby traps, and then headed straight down the side of the ridge. We picked our way slowly beneath deep canopy, edging around one boulder, dropping down to another, hanging onto vines, descending into an emerald green world. Halfway down we broke for a meal in a downpour so heavy that Lurp rations were prepared by simply opening the top of the package and holding it out to the rain. Sitting on boulders and wedged between buttress roots, the men in the column were stacked far up the side of the ridge and out of sight.

We moved out again only to have the column stall. I worked my way back up the ridge and found the problem: One man was threatening the man in front of him with a beating if he moved. Everyone else stared placidly at this scene. Out of breath and infuriated, I railed at everyone — Wyndham for picking on Stone who was half his size and the only man in the company simple enough to take the threat seriously, and everyone else for allowing it to happen. Obviously more than a little retarded, Stone, confused but dutiful, usually got along reasonably well. He should not have been put in a rifle platoon and, at the first opportunity, I sent him to mortars where I believe he com-

143

pleted his tour quite happily, forbidden, as I'm sure was his desire, to have anything to do with actually firing the weapon.

Wyndham's career as a bully went into a decline a few days later when he threatened to stick his fist down Home's throat. Home never even bothered to look up. "Then," he said, "you be comin' out the other end," and returned serenely to his card game. "Wolf tickets," he muttered to his companions, "jes wolf tickets."

Moving again we made good progress until the men in the lead squad suddenly bolted in all directions frantically waving their arms like apes on fire. They had bumped into a nest of large bees. Several men nursed stings and dozens of bees swirled angrily around two M-16s that had been dropped. We stood in a rueful circle and stared at this for several minutes hoping the bees (or hornets or whatever they were) would calm down. They didn't. Someone suggested that a smoke grenade would clear them out but that would give away our position. I knew that Speare would be calling soon to complain about the hold up and I didn't care to tell him the column had been stalled by bees.

He did call but delivered only a few blunt words before he clicked off.

Silence.

"Six, Two-Six, anything further?"

Tex answered: "Be advised, Six had to take a shit and he fell down the hill."

"Oh Jesus! Is he all right?"

"Affirmative, I think so, . . . Yea [giggling now] he's okay. But I think you better get a move on."

So motivated, I darted in, collected the weapons, and ran back out trailing bees for 50 yards. I must have resembled a very harassed bellhop.

Stung six or seven times, my face rapidly swelled to gargoyle dimensions with one eye closed and the other a slit. For nearly an hour navigation consisted of squinting past a Durante nose at the compass and then pointing the direction. I could barely see the ground in front of me. By the time we got off the ridge the swelling had gone down but I still had the heart rate of a jack rabbit.

The valley floor seeped mist. It was cold. A sluggish stream cut through a meadow haunted by a fetid pile of torn and bloody NVA fatigues in which maggots twitched.

Our night perimeter was on a hilltop partially covered with knee high grass. To the east, toward the South China Sea, a dragon tail ridge stretched down to an enormous brown tract of grassland six or seven hundred feet below. As we dug in for the night we watched a couple of chinooks in the distance lazily circling dense columns of black smoke. We were told that barrels of jet fuel were being dumped on NVA positions. It was in this setting that Sergeant Chisholm and Simpson, a gunner from Third Platoon and also a fellow Appalachian, puckishly drew Captain Speare into a discussion of "stump trained mules." I think that's what they called it; you could call it something else. Speare had a puritanical streak which came out in odd ways. He would not, unless very angry, say "fuck." What he usually said was "uck," as in "number uckin' ten." Speare had no idea of what was coming and when this bit of mountain lore was explained to him, he backed away in astonishment. "I don't ucking believe that."

The rain stopped and it grew hot again. We stayed on that homey hill for three days, running daily patrols and ambushes, learning the trails, exploring into the valley, dipping canteens into the streams that chased down the hills and sweating our way back to the perimeter. There were always a few NVA around; perhaps they lived on our hill, or perhaps on a neighboring hill, well down toward the grasslands we supposed. We would hear them below us, try to close, and they would drop further down the ridge. The next day we would find them above us. We would go on line and wait, only to have them sideslip away. Hardoy had the same experience. Such minuets now seemed so normal to us that it was not until the second day that we reported our pet NVA to Speare.

The following day the company filed out along a broad trail that ran north along the hilltops toward a new position about two miles distant. Second Platoon, last in the column, dropped off and dug in—no hooches, brush covering our foxholes—on a knoll just below our old perimeter which still had trip flares in place. Left alone again, and this time in a familiar place, I hoped the assignment would last for several days.

It did not: adventurous or merely hungry, our pet NVA rose repeatedly to the bait of a recently abandoned perimeter. Late that afternoon there was a call from Six. Several NVA had been spotted on the bare ridge that jutted out from our old perimeter. "I've got Cavalier [a scout helicopter and a Cobra gunship from the 1st of the 9th] on the way."

Within minutes Cavalier was overhead with a simple request: "Where are the NVA?" I was much more concerned that they knew where we were and asked if they had our position. After they said that they did, a little testily, I directed them to the ridge. Six cut in: "They're along the military crest of the hill." The scout ship dipped low across the front of our position chattering away with an M-60 hoping to draw fire; it didn't, and made way for the gunship which plastered the ridge and hillside with rockets. Immediately the scout ship returned and buzzed around like an angry bee just above the tree tops. On its second pass the Cobra opened up with its minigun chasing hundreds of rounds along a rocky stream that ran at the base of the ridge. The sound reminded me of someone shaking a tin can full of marbles, only much louder. Then out of ammunition, Cavalier said good-bye and left. The only casualty that afternoon, probably, was a man who burned his hand in the process of setting out trip flares.

We settled into a warm black night. I pushed an LP out towards the old perimeter. Below and only a few yards away from our old positions, the LP was nerve-wracking and produced false alarms. Getting up to check out one of these, an improbable report of whistling, I spilled a cherished Lurp-ration (chili and rice) into which I had poured most of my last canteen. Finally, tired of being disturbed every half hour, I joined Villareal, on the LP. The night was pitch black and the hill above us was ominous. Villareal who looked amazingly like a Mexican revolutionary soldier when he had belts of M-60 ammo draped across his chest, had transferred the fierce loyalties of the Los Angeles ghetto to Delta Company. To him, Vietnam was some sort of enlarged turf dispute. He was an enthusiastic point man but had the disconcerting habit of turning around every five minutes to look back at me for encouragement. He once proudly showed me a snapshot of his girlfriend wearing only her bra and panties. For some reason he would not let anyone take his picture.

I could hear nothing—no movement, no whistling (except the wind), nothing out of the ordinary. After about an hour I told Villareal I would send out his relief and returned to the platoon. Midnight passed but very few of us were sleeping. Momentarily a trip flare blazed on the far side of the hill above us and then abruptly went out. Someone had evidently scuttled it into a foxhole and covered it with dirt. The rest of the company located on a ridge that had our old perimeter under observation had also seen the flare.

146

I called for a fire mission asking for "Willie Peter" (white phosphorous) and Four Six responded within less than a minute, calling out the shot—"Four Six, Two Six, Shot, Over"—although, of course, we could easily hear the round leave the tube. I acknowledged and waited apprehensively for the fall of the round. We were close to the gun target line and, at the most, 100 yards from the old perimeter. The round fell short, blossoming menacingly at the base of our knoll. There was no danger but the thought of being splashed with white phosphorous had me sputtering into the radio, "Jesus, hold it, check fire, check fire," until I realized how foolish I sounded and clicked off. Two Niner Mike India approached me with the formality of an English butler and pointed out what I should have done automatically: shoot another compass heading to the target and add 200. I did this with exaggerated calm and the round, white phosphorous again dropped well to the far side of our old perimeter silhouetting the crest of the hill.

"Four Six, Two Six: drop five zero, repeat three rounds Hotel Echo."

Four Six acknowledged and again within less than a minute called out the shots. The rounds landed in rapid succession just on the perimeter, one of them looping a trip flare high into the air. I dropped six more rounds onto the perimeter and ended the mission.

We waited, expecting that the fire mission had shooed the NVA in our direction. But it didn't. No NVA materialized out of the night. After a couple of hours we went back to our normal guard routine.

In the morning we inspected our old perimeter and, if we had hit anyone, there was no sign of it. We retrieved our trip flares and discovered that the wires to most of them had been cut—with wire cutters, not by shrapnel.

The perimeter was an education because it was not hard to see why the NVA regarded our old positions as interesting places to visit. Despite a call for a police before we had pulled out, the perimeter looked like a junkyard. Food, web gear, a poncho, and two fragmentation grenades were found. None of this would have been overlooked by the NVA.

It had been over 24 hours since our last chance to fill our canteens so we had very little water. I called Six and requested that a water blivet or at least a few plastic gallon jugs be dropped, only to be informed after a ten minute wait "that wind conditions did not encourage a water drop unless absolutely imperative," which meant no. Tex used that stilted phrasing so that I would know that it was someone at battalion and not Speare who had refused the mission.

As I stewed about the times battalion had dumped water blivets on us when we did not want them, Tex relayed another message from battalion. I was ordered to conduct a search for bodies along the ridge where the NVA had been spotted the day before. It came to mind that we sometimes spent more time looking for dead NVA than live ones but I lacked the wit to sit tight for awhile and then call in some vague report about blood trails or maybe even body parts in trees. What harm would it have done? Not a single graph in Saigon would have moved a millimeter. And I know it would have brightened battalion's day; perhaps he (Arizona Six) would have started to like us.

We searched the hillside below the perimeter and found nothing. The narrow, grassy ridge that jutted out from the hill also revealed nothing save a big burned patch where a rocket had detonated. I reported finding "zero bodies" and, since the time and effort involved in producing this statistical tidbit had totally exhausted our water, I reported that also. "Zero water."

It was by then mid-morning and already very hot. Water on such days was like a drug to us and I knew the symptoms of withdrawal as well as any addict. I was convinced that we could not make it back up the ridge, still less reach the company, without medevacking people with heat exhaustion in batch lots. I should have sat the platoon down and screamed over the radio for water. I chose, instead, to head for the nearest water which was only about 500 feet away, *roughly straight down*, in the stream that trickled along the base of the ridge. Getting there would be hard; getting back perhaps a little risky, but the subtleties of duty sometimes took an unambiguous form in the Division. Risk lives or burn shit, at least metaphorically.

I decided to follow the ridge down to where we could get to the stream. Then we could head back along the ridge that paralleled the one we were on and eventually cut the trail that led to Navajo.

A head-buzzing rage mantled the platoon as we plodded along the top of the dragon's tail that drooped down toward the grassland. Equipment disappeared over the side of the ridge and those who still had the energy cursed me, the army, and the Republic of Vietnam. That ridge was my road to Damascus. The god of battles spoke to me out of a bright Vietnamese sky: "Fuck Arizona Six," he said. God meant that I should be more creative in my interpretation of orders.

148

When God spoke to me, the stream was in plain view about a hundred feet below us. But getting to it meant picking our way down the steep sides of the ridge. The First Squad, myself included, made it down by sliding on their backsides for the last 30 or 40 feet. We landed directly in a pool of ice-cold water.

Rapture. Everyone arrived in minutes. Among the last were Bishop, the son of a Baptist minister and a man who took care of his M-60 like a Rolex watch, and Ju Ju, his stocky, sullen, assistant gunner. Burdened by their heavy load of gun and ammo belts, they lost their footing and came flailing down off the ridge to land in a heap, helmets down on their noses, unhurt, and laughing. At this the spirit of Two Niner Mike India, who was normally a prophet of doom, soared.

"I can make it in the field as long as we got guys like that," he sang.

Plunging our heads into the water we drank directly from the stream; we filled our canteens and drank, popped salt tablets and drank more. For half an hour the platoon splashed and played like otters while I nervously eyed the ridge tops. Then we moved out again through head-high grass, skirting the tip of one ridge, and climbing back onto another, heading towards the trail that would lead us home. With the last squad still plowing through the elephant grass, Villareal dropped out with heat exhaustion.

Two Six Bandaid soon radioed that he would have to be medevacked—and quickly. I called Six requesting a medevac; encoding our position since I didn't want our location pinpointed any sooner than necessary. A quarter mile of elephant grass had left us exhausted and now we could only sit, dully baking, until Dust Off arrived. Somewhere along the line, they got the wrong coordinates and spent 20 minutes flying in widening circles until at last they raised us, very faintly, on the radio. I sent in the correct coordinates in the clear as I should have done in the first place.

The scene at the rear of the column was chaotic. On a bed of trampled grass, Villareal was writhing and puking with severe heat cramps, sweat streaming off him, and Sergeant Taliferro was yelling at his RTO to put up the long whip. Livid, my head bursting in the heat, I only added to the chaos by screeching at everyone (Villareal included for not taking his salt tablets) slamming my helmet down, and booting it into the grass. We were all still feeling the effects of dehydration and no one in that kiln of an afternoon was behaving very rationally.

Even though canteen after canteen had been poured over Villareal's chest and back he could not have been far from heat stroke. Finally we could hear medevac thumping towards us on the other side of the ridge and then came the request to pop smoke. A minute later they swept over the ridge and in that flat brown expanse spotted us immediately. The grass was too high for medevac to land and Villareal, barely conscious, had to be strapped into a "jungle suit," a contraption of heavy slatted canvas, before he could be winched into the huey. Moreno, the man who had suffered the flare burn, rode up on the penetrator. His hand was a mass of blisters.

Villareal returned to the company the next day, still weak and wobbly, and with, for some reason, a chronic nosebleed. He must have simply left the hospital and hitched a ride back to the company as soon as he discovered he could walk.

Then began the climb up the ridge. Part of the time we could easily see the company perimeter two ridges over and far above us but they simply could not see us. "We're on the. . .third ridge. We're in a little open area, over." I waited.

"Negative—we can't see you."

"We're looking right at you."

"Negative, can't see you."

It was a lesson in how easily the NVA could operate undetected in the mountains.

Finally I called in our coordinates. I had no intention of just popping smoke and discovering how many NVA were concealed in that area. Speare responded in amazement. "What the hell are you doing there? Never mind. Get out of there. Out." The "out" was ominous. After about a minute Speare came back on the radio.

"I want you back on your assigned route. You are really stepping on your dick. . .do you get my drift?" I said that I did.

The ridge was steep, sinuous, and covered with heavy undergrowth. Two Niner Mike India and probably half the platoon was convinced that we were lost. I kept saying that "we'll cut the trail pretty soon. This ridge has to lead back to the trail." After an hour, I wasn't so sure. "Pretty soon" consumed all of the afternoon and most of our water. We finally hit the trail but much further away from the company than I had hoped.

We moved slowly with frequent breaks, everyone just sliding down on their packs to rest. After each break it was harder and harder to get people back on their feet. No one spoke anymore. With only an hour or so of daylight we came to a little knoll. It was irresistible! Fields of fire were excellent and the digging easy. I called Six and told him we couldn't make it.

"I've got a good position. We're beat; we can link up with you in the morning." Six said no; we had to come in that night. And, as the platoon clustered around me, he lapsed uncharacteristically into a pep talk.

"It's been a tough day," he said, "but I know you can do it. We all know what a tough outfit Second Platoon is." Or words like that; it was pure rotarian boosterism.

Someone, I've forgotten who, started to laugh. Then everyone. Actually, we howled and hooted and screeched; for some reason we found Speare's pep talk, which was intended to goose us back on the trail, hysterically funny. Speare kept saying "Over," trying to get me to acknowledge, but this only prompted more laughter. Gasping for air, I tried to speak with Speare but only managed to transmit a few croaks that may have been audible above a background of maniacal cackling. It was several minutes before I could come back on the radio, still wheezing, to say we were moving out.

It took us several hours, most of it in darkness, to reach the company. We moved slowly along the trail and took no breaks; if we had, I don't think I could have gotten everyone on their feet again. My biggest fear, apart from being ambushed, was that someone would fall behind the column. Sergeant Taliferro guarded against this, encouraging, cajoling, carrying first one man's weapon and then another's.

The column kept stretching out. The only way I could control this was by moving to the front of the column and setting a pace that was virtually a crawl. Gosselin, the best point man in the company, moved well in front. He would search ahead for a couple hundred yards and then wait for us to catch up again. Sometimes he would lose patience and come back to see that we had not lost the trail. Then he would move ahead again. He didn't seem the least bit tired.

When I thought we were close to the perimeter I called to make sure "those people know we're coming in." The strength of the reply suggested that we were very close and I passed the word down the line. Within minutes I could see Aguirre's skinny figure crouched in front of the perimeter like some enormous grey langur. Always the infantryman, he had remembered to open a path through the trip flares.

151

We filed in, some men festooned with extra gear and weapons, and were met by Hardoy who guided us to our sector of the perimeter which was at the point of the ridge. To my relief it dropped off steeply on all three sides; unless the NVA had alpine troops, there was little danger of an attack. All three squads dumped their gear and with very few exceptions fell instantly asleep, literally in a pile.

Keyed up, I joined Speare and Hardoy at the company CP. We talked for some time, nursing coffee. When I returned to the platoon everyone was asleep but Sergeant Taliferro, and I moved well out toward the end of the ridge to keep watch. For the first time I noticed the evening. It was cool and very clear. There wasn't a trace of wind. I could easily see the neighboring ridges on either side and a bright moon washed the grassland far below; beyond, faintly visible, silvered the South China Sea.

We were lifted out in the morning beginning a period of frequent assaults and long marches. We would be inserted into a new area, push to make our assigned night position, push to reach the next night's position, and then be lifted out to repeat the process. Fatigue made us careless. There was always the nagging sense of being behind schedule. I can remember running the point squad down a stream bed in an effort to make time until Six got wind of what I was doing and ordered me back into heavy cover. We had not gone 100 yards before we came across an abandoned ambush site which covered the stream. Two pineapple-type fragmentation grenades were still left in place behind a carefully constructed screen of rocks and logs. How long had they been there? — a week, five minutes? Maybe the French had left them.

Accidents accumulated. I tore a muscle in my leg and hobbled around for days, barely able to keep up. One of the mortar men, the man carrying the base-plate, fell and broke an ankle as the company picked its way down the side of an impossibly steep ridge. Someone in the First Platoon cut his calf to the bone with a machete. Davis nearly blew my head off. He was fiddling with the safety on his M-16, which was stuck (a common problem), and before I could tell him to clear the weapon, Pow! it went off, burying a round in a tree trunk just above my head.

If ever a man looked as though his life was flashing before his eyes, Davis had that look. And, for good reason; Davis had just returned from an emergency leave which he had unofficially extended by several weeks. He was evidently considering extending it for several decades but was apprehended. Once in military custody, he insisted that all he really wanted was to rejoin his unit. The army wanted that too and Davis was returned to Vietnam minus part of his pay and with his tour of duty appropriately extended. Captain Speare's view of this was not charitable and it would not have gone well for Davis had he drilled his platoon leader between the eyes.

I was so exhausted that the near miss neither angered nor frightened me. (It did later, when I thought of the spectacular effect of taking an M-16 round through the head at close range.) And I never doubted that it was an accident. Furthermore I knew that Davis was a good man; if anything he was too aggressive. Davis dug a sump for trash, closing the matter.

Arizona Six dropped in on one of our night perimeters and was greeted with a crude drawing on C-ration cardboard of a Cav patch. But instead of a horse's head, there was a large knobby-toed foot above the diagonal bar. "Foot Cavalry!" This heresy plus the accidental discharge of an M-16 at the far end of the perimeter just as he landed served to convince him that someone had winged a shot at his helicopter. He left in a huff.

A few days later, several hours into a long, hot patrol, Gonzales from the Third Platoon, announced that it was too hot to continue, dumped his gear, removed all his clothes and simply sat down. He wouldn't move. "He seems okay," reported Hardoy, "no heat exhaustion; he just won't move."

"I'm coming down [to Hardoy's location]," said Speare, "And, you tell that man he better fucking be in gear before I get there . . . Out."

After a few minutes of ominous silence, we could hear Speare thrashing through the underbrush as he worked his way toward the rear of the column. More silence. Then came a shrill, piercing, almost bird-like cry, "I'll Kiill Yooo!" followed by a thick metallic sound. Speare had picked up the man's helmet and fired it at him skulling him on the side of the head. Then came a series of yelps and howls so inhuman that I could not tell if they came from Gonzales or Speare. For several minutes both men gasped for air and then the column began to move again. That evening a huey landed, two MPs got out and took Gonzales away in handcuffs and leg chains.

After a long march we dug in on a high ridge topped with dead, grey, curiously limbless trees. An air strike had hit the ridge, it was cratered everywhere, and some of the bombs had not exploded. Each dud left a deep shaft about a foot in diameter where it had spiked into the ground. At first I was apprehensive, especially when I discovered someone dropping stones down one of these holes to see how deep it was, but the first sergeant was unconcerned. He knew that it was part of God's great plan for the air force to drop an occasional dud bomb so that the infantry would not have to dig trash sumps. It was just a matter of world-view.

As the engineers, who now traveled with us, lugging their chainsaws and gas cans, carved out an LZ, a recon helicopter radioed that it had spotted a bunker complex a couple of miles from our perimeter. Speare said he would like to take a look at it and as soon as the LZ was opened the little chopper hovered down. Speare wedged his big frame into the machine and it flitted away. After about 20 minutes the scout ship returned, bobbing up from the valley beneath us like a beach ball held under water, and deposited Speare, a little glazed in the eyes, on the LZ. The bunker complex was small, reported Speare, and "apparently unoccupied," which meant that no one had shot at the helicopter.

Hot chow arrived that evening, the first in a long time, and also a captain in spanking new boots and bright green fatigues. That was the first thing I noticed about him; the second was the black leather glove he wore on his right hand. Speare introduced us and explained that he would be spending a few days with us to settle into the field before he took over Echo Company. This was standard for new company commanders; Speare had spent a week with Commanche before he joined Navajo.

The new captain had just returned from two months in the hospital. Why he had been sent there he did not say except to mention that the scars on his hand bothered him. That's why he wore the glove. He regaled us with hospital stories: men in complete body casts being wheeled down to the bar, and so forth. It struck me that he was a lonely, uncertain man and unfairly, I suppose only because he was an outsider, I disliked him.

In the morning Speare took Second and Third platoons out to investigate his bunker complex. Sure of our route (having seen it from the air—a rare luxury) Speare led us rapidly along an ashy defoliated ridge as two gunships eagerly cast back and forth ahead of us like airborne bird dogs. They gave the impression of being annoyed that we couldn't keep up. Speare seemed intent on trying. We quickly worked our way across a hot scrubby valley and with relief climbed onto a ridge that was under deep, cool canopy.

As we labored over the top of the ridge, raindrops began to splatter heavily into the canopy above us. Or at least that's what it sounded like, rain, but before I realized that I hadn't seen a cloud all day there came the buzzing roar of a gunship's minigun. Leaves, bark and twigs trickled down as the gunship swept overhead, cascading brass which pinged and clattered through the branches.

Too stunned to take cover, I yelled at my RTO, "Jesus, they're shooting at us. Tell Six they're shooting at us."

"I think he knows that, sir."

The front of the column was already blossoming red smoke and nearer to us men were clutching smoke grenades off their pack straps and pulling pins. We did the same. In all we must have popped 15 smoke grenades in the span of 10 seconds as Speare scrambled to call off the gunship. The rest of us could only wait, tensed like rabbits, for the smoke to filter up through the canopy. The pilot who had probably not been shooting at us at all (but that was no comfort) was soon rewarded with what must have been an amazing sight as acres and acres of forest began to emit softened hues of red, green, violet and yellow.

After several minutes, we moved out again, through a colorfully hazy forest, and dropped down into a broad, flat valley, deep in elephant grass. Threading all through this grass were trails along which commo wire was laid (meticulously spliced, I noticed — the splices sealed with hard wax). Apparently all the surrounding ridges are in communication.

For a time we sloshed along a sunken stream bed unable to see the gunships circling above. We couldn't see anything; the grass on the overhung banks on either side of us was eight-feet high. Suddenly one of the gunships dipped very low over the grass and fired a brace of rockets right over our heads and up toward a ridge on the other side of the valley. This sent us all sprawling into rocks and mud. Speare had asked one of the pilots where the bunkers were and that was his way of pointing them out. Then low on fuel, the gunships lifted out of the valley and turned toward Evans and cold beer. We listened to them depart with mixed feelings.

We shoved our way through the grass, accumulating the usual multitude of annoying little cuts, and climbed onto the ridge which was covered by nothing more than thin scrubby trees and brush. But underneath this, connected by barely perceptible paths, we found seven large and very deep bunkers, plus a storage pit, and three big hooches. Something else: the entire ridge stank of shit and dead bodies.

We had found an NVA hospital. From out of the bunkers came rolls of bandages and bottles of pills. Other bottles contained liquid. We also found the graves of two decomposed men. Actually we found several more graves but Speare chose to ignore them. The complex must have been abandoned soon after the scoutship found it, and quickly, because we found five or six NVA packs lying about. The packs contained uniforms, peasant pajamas, a few Chinese stick grenades, two diaries, and—heady stuff to us—a brassiere (albeit remarkably small) which was later presented to the battalion commander.

The storage pit held perhaps a dozen large bags of rice. Getting rid of all that rice presented a problem; we certainly weren't going to carry it back with us. There was some discussion of "marine methods" which we all believed consisted of shitting on enemy perishables, but we contented ourselves with burning the thatch and dumping the rice into the bottom of the pit.

We were lifted out the following morning, into an old Montagnard field, and then moved down a forested ridge. Second Platoon was in the lead. By early afternoon the ridge had narrowed to a knife-edge and we followed the trail that led along the top. The trail was broad and well beaten but showed no sign of recent traffic. It led us directly into a bunker complex.

The point man froze and then recoiled, wide eyed, back into me. Tired, dehydrated, plodding heavily downhill, some of the men in the trailing squads continued on, unaware, until they bumped into the men in front of them. Keystone Kops was all I could think of—we must look like the Keystone Kops.

Hissing orders, I sorted the platoon back into squads. We worked our way along either side of the ridge and then swept through the complex, shooting into the bunker entrances and following that up with frags on the off chance that there might be a few (and very stupid) NVA still hanging around. During these fireworks I caught sight of our transient captain, black glove and all, advancing on tiptoe towards one of the bunkers. He was about to toss a grenade into a bunker that had already been fragged twice over.

I cannot explain what followed. I began bellowing at him insanely.

"What are you doing? Who said you could throw a goddamn frag? Get out of my assault. Get out of my assault. Get out of my assault!"

The man stood by forlornly, his hand glued to his grenade (he had already tossed the pin away), until finally I gestured toward the bunker indicating that he could dump his grenade. Still raving like a bus station lunatic, I stomped off towards the far end of the complex where I ran through a couple of magazines for the pleasure of chasing tracers around the interior of one of the bunkers. By then everyone was gaping at me and I was the only one shooting. I headed on down the ridge, out of the bunker complex, Ti Ti, concerned, a little distance behind me. About 200 yards down the trail we came to a small security bunker into which I shoveled a grenade. A hole appeared in the bunker's roof, right beside my foot. I ignored it. Ti Ti had had enough and actually began to pull me back up the trail by my shirttail.

The walk back to the complex restored some equilibrium. Later I sought out Black Glove and apologized. "No problem," he said after a long pause. "I think I understand." He eyed me strangely.

If the NVA had a recruiting brochure, this bunker complex would have been featured. Of about company size, with eight or ten large, and dry bunkers, it was located on a flat, expanded portion of the ridge that I was surprised to see actually showed on our maps. The ridge dropped off steeply on either side and the only possible approach was the trail that we had just blundered along. Shielded from the sun, the ridge was cool and pleasant. The ground around the bunkers was smooth and looked as though it had been raked. In the center of the complex, as was standard, there was a large command bunker which opened onto a conference area, a pit about 10 feet by 15 feet and perhaps 5 feet deep. A thatch roof constructed on a frame that was joined and lashed together in a way that would have made a cabinetmaker proud protected this. We found no burials and no equipment—nothing but a few bones (pig bones we guessed) around the command bunker. Later I heard that one of the bunkers had produced a stack of documents, of what value to us I don't know.

That evening, as the rest of the company settled in among the bunkers, we pulled an ambush on the trail that led along the ridge, and in, I'm quite sure, exactly the same location that the NVA had placed their security. Easy, ribold banter softened the chore of digging in. We put enough claymores out to stop a buffalo herd. It did not rain and, cradled in the buttress roots of a giant mahogany, I slept like a baby.

We returned the next morning and worked on destroying the bunkers (an exhausting waste of time without explosives) while the engineers cut out an LZ with chain saws. In the meantime Third Platoon, Six with them, explored into the valley below.

By afternoon the engineers had produced a ragged hole in the canopy. A huey soon arrived over the ridge, dancing in the wind like a dragonfly, hovered and began its descent. Standing just below, I could see the look of irritation on the pilot's face as the huey's big sweeps started clattering through some overhanging bamboo. He pulled up, came around and made it on the second try, delivering the battalion commander and a chaplain.

"This means you, sir," said Honeywell, meaning that as the only officer present I was the one who had to report. Honeywell knew just how much I enjoyed the company of field grade officers.

After squiring Arizona Six around the bunker complex in a manner that may have suggested that I was trying to sell it to him, he sheared away from me and fell into small talk with Sergeant Honeywell. Much of this centered on how difficult it was to get "extra" air medals. While Honeywell and Arizona Six chatted amiably in the shade, as though on a picnic, I put out security and made a show of pulling apart the bunkers. After perhaps an hour, Third Platoon filed into view along the trail that led into the complex from above. Speare bounded over to Arizona Six and delivered a crisp airborne salute. A map soon absorbed their attention.

The chaplain, whose smile faded whenever he was more than ten feet away from Arizona Six, had come to hold a memorial service for Stanhope. He seemed anxious to get it over with and finally set things in motion by requesting an M-16 with a fixed bayonet which was soon provided. The chaplain, now professionally somber, walked to the patch of sun beneath the opening in the canopy and carefully thrust the weapon into the ground. I believe he placed his own helmet on the stock. Three men, web gear and helmets on, and armed with M-16s, took position near the solitary rifle.

The symbol of a dead American infantryman, now three wars old, announced the chaplain's purpose and the company assembled on the slope that overlooked the bunkers. We were motioned to sit down. Behind us an M-60 crew on security continued to stand, now and again looking over their shoulders to check the trail. Eulogy and prayer were brief. Speare tried to speak but found after a few words that he could not. Voice keening, he called the company to attention and was instantaneously obeyed. In dappling light, the firing party shot three volleys through the canopy and came to present arms. There was no bugler.

Dismissed, we drifted back to our positions. Speare and the battalion commander returned to their map. Later someone quietly reclaimed the rifle from the red earth.

CHAPTER 9

*"We're going to miss Big Man.
It isn't going to be the same without Big Man."*
—Two Six Bandaid, Late September, 1968

With Navajo's officers stiffly in attendance, Arizona Six boarded his huey and lifted through the canopy. Tableaux vivant from a Methodist Sunday School book: the disciples are gazing uniformly aloft as Christ ascends to heaven on a small, dense, apparently jet-powered cloud. We did not hold that pose for long. Before the sound of the colonel's huey had started to fade, Speare wheeled and ordered me to "Police up that pig pen of an ambush site you left up there. It's got trash and crap all over it." Second Squad, a little bemused, went with me. As I expected, we found nothing on our old night position that would have been useful to the NVA. The chore was punishment for revealing an unmilitary appearance to the battalion commander who had probably made some comment. I kept up my end of the ritual and called in a list of what we did find.

"...empty cans, C-ration, 6 each; cigarette butts, 15 each, cardboard boxes, type C-ration, 7 each; turds, human, 4 each..." and so on.

"Clean as a hound's tooth?" said Tex, relaying Speare's response.

"Affirmative, anything further? Over."

"Negative, return to base. Out."

Speare was genuinely angry and had more time been available he would probably have ordered me to fill in the holes, rake the ground in an "eye-appealing manner," and line the trail with white rocks. Stranger things have happened to me in the army. As it was, however, there was no time for that.

We were lifted out that afternoon and deposited beside C Company just outside of LZ Juliet. Two other companies were already digging in. Our combined perimeter ran along a line of foxholes that bulged out from Juliet's greenline with Navajo sandwiched between Commanche and another company, and in front of us was open rolling grassland interrupted by patches of brown, half-defoliated woods.

Seeing the entire battalion assembled impressed me enormously. For the men of Navajo who lived in the mountains and seldom saw another company, and then only in passing, this was like the Rocky Mountain Rendezvous. But I was wrong about the battalion; I would never see it assembled, not once. The First Cavalry treated rifle companies like individual Legos to be combined and recombined to suit the needs of a particular task. The other two companies were from another battalion, the 1st of the 5th, and we were now under the command of someone identified as General Motors Six.

It was a pleasant sunny day and after digging in there wasn't much to do. The battalion's cooks were merrily grilling steaks over bisected 55-gallon drums. And, there was beer, two cans apiece which we didn't even have to pay for. New ammunition was issued. Everyone was also to get new boots which most men didn't want because they had grown attached to their old, scuffed, smoke grenade-dyed boots. A few men drew new boots, discarded them, and kept only the laces.

No one speculated, except privately, on the operation to come and the only rumor in circulation was an old one: a bulldozer clearing brush outside the greenline had suddenly dropped out of sight into an enormous bunker. I had heard it before at Camp Evans and then again at Wunder Beach. It was a standard rumor. It was a standard rumor because bulldozers did sometimes drop out of sight into concealed bunkers.

Even more than the new ammunition, the sizzling steaks presented a clear forecast of trouble. The new ammo *might* be a routine issue, but a steak dinner for nothing? "Never fucking happen." I made a show of cleaning my rifle and breaking down each of the 20 magazines I carried, wiping them clean of sand. My theory is that M-16s often jam because the magazines are dirty; Aguirre's theory is that cleaning your rifle is bad luck. On this we disagree.

As I was thumbing rounds into the last magazine, Speare called me to the CP. Motor Six, explained Speare, wanted a squad-sized patrol sent out to ensure that an attack was not launched from a wooded

162

area located about 1,500 yards to our front. And the patrol is not to leave the perimeter until midnight. All my huge, salivating anticipation of a steak dinner vanished as did all prospects of a night's sleep.

The evening was warm and clear. Darkened gunships came out to prowl the grassland. Around 10:00 a company somewhere along Highway One several miles away came under attack and erupted in a spray of red tracers. After a few minutes Juliet's 155s banged out in support and had us all diving into our holes when someone mistakenly called "incoming!" Just as quickly we were back out again, feeling foolish. A radio was put on the frequency of the company under attack and for an hour we had a grandstand seat. In the darkness, the distant perimeter seemed to float in space as rockets and artillery exploded all around it. Gunships made several runs with miniguns, each time producing a thin, red, uninterrupted beam of light (tracers) that ended in a molten flower.

"Good, good; that's right where we want it," said an excited voice over the radio. We gathered that the NVA or VC (around Juliet it could have been either) had broken off their attack and that the company commander we were listening to was calling the mission in on their line of retreat.

A little before 12:00, I walked over to the CP to double check that all companies had been informed that a patrol would be operating to their front. If we were mistakenly fired on, every position on the entire sweeping perimeter would probably start blasting away within seconds. Red splash! And even if the other companies had been warned, and warned again at Speare's insistence, the only part of the perimeter that I could trust not to open up was Navajo's.

When I got back, Third Squad had their gear on and was waiting for me. They were nervous. It was plain that they thought the mission was stupid because the chances of crossing all that open grassland undetected on a moonlit night were very small. We should have gone out earlier and shifted position after it was dark.

"Canteens full?" All nodded; in an hour we would be soaked in sweat, as wet as if we had jumped into a stream. A few men rocked abruptly up and down on the balls of their feet to check for loose equipment, for something that made noise, but anything like that had been eliminated from our persons months or weeks ago. Navajo men, many of them, were set apart by the dog tag laced into their left boot. Aguirre had told me to do that within minutes of my arrival at the bridge. "No noise," he said, "and they won't send that leg home in the wrong fucking box." I had spread the custom to Second Platoon.

I told my RTO to inform Speare that we were leaving the perimeter.

"Navajo Six, Navajo Six, be advised: the suicide patrol is leaving the perimeter."

"No more of that shit," I snapped, genuinely irritated.

"Roger on the suicide patrol," replied Tex matter-of-factly. He had heard complaints about "suicide patrols" before and with more justification.

We left the perimeter as if shot by a bow, the little column heading straight out for the first 200 yards because I wanted to get beyond the point where we could be seen by any of the guard positions as quickly as possible. When we had a slight rise between ourselves and the perimeter, I called a halt. For 15 minutes we sat and soaked in the environment. Then we moved again, this time slowly. Another halt; I sipped a beer and tried to figure out the least exposed route to the woods. The route that had looked plausible in the daylight had melted into shadow. For two hours we moved across a grey indeterminate landscape, slipping over one rise after another, stopping every 200 yards or so to listen.

Tex at intervals would call. The radio was a necessary evil. Even with the volume turned down, it sounded as though we were broadcasting our position for 500 yards. Probably we were; but Tex was keeping Juliet's night-stalking gunships from "dumping the world on us," as he put it, and we had to be ready to give him our position when he requested it. He sounded tense over the radio.

"You're a good scout," I chided, "bless you."

"Fuck you...Over."

Actually, Tex squelched the first word but I knew what he meant. Sitting among his radios, a crescent of pack strap sores on each skinny shoulder (his badge of rank; he always had them), Tex was spending another sleepless night and wasn't happy about it. But I was very grateful that it was Tex and not someone else who was doing that chore. My gratitude increased every time one of those darkened gunships came near. With or without their night vision gadgets, it was all too easy to make a mistake. The sound of a huey's big sweeps would grow louder, pinpoint cobalt blue lights would appear and then the black outline of a gunship. After a few seconds, it would glide away,

164

like a disappointed wolf. The disappointment I knew from talking to gunship pilots was genuine. "A whole squad of infantry in the open and they happen to be ours—shit." As we drew near the woods, a cobra gunship came slanting toward us, nose down.

"Tex, it's coming after us!"

"Roger that, I'm talking to them now. Out."

The gunship turned away.

I had no intention of blundering through a bone-dry and probably booby-trapped woods in the middle of the night. We skirted the woods, now an enormous menacing ink blot in the center of a shallow grassy bowl, and worked our way behind it to a point where we would catch anyone trying to slip into it. The squad lay sprawled in the grass just below the crest of an all but imperceptible rise some 100 yards from the trees. I crawled to where I could get a clear view. Gosselin was beside me.

"We aren't going into that dry whore of a woods are we?"

"Fuck no."

It was one of those humid, windless nights when the air seems to carry sound like water. We would hear anyone moving through that brittle forest, just as they would hear us, and now, in position, we could spot anyone trying to get into it. I didn't want 11 heads bobbing above the rise, so only two men at a time kept watch. I gave Tex our position and then ordered the radio turned down—way down. An hour passed in silence; I rolled onto my back and studied the bright sky. No one slept. Another hour passed. Another. It was near dawn.

I called to tell Tex that we were coming in. We did this by stages, cautiously, most of the time uncertain of our position except that the ink blot was behind us and the perimeter somewhere at an undetermined distance to our front. The danger now lay in hitting the perimeter in the wrong place—in front of the wrong company.

We closed on the perimeter sooner than I expected.

"That's Commanche over there," hissed Gosselin.

How he could tell that I don't know; the perimeter was invisible to me. We changed course and soon a shadowy stretch of fighting positions materialized. The patrol padded into Navajo's sector, past a silent, apprehensive guard, and then dissolved as men shed their web gear and sank to the ground for a couple of hours sleep.

The sun was up when I awoke. Two companies were filing through the chow line; the others, burdened with several days' rations, were already heading towards the pick-up zone. Trash was burning here and there, and our foxholes had been backfilled. Speare told me that we were going into an area that had produced heavy indications of NVA activity. Just what these were he didn't say. Each company would be inserted into one of two LZs located in the vicinity of a small fire base, LZ Barbara, which I had never heard of, and then move out in parallel columns. Phase lines, said Speare with heavy emphasis, would be used to coordinate the operation and being out of position risked being clobbered by one of the air strikes that had been ordered onto suspected bunker complexes or for "LZ construction." The idea was that we would stir things up and "flush" the NVA out onto the grasslands around LZ Barbara. Tactically, I gathered, the whole operation was conceived of as a pheasant hunt.

Lifts of both hueys and chinooks showed up and the staging area was empty within less than an hour. As I looked down I could see nothing but trampled grass, patches of turned up earth, and scraps of white and brown windblown paper. It looked like a county fair had just left town.

I didn't like being in a chinook because they are vulnerable to ground fire (a big target crammed with hydraulics and all sorts of connecting parts) and for the less substantial reason that they reminded me of a school bus, which is what they resemble, a flying school bus. The entire platoon seemed subdued, as I was, by that sinking feeling associated with your first day at a new school. The gunner who sat behind a .50 caliber machine gun aimed out of the rear of the chopper had the air of a self-important hall monitor. Probably he had been, I decided.

Commanche was said to have taken some fire from a heavy machine gun but the LZ was secure when we landed. Navajo was soon heading down a trail with Third Platoon on point. We were behind them and First Platoon took up the rear. Hardoy was staying on the trail but that was his business. An air strike went in, far ahead of us by the sound, but the ground trembled beneath our feet.

We settled into the routine of following the platoon in front of us. Stop, start, stop, cloverleaf; start again. Everyone was going through their water very fast. After a couple of hours a break was called. Some men shed their packs to knead sore shoulders, adjust sweat towels, pick at jungle rot. Others just sank to the ground and dreamily examined their feet. Insects buzzed.

166

There was a long shattering M-60 burst at the rear of the column and then a couple of "I love Mary" bursts of six. Then some M-16s on automatic.

"Six, One Six, we gotta couple of KIA...a couple of KIA. They walked right into our rear security."

Speare acknowledged and said he was heading back to take a look. Ten minutes later he returned to say that a small squad of NVA had walked right down the trail we had just traveled and smack into the muzzle of an M-60. The long burst had cut down two men. Before we started moving again an embellishing tale leapfrogged its way up from the rear of the column: The NVA had been carrying a man on a stretcher. It was the stretcher bearers who had been killed as the patient made his escape ("No shit, the gook on the stretcher ran off like a fucking deer."). It was just the sort of event that an infantryman's swollen sense of irony would emphasize—or invent—and I don't know the truth of it. No one does anymore. More concretely, a quick search of the area found blocks of plastic explosive, a U.S. grenade, AK-47 ammo, a bundle of new NVA uniforms, and several bags of rice. All this seems like a lot for two stretcher bearers to be carrying but the "gook on the stretcher" story persisted because it was so funny.

We moved out again and after a few minutes Speare radioed for me to take point. As we slipped ahead of the Third Platoon it started to rain and we were soon soaked and miserable. I moved the platoon off the trail into heavy second growth making everyone even more miserable. It began to rain harder. With visibility down to perhaps 30 feet, the point element slowed to a crawl.

I moved up behind Gosselin who was on point. It is easier to navigate at the head of the column—"you can't push a string"—but there the radio nags at you all the more because you should be helping the point man, not talking on the radio. I tried keeping Jerome, RTO that day, a couple of men back but every few minutes he would come bounding up the line with a call from Six who insisted on talking directly with me. We pushed on like that; the rain drumming into the vegetation.

Six called again. I had only part of the message before Gosselin cut loose with several rounds and then looked back at me.

"I just shot a gook," he announced.

I blurted something about "bushrake" and we both went on full automatic. I could see nothing and just hosed the area down.

"Where?" I yelled.

Gosselin pointed. After a couple of steps I could see a small man in dark green NVA fatigues lying on his back. A thin dark poncho covered most of his upper body concealing his hands. Gosselin was beside me.

"Should I kill him, Sir?"

I hesitated, then said no. I pulled the man's poncho off; no rifle, no grenade. I knelt beside him. Still alive, he had been hit several times and there were big exit wounds in his chest and shoulders. It struck me that there wasn't much blood. His eyes were open and they searched my face.

I got back on the radio to Six. "We've got a WIA, an NVA."

I told Six that I was going to try and get onto the hill to our front and sprinted off too excited to wait for his reply. The hill, which I could just make out through the rain, was small but beetled above us, dominating everything. Possibly 30 seconds, but probably less, had elapsed between the time Gosselin had fired and I was back on the radio. No one but Six and Third Squad had any clear idea of what was going on. I plowed back through the underbrush to grab Second Squad which was still mired emotionally in the wet cold woods. They were stalled because several men were busily engaged in removing leeches from their face and neck. I bellowed at Sergeant Taliferro, "We got contact, get your people up here," and scrambled forward with Third Squad. After 50 yards we came to a well-travelled trail running along the base of the hill. I ordered a few bursts fired down the trail and grabbed a couple of men to keep watch in case some NVA came barging into us. They seemed to be running all over the place.

By then, Third Squad was already moving up the hill. Jerome and I followed on their right, slipping and sliding, and finally completing the climb on all fours. If there had been any NVA ahead of us, they were not on that hill. Third Squad, out of breath and apprehensive, searched around carefully. They were adamant: "There were three gooks—right up ahead of us." Jerome gave every sign of having enjoyed the whole business and was hopping around and laughing with nervous excitement. "Some slippery ass climb, huh, Sir. You shoulda seen your face when Gosselin said he shot that gook; plumb white." The truth is, if it hadn't been raining, Jerome might have had a lot more to laugh about.

The rest of the company climbed the hill and pushed out a perimeter in workmanlike fashion. Two Six Bandaid arrived with the tail of the column. He had stayed behind with the wounded NVA soldier.

"What happened to that guy?" I asked.

"KIA," he said laconically, "never had a chance."

I think he anticipated my next question.

"Anybody find a weapon?"

"No."

Gosselin joined us, still out of breath.

"I thought Top was going to kiss me," he said. "He made every lazy dick in this company walk by that dead gook; now maybe they won't be so slack. Top told me, 'You've done a wonderful thing,' he told me that—no shit."

"Anybody leave a Cav patch on him?" someone asked.

The man had jumped up in front of Gosselin no more than ten feet away and turned to run. It was then that Gosselin shot him, hitting him at least once and knocking him down. He was hit again, three or four times, as he lay on the ground. I suspect that Speare thought that we had deliberately shot the man as he lay wounded, finishing him off, but he said nothing to me.

It was already late afternoon and Speare announced that this would be our night perimeter. Each squad turned in on itself to cook and dig in. By evening the rain had stopped.

Speare, who of course monitors most of what comes across the battalion net (Tex hears it all), told us that the 1st of the 9th had been "getting shot at all over the place," and that Bounty Hunter, the 1st of the 5th's recon company, had ambushed an NVA squad. But when they checked the area for bodies, they had been ambushed in turn. The exchange of ambushes had taken the life of one North Vietnamese and one American.

An LP went out that night. A real LP this time: two men and a radio sit out the night two or three hundred yards beyond the perimeter to give us warning of an attack. It is the worst job there is but at least they will be too terrified to fall asleep.

We linked up with Commanche the next day and established a large paramecium-shaped perimeter in a grassy field. The wreck of a huey lay in a ravine not far away. I walked over to Commanche's sector to make sure that the perimeter was closed, that we were tied in, and talked briefly with the men on the position next to us. I didn't recognize a single face; they were aliens, as we were to them.

A call to the CP: Speare explained that intelligence expected that some NVA might try to surrender. I was to get the word out not to shoot if someone came out of the tree line with their hands on their head or holding a weapon in the air. A lot of Chieu Hoi leaflets, he said, had been dropped over this area. I stopped at each position with this information and was told directly by a couple of men that they intended to shoot regardless.

Big Man, scuffing around in the grass, came across an issue revolver—the kind pilots carry. The cylinder was smashed; hit by a round that came in directly from the front. Evidently one of the pilots had survived the crash of the huey, made it to the field hoping to be picked up and then in the end had decided to shoot it out rather than be captured. Looking around it was easy to picture the field empty except for the pilot, standing where we were, waiting for the NVA to close in. How long ago had that happened, I wondered—a week, six months? The serial number of the weapon may have linked this lonely event to someone listed as missing and we turned it in to Speare. We all regretted the loss of so valuable a souvenir.

Just before twilight a small plane cruised back and forth, not very high up, broadcasting in Vietnamese. Interspersed with the message, whatever it was, were long banshee wails that floated over the perimeter. It was psy ops tucking us in for the night.

No one surrendered, or tried to surrender, that evening and the following morning the two companies renewed their independent lives. Under cold, drizzly rain, Navajo's platoons now moved in parallel columns. Fearful of encroaching on one another, we humped through tangled second growth as we tried to keep to phase lines marked on wet, blurred maps. Around midday, Third Platoon found a downed gunship with a full load of rockets. There was no sign of the crew. Six called battalion and asked if they wanted us to secure the area so that the bird could be hauled out as salvage. Answer: blow the rockets and proceed to the next phase line. On a narrow trail that curved around huge boulders and along the side of an open ridge we encountered several traps in the form of grass-covered depressions filled with short punji sticks. We just scuffed them aside. I'm sure that Speare would have court marshalled anyone who claimed injury by one of these arrangements. The trail led us into a sleeping position for 15 men that had been used only a day or so before. Further on, a booby-trapped unexploded bomb was also discovered, given a very wide berth, and

170

finally blown by the engineers. In fact, one of the engineers later told me, it was not a bomb at all, just a bomb case. The explosive had been removed and the empty casing rigged to a pressure release device which the engineer had detected just in time. He did not seem to be at all affected by that experience.

At one point, our route was blocked by a swollen stream — chest deep and dangerous. Our more confident swimmers linked arms, wrist to wrist, Indian fashion, and stood in the water while the rest of us worked our way across. Six, who was several hundred yards downstream, requested that a rope be dropped. A hundred feet would have done it, the stream was only about 40 feet wide; but after a long wait a chopper delivered an enormous coil of heavy nylon rope along with the order that the rope could not be cut. "We'll pick it up in a couple of days," said the pilot jauntily. After all, what's another 50 pounds to a bunch of donkey grunts? I was told that after everyone had crossed, Six dumped the rope into the stream.

A few game trails, less than a foot wide but almost eight inches deep, laced through this country. We kept coming across isolated bunkers, looked to be long abandoned. The sky continued impenetrably grey and all color seemed to be seeping out of the landscape. The night perimeter was in cold, wet, cheerless scrub. No one slept.

The next day we moved through Commanche sitting moodily on a hilltop. Not a word passed between us. Navajo pressed on through cratered scrub. Down toward the floor of a meandering valley, we picked up a trail. It was broad and packed hard and we stayed on it because we had a phase line to make. After a few minutes a herd of pigs clattered and snorted off ahead of us. "Good," said Ti Ti, "let Porky Pig trip the booby traps." He had his helmet on backwards; he didn't like the lip down in his eyes when he was on point.

The canopy was not far above us and in places branches had been tied together. Once again, there were barked trees; but here the signs were written in black marker and they were fresh, unfaded. Our porcine point soon outdistanced us and we slowed down, slipping on and off the trail. Cloverleaf: one squad was slow in coming back and I was getting pissed — and nervous. Where were they? A few minutes more and they returned with several teeth the size of half a brick. "There's some huge bones over there, piles of em; fucking huge!" They are really excited by their discovery. Elephants probably, and probably they were killed long ago by gunships.

171

When we had finished digging in for the night, Speare told me to send out an LP. I protested: "They'll never stay awake." I was just as worried that the perimeter guards, knowing that there was an LP in front of them would go to sleep, and, that if we were hit, the men on the LP would be killed trying to get back to the perimeter. The LP went out.

Earlier that evening a company from the 1st of the 5th about a half mile away was hit as they moved into their night position. Two men were killed and four wounded. The wounded were medevacked shortly after dark but the dead remained inside the perimeter until morning to be taken out by the log bird. At dawn, the company was hit again by grenades that came in from all around the perimeter and lost another man.

The following day we plowed on. Keeping track of the platoons beside us was always a problem. There was no way of knowing if they were 400 yards away or 75. I got ahead of the phase line and had to double back. At one point, Six told me to link up with First Platoon and for ten minutes I argued over the radio with Tompkins, a newly arrived lieutenant, about his position. I was certain he couldn't be where he said he was. In fact, we were only about 150 yards apart but it took us 45 minutes to find each other. That evening Honeywell and I got into a dispute over how much of the perimeter our platoons should be responsible for. Speare had to intervene as we both stood and yelled at each other across the perimeter. Another sleepwalking LP went out. We learned that an air strike which we heard go in far off on our flank had landed on a bunker complex. C Company (1st of the 5th) searched through it and tabulated the body parts found in the general vicinity. The estimate was ten KBAs (killed by air). The 1st of the 9th, flying hungrily overhead, had located or produced half a dozen more. Another company found a foot — just a foot. Battalion, said Tex, wanted to know if it was a right foot or a left foot. It was a left foot.

The day after it stopped raining. We pushed on as before, not daring to set out flank protection for fear of the platoons beside us. I knew that they were no more than 200 yards away but for all we could see or hear, they could have been on the moon. Several South Vietnamese dive bombers attacked along a line about a mile ahead of us. Prop planes (they cruised slowly around like gulls) tipped over on their noses and dove straight down. At what, I never learned.

Early that afternoon the company broke into open grassland. We pulled up, formed a perimeter...and sat. Away from the trees it was blistering hot. Headaches were universal and everyone was fatigued past the point of surliness. Speare ordered me to send a squad to secure a small hill that dominated our perimeter. I trudged up with them. From the top we could see the grassland, brown and hot, extending off for miles. Just above it gunships skated on heat waves, like water bugs. One of the gunships, all shark's teeth and rockets, swept low toward our position. Slowing almost to a hover, with a little left pedal that presented us a three-quarter view, the pilot guided his big weapon down the length of Navajo's perimeter. Helmet visor down, one of the men inside waved us a faceless greeting.

Six called. No need to be up there so long as gunships are around. A huey kicked off C-rations and we ate a shadeless, hurried meal. Another huey, said Honeywill, would bring water, which we desperately needed, and pick up mail. Many of us used the top of C-ration boxes as postcards. That was a common practice since the brown cardboard meal containers were often the only dry paper we had. Mine said, "We are very busy now but I'm okay." I could manage nothing more.

Big Man, grown silent these past days, sorted through his gear, gave a few things away, a knife, a few extra magazines, a can of C-ration fruit cocktail, and quietly began shaking hands. Eleven and a half months in the field, he was going home. When the chopper returned, Big Man crouched below the sweeps and boarded the ship. He sat between the door gunners, his pack still on his back, head down, not believing. The chopper lifted off, circled the company as Big Man stared down at us — he didn't wave, he just stared — and then turned east, away from an advancing line of grey clouds. Two Six Band-aid and I watched the huey getting smaller and smaller over the grassland as it whirled Big Man along the first stage of a journey that would take him to the other side of the earth.

"We're going to miss Big Man," he said. "It isn't going to be the same without Big Man."

Speare called the platoon leaders together to tell us that we would be lifted out in an hour to begin another part of the operation. He spoke urgently about phase lines saying that the Motor Six had been giving another company commander hell for "not keeping up." Speare used that phrase as though it identified some terrible perversion. "He was going crazy over the radio," said Speare who obviously wanted to avoid that treatment. It began to rain as the slicks arrived.

Raindrops whipped past the open doors of our slicks as the pilots dodged low lying clouds. In places the sun still warmed the landscape unrolling beneath us and the rain seemed to have brightened every color. Our formation canted around a dark towering cloud and then dove into a valley meadow. The slicks flared sharply to slow our descent, jamming us against the cargo deck, and came to a hover just off the ground so that the skids combed slowly ahead through knee-high grass. We jumped out, our forward movement tipping many of us off our feet, and the slicks boiled out of the valley. We were soon alone, eyeing the ridges above us. The meadow offered no cover whatsoever and there had been no artillery preparation; either because the artillery had fired on the wrong grid or because, in the interest of surprise, none had been ordered. I suspected the latter. The LZ was green but the "pucker factor" remained very high until the rest of the company joined us.

Two gunships circled above while a scout ship flew low between the ridges and popped away with an M-60 that kept jamming. Apparently it was trying to draw fire which did not seem necessary with a whole company of infantry standing in the open. The gunship commander called for smoke to be tossed to mark our position and then the FO called in rockets onto the ridge above us. The gunships came in almost parallel to the ridge and looked to be heading right for us. The rockets burned toward us, it seemed, and then at the last instant appeared to veer into the ridge 100 yards away—a safe distance, but only just. This illusion was repeated twice for our benefit. We could have done without it; the ridge was unoccupied.

A command helicopter landed and disgorged a neatly pressed colonel. In his middle thirties, Motor Six was a lean man, not quite six feet tall, and his manner was pleasantly avuncular (an acquired skill) as he briefed us in detail on the operation. He identified the unit we would be facing (the K4 Battalion of the 812 Regiment) and said that it was down to less than half strength. He mentioned that they had been located by a highly classified method that even he didn't know about (Speare said later that their radio traffic was being monitored) and that it was known that they still had their heavy weapons, especially 82mm mortars. He offered a bit of practical advice. Lately, he said, they had encountered people in the trees with B-40 rocket

174

launchers. "Putting some artillery in front of your line of march should discourage that sort of activity."

"Well," he said, "we'd better break up this little huddle before somebody gets shot. I don't want Captain Speare to get mad at me." We all chuckled on cue.

The colonel wanted that NVA battalion, had wanted them for a long time. And now he knew roughly where they were. In the morning he would extend his column tentacles into the forest to probe beneath the canopy, the way a hungry octopus searches along a coral reef. Fatigue conjures up odd images and I wondered: does the colonel change color when he is frustrated, like an octopus?

After the colonel departed, Navajo filed out of the valley, onto a low cratered ridge where we dug in for the night in a dispiriting rain. Part of our perimeter was exposed to a high hill several hundred yards away. Speare glared at the hill and ordered me to move Second Platoon onto it, which was absolutely the last thing I wanted to do. Then, as we got ready to move out, he checked with battalion. "No need," he said, "forget it." A few minutes later a light plane began buzzing around the hill like a fly. It shot in a white phosphorous rocket to mark the position and flew off. Shortly after that, eight inch shells began methodically hitting the hill, sending up plumes of black smoke and, once, spectacularly, a tree trunk that had been snapped off at the base.

With the little plane still overhead on its fly errands, someone accidentally popped a trip flare which began giving off a thin column of white smoke—the same color given off by the WP rockets the spotter used to mark targets. "Kick it, put it out, kick the goddamn thing!" The culprit booted the hissing flare around until it burned out. We waited apprehensively for the smoke to dissipate.

Toward evening, I stood on the perimeter and nursed warmth from a sugary cup of C-ration coffee. Honeywell joined me. "Ever notice," said Honeywell, "that there are only two kinds of field medics?" He inclined his head toward a wan young man who was wading like a fastidious cat through wet, leech-ridden underbrush to hand out malaria pills to a few men who were still setting out claymores and trip flares. He had only just joined the company and was obviously beset by the cold, grey, frightening world he now inhabited. Honeywell didn't care about that; it would pass and the young man would do his job. "Or," said Honeywell, "they're like Doc [our chief medic]; he's a frustrated rifleman. He'd carry a shotgun if the captain would

175

let him." Doc was a big, strapping kid from rural Georgia who resembled no one so much as one of Winslow Homer's Confederates as he painted them in "Prisoners from the Front," except that they were better dressed. It could be imagined that someone had mistakenly delivered a draft notice to the Cleveland Art Museum and that Doc had stepped out from Homer's painting, strode down Euclid Avenue to the induction center to be examined, given a meal ticket good for beans and franks at the diner around the corner, and then sworn in.

"I had to break him of shooting," confided Honeywell without elaborating.

On the face of it, there surely was something to Honeywell's typology but Two Six Bandaid did not fit into it. Maybe that was because he had so much of what all medics share. Neither reluctant nor aggressive, he coldly, rationally detested the field. We all hated being in the field. Two Six Bandaid hated *the field* as though it was a loathsome disease that killed and maimed adolescents. And so it is, I suppose; anyhow he handed out pills and salve and bandaged cuts in the same controlled, determined manner that he risked his life. In the end, the disease, his personal advisary, would kill him.

That night the colonel changed color. The company that had failed to keep to its phase lines, had not kept up, was ordered to Charlie Alpha onto a ridge close to ours — at night. It had never occurred to me that anyone would order a night Charlie Alpha or even that it could be done and I was immensely glad that it was another company and not Delta Company that had been given this mission. The FO's view of night assaults was far more lighthearted. "Wait till you see those eight inch flares," he said, "It's like daylight. Those things are amazing." It was obvious that he was looking forward to the show.

The assault took place several hours after dark. Without warning, big flares popped softly about a half mile away bathing the hills in brilliant white light. The world seemed scrubbed of all natural color. Obviously the gunships and slicks could make out the LZ but from where we were it was impossible to see. Rockets, grenade rounds, and tracers focused on an arbitrary point in the distance from which the tracers arched back into the sky. A cone of light appeared, the spotlight of the first slick; it flashed around and then pointed almost straight down. The cone descended and then winked out. Another cone of light did the same, and then two more. It looked like gigantic neon dunce caps were being gently dropped on the dark hills. We waited for the spray of green tracers that would indicate that the lead platoon was in contact. None came. Finally, after the remaining platoons had been ferried in, a last lonely great flare spiraled down and went out. The hills went black.

"What did I tell you about those flares," said the FO.

Speare and I stood together, ignoring the FO's happy chatter, and stared glumly into the darkness. We both understood that this assault had been the colonel's retribution for not keeping to the phase lines and that there would be a repeat performance if any company failed to make their objective tomorrow.

Speare had already told me that Second Platoon would take point in the morning, something that I had anticipated. Hardoy was back at Juliet taking care of some task that normally would have fallen to the XO, except that we didn't have an XO any longer, and Tompkins, only three days in the field, had no business running the lead platoon. I suggested, and Speare agreed, that the mortar platoon dump its basic load along our route of march. That, at least, would make life in the trees unpleasant but I had no illusion that it would accomplish much else. Dead tired, I turned in early that night, nestling in a shallow crater beneath the roots of a bomb-toppled tree. Cold, wet and scared, I slept very little.

In the morning, Second Platoon moved out, past clusters of men sipping morning coffee. The mortar platoon had already cut their charges and was contentedly banging rounds in the general direction of our objective. They would tack onto the column with the last platoon. We struck a trail, followed it briefly and then pulled off it — too dangerous. After a couple of hundred yards, I decided to pick up the trail again because we were making very poor time.

The trail paralleled a stream bed which soon revealed a huge dud shell. It was rusty, evidently very old, and seemed to have eroded out of the bank (left over from the French?). It was easy to see why it had not exploded; the shipping plug was still in it. I reported this curiosity to Six and left it for the engineers.

Gosselin who was on point (again) came back down the column and said there was another stream ahead. I halted the column and moved up to take a look. The trail picked up on the other side of the stream which was broad, sluggish and maybe waist deep. The logical place for an ambush.

Two Niner Mike India was with me and I told him that I wanted some artillery. He called in the mission and got a flat refusal. The battery was short on rounds and wasn't going to waste any on a recon by fire. Two Niner Mike India insisted, making up some lie about why we needed the rounds. What he said, I've forgotten but it was creative and after a brief wait we were told we could have a few 155 rounds. We pulled back a short distance. The first round landed about 200 yards beyond the stream judging from the sound. . . not close enough. Two Niner Mike India dropped 50 and then 50 again; still not close enough. I wanted it dropped again. Two Niner Mike India handed me the radio. "You call it in."

I called in the mission, remembering to say "danger close" since I guessed the round would land just on the other side of the stream. Head down, hands to ears, mouth open, it was hard to judge how close the round landed but I was sure that it was too far away to do any good. "No more rounds," announced Two Niner Mike India. "They cut us off." So the fire mission was largely a waste of time but it did wake me up. It was stupid to try and cross at that point and I should never have considered it. I should never have been on the trail.

Off the trail again, we moved downstream thumping out a few grenade rounds in the hopes of drawing fire. We didn't. Gosselin waded across and snooped around. The other side of the stream was clear.

The column moved ahead rapidly for a few hundred yards allowing everyone to cross. First Squad went out perhaps a hundred yards on our left flank and reported a trail, probably the one we had been following. I wanted no part of it. We plodded cautiously ahead through heavy cover like a ship in the fog. I kept moving up the column until I was directly behind Gosselin because, as always, it was impossible to control the column from any other position. Six called to encourage our progress but there was nothing in his voice to suggest that the Motor Six was dissatisfied.

Tex called to say that the timed charge the engineers had set on "that object" (the dud shell) was about to blow. A minute later it did, thunderously, tossing rock and gravel high into the air to spatter down on the canopy all around us.

A light rain started to fall but did nothing to destroy my mood. At this pace, I thought, we'll be in the perimeter by mid-afternoon with plenty of time to dig in up to our eyeballs. Moving down the column to check with Sergeant Taliferro, another domestic thought intruded, mundane but important: dig a latrine inside the perimeter.

"No one from Second Platoon is going to be killed taking a crap." Sergeant Taliferro received this edict solemnly.

Cloverleaf: Third Squad returned to say that there was a stream off to our right. I went out to check and found that the stream slipped around the base of the hill we were on eroding a cliff perhaps 100 feet high. From the top of it I could look out across a tranquil, forested valley. It was a peaceful, engaging landscape but somewhere beneath those trees there was another column of infantry and somewhere in front of that column or in front of us, if intelligence was correct, an NVA battalion.

I checked my wrinkled map. A stream, almost certainly that stream, was indicated. I called Six.

"There is a little blue on our right flank. Looks like the one on the funny papers. We should be home in a couple of hours."

"Roger Roger, I see it. Looks good to me. Continue to march."

And so the remainder of the day advertised itself. And so briefly it went.

A call from Tex; Six wants me back at his position. Speare was on battalion frequency when I arrived at his location. He soon clicked off. The company beside us had been ambushed.

"They blew a claymore on them," said Speare in a flat, measured voice. "Took out the point squad...all of them. Bad...five men KIA."

The operation commander had ordered a change of course and Speare told me to take the company directly to the summit of the hill we were on. News of the ambush outdistanced me as I headed to the front of the column. As we approached the top of the hill the trees thinned and light splashed here and there through the canopy. We came to a small opening. I called Six.

"There's a clearing just ahead. I'm going to shoot the place up a little."

Gosselin sat on his haunches, peering ahead while I wriggled out of my pack, moved back down the column a few men and beckoned to Bishop and Ju Ju. Once in position, we all cut loose together: Gosselin, myself and the M-60 crew—I wanted it to sound to any NVA on the hill as though we were really engaging, as though, if they were there, we knew it. Nothing; no return fire.

We moved onto the hilltop and immediately came across a shallow foxhole. It was only a few hours old, if that old, and had been hastily dug, not up to the usual high NVA standards. In the dirt around it was the fresh imprint of a Ho Chi Minh. I told Six of this while the point squad, crouched and anxious, fanned out over the hill.

Shots: sharp and alien. A few seconds of silence and then everything started to crackle. A shouting voice told me that Davis was pinned down. Probing down the side of the hill, he came under fire and now lay sprawled face down in the brush.

"Davis, are you okay—Davis?"

Second Squad was shooting in the general direction of where the shots came from, but high for fear of hitting Davis.

"Davis? Davis?" I was convinced he had been hit. Ti Ti, the old hand now that Big Man was gone, was beside me.

"He can't answer you, sir. He'll give away his position."

Of course.

Rounds were snapping back and forth as Davis lay hugging the earth about 20 feet from an NVA position. As long as he doesn't move, they can't see him without exposing themselves.

"Don't move. Lay still. . .Goddamn you, Davis, lay still!"

More shots. Then silence. Suddenly, Davis came pounding up the side of the hill, all arms and legs, running out from under his helmet. He was unharmed.

The shooting confirmed the rumor that had bounded from squad to squad back down the column which still stretched a couple of hundred yards along our path: "There are gooks on this hill." I started yelling to the other squads to get into position, pointing to where I wanted them to set up. But visibility was so poor that any real control was impossible. Second Platoon closed in on the NVA without much direction on my part.

The NVA, well below the crest of the hill, about halfway down, were shooting high and so were we, most of us. But not all; hugging the earth a few men would creep forward and then bob up to fire. . .at what I could not see. There was a flurry of shots followed by a piercing scream. Gosselin had hit one of the NVA. They shot back.

The spoon of a grenade tinged off and everyone on that side of the hill hunched low. One, two, three more grenades followed in succession. Several men were trying their hand at getting a grenade into what they said was a bunker. The NVA were still firing. I pitched a grenade in the general direction of where everyone else seemed to be throwing them but I could see no bunker.

Aguirre, T-shirted and skinny-armed, stooped in beside me.

"La dai," he shouted, "la dai [come out]." That had not occurred to me. Maybe they'll surrender.

"La dai."

We called for Van who slipped dangerously a little forward of us and called out in phrases I did not understand. The NVA did not answer, nor did they surrender, nor did they shoot. (Throughout all of this it bothered me for some reason that I did not know where my pack was. I had ditched it as soon as the shooting started.)

The rest of the column was moving onto the hilltop very rapidly and the result, since no one could see more than 50 feet in any direction, was something like dropping a long strand of spaghetti into a tea cup. Speare stood in the middle of this talking on the radio with Motor Six, and waving men into position with his free hand.

I reported to Speare while platoons and squads quickly sorted themselves out. Men would look around nervously, find their squad, and with obvious relief join the men they were most comfortable with. The perimeter was rapidly taking shape. I told Speare what I knew: a small group of men ("Maybe there's a squad down there, maybe less") were shooting at us from below the military crest of the hill. I did not report a bunker because I had not seen one.

"I don't know, maybe they've pulled out; but I'm not sending anybody down there."

Speare informed me that I was.

"We've got to push out this perimeter. Send a squad down there to clear that area out."

I hoped that the NVA had pulled out; they had had every chance. But the NVA, I knew, were trained to "hug" American positions to avoid our murderous artillery. If that's what they're doing, I realized, someone's going to get hurt.

I stooped over to Second Squad and told them to go on line. "We're going down the hill." A few men clicked in fresh magazines. When I stood up, they stood up. Two steps and I could see well down the hillside.

"Shoot, shoot!" No one was firing. I got off a couple of rounds before everyone else opened up, firing as I did into the ground about 15 yards in front of us. There were no obvious targets; I could see no bunker, no position of any kind. Breasting through the scrub, for 10 steps, maybe 15, shooting all the while, we moved down the hill.

There was no return fire and I was mostly concerned that the assault line would get tangled up in the heavy cover. Then there would be a real danger that we would start shooting each other.

Bunker! There was an isolated shot and red dust spouted from the entrance just in front of me. My rifle and helmet simply disappeared, by what mechanism I didn't know, and my right hand stung viciously. It was easy to see why; the fingers were hanging at odd angles and much of the meat had been blown off the palm. I managed a couple of steps to my right, fell on my face, and rolled over onto my back.

I next remember trying to focus on the tracery of leaves and branches above me which for some reason had become the most interesting things in the world to examine. Then, from somewhere nearby I could hear Speare roaring at Second Squad to keep shooting. The firing picked up amid a chorus of shouts which seemed to include my own disembodied voice. "Shoot him, shoot him, kill him!" A dozen men were alternately screaming and shooting.

"Medic!"

Suddenly terrified, I tried to get back up the hill. All this time I had been blinking like an owl but everything remained blurred and flat, a bad watercolor. Confused, unable to see clearly, I ran directly in front of the bunker and there, I am told, I sat down. The shooting continued, but at what I didn't know. Two Six Bandaid arrived at my side and in a voice that suggested that he was about to escort an old lady across the street he asked me if I could walk. I said that I could and he led me up the hill and into the hands of the company medic.

"I'm hit in the eye, Doc. I can't see." I could see, but not very well.

"It's nothing," the standard answer.

"It hurts."

"Hold on. Hold still."

"There's a hole in my eye."

"Hold the fuck still, sir."

More grenades. I could hear someone saying that there must be a cut-off in the bunker. Doc ripped open a first aid packet and carefully applied heavy gauze bandages to my left eye. "Don't move your head." More bandages encased my hand which was then buttoned Napoleon fashion inside my fatigue jacket. An elastic band was around my wrist. Doc gave me a shot of morphine; then ran the needle through my collar and bent it over. An IV containing something Doc described as "blood expander" was started.

182

Before he was finished there were more cries for a medic. Canfield had been hit and was carried yelping up the hill by Two Six Bandaid and another man. They said he had tried to enter a second bunker with a .45 and had been shot in both legs at point blank range. He was bleeding very badly.

I could hear hueys overhead. Gunships. Braces of rockets started slamming in very close to the perimeter while both medics worked frantically, trying to stop the blood that was streaming out of Randy's legs. Each time the rockets came in, the two men would wince, duck low over Randy's body and then go back to work.

Sergeant Honeywell came over to see how I was doing. I said, "I've had better days." The morphine was taking effect. "Stay away from the lieutenant," Honeywell barked at a couple of men peering over his shoulder. "You wanna draw fire?"

I had other visitors who brought news of what had happened to me and of the brutal little fight that was taking place about 75 yards away. Those men in the bunkers would soon be killed; it was now only a question of whether or not anyone from Navajo would die in the process.

"Your rifle is smashed to shit. Fucking round hit it. Fucking forepiece is gone."

"Fucking Randy went right in after those gooks...struck the muzzle against his leg."

"You're lucky!" A cheerful voice announced.

A mangled 7.62 round was held close to my face.

"We got this out of your helmet, in between the liner. It hit the lip [of the helmet]. ...You want it?"

"You keep it," I said.

"Thanks."

The firing picked up again. A grenade..."Medic." A few seconds later Gosselin appeared. He asked how I was doing and then held up his left arm. A grenade fragment had gone through the bicep. "How long is that good for?" he asked Doc who examined it with a professional eye.

"Ten days," said Doc, "maybe two weeks," meaning the time that Gosselin would get in a rear area. Gosselin looked pleased, wished me luck, and returned without bothering to get his arm bandaged.

Rounds popped intermittently as the gunships continued to orbit overhead. I could hear Speare shouting. Almost immediately the

183

rockets came in again, 10 or 12 of them, very loud and very close. There was a momentary, ringing silence. The firing picked up again, briefly; then it stopped.

"How long before medevac gets here?"

"They're still busy with the other company. . .four, five guys hurt real bad."

Jerome came up to tell me that they had finally blown the roof off the second bunker and killed the men inside. Three men he said, and there had been one other killed outside of the bunker.

"We shot the piss out of them. You should see them."

A huey was briefly overhead. A jungle suit was dropped and I was quickly strapped into it. It was like being in a mummy case.

I was carried back and forth. I can remember being put in a place where the sun was in my face and feeling very hot. I dozed. I was moved; then moved again. There was a huey overhead and I was conscious of a lot of activity around me. Then a tug and I was upright with a slowly revolving green world falling away beneath me. Above the canopy the sun was very bright. I was pulled into the chopper and the jungle suit quickly removed. The man in the door was peering intently over the side watching the cable head back down. I crawled over to him.

"Toss some smokes down; we're out of smokes." I knew the company was nearly out of smoke grenades. We were low on them when we moved out that morning; Sergeant Honeywell had been worried about that.

"Get back over there, get out of the way." The man pointed to the other side of the chopper.

"We need some fucking smokes."

"Get the fuck away from me!" he shrieked.

Someone pulled me out of the way. I sat propped against the pilot's armor plate and squinted at the medic as he carefully guided the cable back up. Randy was pulled into the chopper and dragged over beside me. The cable headed back down with the penetrator on it. By this time the chopper had been hovering just over the company for several long minutes. Goggins rose into view on the penetrator and was pulled in. He was smiling broadly.

The chopper nosed down slightly, picked up speed, and soared to altitude. Only then did the man at the door relax. He cupped his hand next to my ear. "Didn't mean to yell at you," he said amiably. In places the deck of the chopper seemed sticky; in others slippery. Blood.

CHAPTER 10

"What happened to you?
Where do you hurt?"

The chopper took us home — to Juliet, where we were put on stretchers and moved to the first aid tent. News that Navajo had taken casualties brought several men to the tent including Father Grayson who said a brief prayer and then asked if there was anything he could do for us. Randy was afraid that someone would steal his tape recorder. Father Grayson, without any trace of surprise that I could detect, said that no one would; he would see to it. As for me, I was scared and seeing that, Father Grayson put his cross around my neck.

I doubt that the hospital at Quang Tri (I remember nothing of the flight over) was experiencing anything other than an ordinary day, but to me it seemed to be in chaos. There were patients in the halls and in the room I was in several men were being worked on at the same time.

"Jesus, make them stop! Jesus, make them stop!" someone kept pleading.

"Jesus, make them stop. Jesus, make them stop"; loud desperate cries.

A face appeared in front of me.

"Head wound," explained the face. "They sometimes make a lotta noise."

A doctor swam into view, looked briefly at my eye, turned to the person beside him, said a few words and moved on to another patient. After the doctor left a young chaplain examined my dog tag, the one around my neck, and announced that we were going to pray.

"I already did that at Juliet."

He clasped my unbandaged hand in his. "We shall pray again. God is always..."

"Leave me alone."

I was taken to a hallway and left there with five or six other wounded men. A few minutes later I was moved again, along with the others, outside, where I could hear a helicopter. It was raining. Then I was returned to the hallway and left alone. "Chow time," I thought. "Fucking orderlies, they're going to forget me. I'll bleed to death." After less than half an hour, the chopper returned. I was placed aboard (I remember fretting that it was an old Marine H-34) and told that I was being flown to a hospital ship, the USS *Repose*.

"Where do you hurt?" I was lying stark naked on a metal table beneath an X-ray machine and several people were leaning over me. One of them was yelling at the top of his lungs. "What happened to you? Where do you hurt?"

When I woke up there were bandages on both eyes, a cast on my right wrist and forearm and a bandage on my left hand where the bullet had grooved a knuckle and taken off a patch of skin. Idiotically I complained to someone, a nurse I suppose, that my right earlobe hurt. It had (has) a small piece of metal in it.

Over the next three or four days, during the odd moments that I was awake, a variety of voices explained in bits and pieces what had been done to me. Someone told me that a few metal fragments had been removed from in and around my left eye. "The less you move your eye, the better the prognosis; fair to good I'd say. Both eyes work in unison so we've bandaged both eyes. We'll know in a week or so." It was an optimistic voice. "Your medic," continued the voice, "did a beautiful job...probably saved that eye."

"We've amputated your finger [this was another voice], what is it?...the middle finger, anyway one of the long ones."

I couldn't have cared less; besides it was already gone.

"Your wrist was really smashed—we had to fuse it. Okay, now those pins [two long threaded pins stuck out from the cast] are to keep your arm from shrinking too much as the wrist heals...try to move your fingers as much as you can."

"Had to clamp an artery." The voice didn't say where the artery was.

As much to keep me quiet as for the pain, I was given heavy doses of codeine which provoked vivid dreams about the breasts of a girl I

186

had known in junior high school. I returned to this theme repeatedly, never progressing to other parts of her anatomy. When awake I would remember that she was very myopic and that she wore thick glasses, which no longer seemed as important as it had ten years before.

Once a day the room would be darkened and the bandages removed from my eyes. A doctor would peer into my left eye, tell me that I was doing fine, and leave. Then the bandages would be replaced. These interludes allowed me to attach faces to the two voices that were occupying the room with me.

Roommate number one was a marine lieutenant whose testicles were enormously swollen; the size of tennis balls the nurse said with no hint of amusement.

"I was on LZ Carrol—on patrol—daylight patrol, you know just fucking around. We saw this gook and I took off after him."

"Why?" I asked.

"Anyway, I jumped off this rock—maybe ten feet...must have been more. We never got him. The next day my nuts were this big." He demonstrated with his hands. "Hurt, Jesus. I had to make it up to the log pad on my own; nobody helped me."

Treatment involved staying in bed and lying as quietly as possible. The lieutenant followed these instructions faithfully.

Roommate number two was a 21-year-old helicopter pilot, a captain. "We were flying supply missions into a Yard village. There was nothing to do so I went down to this shack where the Yards were drinking beer. I had a couple. This Yard was eating C-4...I swear it, rolling it up in a little ball and eating it. So I tried it. Right away I got sick. I guess I blacked out on the way over here. They pumped my stomach; I'll be fine in a couple of days."

He paused.

"They sent this other doctor around to ask me why I ate C 4...I swear the gook was eating it."

My roommates' medical problems were not typical. The *Repose* steamed back and forth just off the coast of Vietnam taking the overflow from field hospitals and "tricky" wounds that the field hospitals did not feel they were equipped to handle. Wounds to the eye, even if they were fairly minor, as in my case, came under this category. Helicopters full of wounded men arrived several times a day and would be announced by a bosun's pipe. Then there would be a scamper of stretcher bearers who would take the patients, some still screaming, down through the passageways of the ship; first to X-ray—"where do you hurt"—and then, as a rule, to surgery. Amputations were common and large areas of the ship were set aside for intensive care. Several decks below was a refrigerated room for those who did not survive.

I began to piece together what had happened to me. After the first several days bits of metal, some bright and coppery, began working their way out of my face. The round had struck the lip of my helmet which had shaved off some of the gliding metal. Evidently the bullet had lost enough steam plowing through my rifle, and my wrist, and the front of my helmet, that it had been deflected by the fiberglass helmet liner. Otherwise, at a range of eight or nine feet, it would have gone through my helmet and my head like butter, leaving a disagreeable tooth-cluttered stump—a "head amputee." I had heard it called that. I must have had my rifle to my shoulder, must have been taking aim at something or someone when I was shot. That would explain why I had also been hit in the left hand which would have been grasping the forepiece. Was I shooting at the man who shot me? I had (and have) absolutely no recollection of anything like that. Had we shot each other?

After ten days the bandages were removed from my eyes and following a few tests I was pronounced hale and hearty. And I found that I was strong enough to walk. It had been months since I had last had a hot shower and that was the first thing I wanted. I think I still must have smelled vaguely like an incontinent badger because it became obvious that the nurses wanted me to have a shower even more than I did. I was provided with a towel, a plastic bag to cover my cast, a sponge and a big jar of surgical soap. "Use *all* the water you want," I was commanded.

The *Repose*'s communication system somehow patched into a network (HAM radio operators were part of this) that allowed calls home. I gave this a try and got through. My mother answered. "How's your eye?" she asked without missing a beat. "Fine," I said, "everybody okay at home?"

"They're fine...okay. We're just waiting for you to get home."

And so forth. Not much was said because the calls could be only a few minutes long. And because I was so full of codeine that I kept forgetting to say "Over" after each transmission so there were a lot of 20 second pauses between sentences. Somewhere along the line, I was driving a radio operator nuts. "You have to say 'Over' when you are done," he kept saying. I can remember the sound of an infant squalling in the background — my son.

Periodically the *Repose* transferred those among its cargo judged to be on the mend, or at least stable, to the hospital at Da Nang; from there to be sent back to the field or to Japan. The first indication that I was leaving the ship came when I was told to report to the supply room. A little wobbly, I made my way several decks down into the sour smelling ship to line up with other ambulatory patients in front of a fat and floridly cheerful supply sergeant. He had a joke for every man in line. To my horror, his office was just across from a huge refrigerated locker that contained corpses. I held out against a clammy sepulchral nausea long enough to draw a pair of boots and two sets of Stateside fatigues, then fled topside to air and sunlight.

In the morning two stretcher bearers reported to me. I told them that I could walk but they insisted that I be carried since that was their orders. We arrived at a compromise. When I left Quang Tri all that I had on me — wallet, Swiss Army knife, company roster and a list of radio frequencies (my map had been removed from my pocket before I had been medevacked) — was placed in a cloth bag which had gone with me on my stretcher to the *Repose*. The knife I gave to the marine who was well on the mend and, I gathered, anxious to avenge his battered testicles. Everything else plus a razor and a toothbrush, courtesy of the Red Cross, I returned to the cloth bag. So, after brief goodbyes, I walked to the helipad while the stretcher bearers, pleased to the point of smirking over the agreement we had negotiated, followed with my possessions.

The *Repose* was steaming under a drizzly rain that did nothing to dim the spectacularity of the entrance to Da Nang Harbor. Brightly washed green hills soared above the ship on both sides. I stood around with the stretcher bearers for a few minutes taking this in until one of them salaamed, motioned for me to lay down, and I was carried aboard the helicopter. Watching those green hills slide by I had the feeling that so beautiful a place could not have been at war but once inside the helicopter that illusion left me.

The evacuation wards in the air force hospital at Da Nang had television. For the two days I spent there the bed beside me was occupied by a black marine who had lost both of his legs above the knee. When I arrived he was watching a football game and for some reason I kept getting in front of the TV.

"Get outta the way, you donkey."

Rank doesn't mean much to a double amputee.

Mines and medevac had filled that ward with such men. The mines had blown them to pieces and medevac got them to the hospital before they died. So they lived. And they hurt. The marine lived in a fog of Demerol which every twitch and shift of position cut through. He broke into a sweat at the site of a bed pan.

That evening a red-haired starlet, we supposed from the Bob Hope show, toured the ward. Incomplete, sedated men stared as a smiling air force captain convoyed the frozen-faced woman to likely looking patients. The entire time the woman said not a word. She just stared, wide-eyed, working her throat up and down.

The flight to Japan was my first experience with the Medical Corps' version of a Middle Passage tight pack—four rows of stretchers, three high, running for much of the length of the aircraft. Ambulatory patients rode toward the front of the plane but I was no longer ambulatory. As I was being carried up the loading ramp, I caught sight of a formation of marines on the far end of the tarmac; they had just arrived in-country.

I spent a week in Japan, at Camp Drake, on a large ward of seriously wounded men, not all of whom could be expected to go home. If a man still had all of his arms and legs and could be expected to heal much before his tour of duty was up he would often be sent back to the field. It was up to the doctor: Mine sent me home. It was rumored that he sent everybody home.

At the time patient flow was a priority. Fix them up or get them out. Otherwise patients stacked up in the hallway, soiled laundry faster than it could be washed, and drained the supply of whole blood. I really believe that if it had been technically possible the army would have put every patient on a conveyor belt so that wounds could be dressed and stitches taken out as they moved along at the administratively set pace. After a few weeks, as strong and as healthy as mules and nothing in their heads but grunt-gratitude for time out of the field, they would come to the end of the belt and drop into a deuce and a half. It wasn't technically possible though. You might think that standardized weapons would produce standardized wounds; but it isn't so. And, there were relatively few "it's only a flesh wound, ma'am" wounds which is what kept the starlet swallowing her puke during her tour of the hospital in Da Nang. The kid in the bed across from me had been

190

shot in the back of the knee. The leg was fine except that it didn't have a knee joint any longer. There was a little window in his cast, in the front, where the knee had been, and twice a day the doctors would take a peek. What to do?

Amputations, on the other hand, suited assembly line care. They are all pretty similar. Start at the foot and work up, or start at the hand and work up; but wherever you cut the result is the same: a stump. And the military has accumulated a lot of knowledge on how to produce a "good stump."

The first stage of producing a good stump I got to see a great deal of because the man beside me, a Chicano kid from Arizona, had lost his foot. His leg ended just below the fat part of the calf and from the front looked like a small canned ham; not a very original observation, I suppose, but that's what it looked like. An elastic sock fits over the stump and is used to gradually pull the skin down over the amputation to close it and pad the bone. This sock has to be tended daily and it's very painful. The Chicano kid endured this stoically, cursing and begging softly in Spanish. Not everyone reacted that way. Even lying on my back staring at the ceiling I could follow the progress of the nurses and orderlies around the big ward as they tended the amputees.

Just about every day an attractive well-dressed woman in her thirties — a doctor's wife I guessed — stopped by the ward to write letters for those men who could not see or use their hands and to run errands. I had about $80 worth of MPC in my wallet so I asked her if she would buy "some kimonos or something." She smiled because that's what every busted-up, sedated GI said: "Kimonos." She had probably purchased, packaged, and sent home kimonos to half the states in the Union. The next day she was back with three exquisite kimonos to show me. She wanted to be sure that I thought I was getting my money's worth.

At night a solitary medic sat in an office just off the ward and kept watch. Sometimes during the night the men beside me would call over and ask me to get him: they needed a bed pan, they needed a shot, their bed felt wet and they were afraid they were hemorrhaging. One night it was the kid with the exploded knee. He seldom slept and often just quietly cried.

"Please, I think it's time for my shot. I can't stand this. Please!"

I teetered over to the office to find the medic yawning over a stack of forms.

191

"What can I do for you, Lieutenant?"

"That red-headed kid on bed [whatever the number was] is really hurting."

"Yeah, I know; the Knee, the kid with the fucked-up knee. It's not time yet. He knows that."

The medic thought the Knee complained too much. He paused while I hung on the door jam like a drunk.

"Well, okay, but I'll have to get the night nurse and she's gonna have to contact the duty officer and by then..."

The kid with no knee was waiting for me.

"He's gonna get the night nurse," I said.

"Oh God, thanks; thanks a lot. God, you know, it never fucking stops."

Later, maybe a little before it was time, a nurse came by and gave the kid a shot.

It took me a while to realize it but night after night the medic sat in a windowed room overlooking rows of dismembered, wracked young men. In a week, ten days, three weeks, there would be another group just like them. He had to think in terms of knees, eyes, legs, colostomies and amputations. He had no choice. And what about the supply sergeant who worked in the bottom of the *Repose*? If he ever let up on his joking, if he ever stopped jabbering away, then he'd be staring across the passageway at a refrigerator full of 19-year-old stiffs.

Somewhere along the line I was told that I would be going home but I don't think I believed it until I found myself in a long hallway with about 100 other stretcher patients. We were all lined up in a column of twos with the nurses patrolling up and down checking names and medication. It reminded me vaguely of a Charlie Alpha except that we were loading into ambulances instead of helicopters. The double line of patients, some awake, some sleeping, some unconscious, stretched down the hall, and ended in the parking lot where a group of eight or ten "ambulance stuffers" were working. Ambulance stuffing is not an official Military Occupation Specialty (MOS) but in 1968 it should have been because a lot of men did that full time.

Loading a convoy of 15 or 16 ambulances (six men to an ambulance) in something less than an hour takes skill. The stretchers hang three high from the roof of the ambulance from steel rods about 18 inches long which have rings on both ends. First, four rods are hung from hooks in the roof of the ambulance and then the handles of the top stretcher fit through the bottom rings. The next set of rods slip over these same stretcher handles and suspend another stretcher below that—and so on, until there are three tiers of stretchers and, altogether, six men, hanging inside the ambulance. It was a very efficient system that was literally pinned together by stretchers.

Ambulance after ambulance pulled up and the stuffers, chattering away and sometimes laughing, swiftly constructed these six-man rigs. The nurses would occasionally tell the stuffers to slow down for fear that they would drop someone.

The flight home in a C-141 cargo jet set up as a hospital ward took many hours. My hand was by then badly infected and was swelling inside the cast. The nurses were powerless to increase the set dosage of pain killer during the flight and so it was a prolonged misery. When I was not involved in my own "discomfort," which I gathered was the correct medical term for what I was experiencing, I took stock of the patients around me. The man above me seldom moved and did not speak. Nor did the man below me. Across from me, in a stryker frame, was a "head wound," not really a person or even part of a person anymore. His head was shaved and a huge flap of yellowish skin had been stitched back over his skull. Except for fitful, bubbly breathing he showed no signs of life. The nurses cared for him tenderly, emptying his catheter bag and carefully wiping the saliva and mucus from his waxy mannequin face. He had been very young.

After refueling in Alaska the plane landed, as softly as a feather, at Andrews Air Force Base in Washington, DC. A marine major boarded and welcomed us back home. The Stateside ambulance stuffers quickly went to work and within an hour we were on our way to McGuire Army Hospital at Fort Dix. I had gone through advanced training there two years before but it seemed much longer ago than that.

At McGuire Hospital I was able to call home on a phone that didn't require me to say "Over" and after some complaining was given a shot.

"You shouldn't do that," said the nurse after she gave me the injection. "There are people trying to sleep here."

"Do what?"

"Bang your head like that."

It developed that I had been methodically banging my head against the headboard of the bed.

The next day I was taken to Valley Forge Army Hospital which was only a few miles from the site of Washington's encampment. There, I made some discoveries. I discovered that there was an eighth of an inch to a quarter of an inch of brown, dried callous on the soles of my feet—"I thought you guys just rode in helicopters." And, I discovered that I had lost 30 pounds. Hospital pajamas, cast, and all, I weighed 129 pounds. I am just under six feet tall.

Valley Forge Army Hospital was a huge complex of three-story wooden buildings connected by miles of sloping hallways. When I was there it was full. Constructed during the Second World War, it had not emptied of patients much before the Korean War started. Vietnam filled it with patients once again and kept it filled for another ten years. Valley Forge was primarily an orthopedic hospital and a very good one. It was also another world; a world of amputations, shattered bones, colostomies, and missing faces. I lived there for seven months, undergoing minor surgery and regaining, to my surprise, much of the use of my hand.

After about a week, the old cast was removed, and the pins through my hand and forearm were removed. My hand had swollen to the size of an inflated surgical glove, the palm was as round and as big as an orange, and from this a long toothpaste-squeeze of yellow pus was pressed out by the surgeon. To his and everyone's surprise, I yelped unashamedly during the entire procedure. I got a new and more roomy cast and after that the pain and the infection gradually subsided.

Still, it was a long time before I could sleep for more than a couple of hours at a stretch. I would pass the early morning hours pacing up and down the ward with my right arm held above my head to reduce the pressure. Usually I had a companion, a stocky kid who had been shot in the forearm attempting to escape from LBJ, the army stockade at Long Binh (LBJ stands for Long Binh Jail). He walked up and down with his left hand over his head.

Seven months was not a long stay by Valley Forge standards. My hallway companion was there when I arrived and would be there when I left. Most of his forearm was gone. His doctor told me that it was the worst trauma he had ever seen that did not require amputation. A captain on that ward had been there for two years undergoing vascular surgery so that he could keep his leg. There was still some doubt as to whether he could or not. It was those men undergoing plastic surgery who held the records for longevity. For years they endured operation after operation. They waited for weeks as still as possible, while tubes

194

of skin grew up from their neck and chest to renew their faces. If the graft did not take, they started over.

The staff at Valley Forge carried a heavy patient load but there was time to attach faces (if there was one) and personalities to stumps, hands, eyes, and colostomies. The concern was genuine — if distant. Young bodies make for good patients; that is, they heal. But the men at Valley Forge were also baggaged by all sorts of intractable problems. Often they had massive infections. One night a shaken nurse came into my room. She had been rolling a patient over to change his sheets when an enormous abscess burst drenching her in pus.

"My last uniform," she said distractedly. "I can't go back on the ward like this. I had no idea."

A man who has spent nine months with the LRRP team in Vietnam is not likely to take a bullet wound to the lower leg very seriously even if there is massive tissue damage. If he feels like walking on it, chances are he will. If a cast covering an open wound itches, the owner may dump a can of talcum powder down it. If he's on pass and feels like going swimming, he may do that as well.

Accidents while on pass were common; usually just ordinary accidents, but there were a lot of them. Men who should not get into fights frequently did. One of the men on the ward was from the 101 Airborne. Joe would leave on pass Friday afternoon and, by Friday evening, would have often gotten drunk, picked a fight, and lost it. By Saturday he would be back on the ward with loose teeth, black eyes, and once, a broken nose. He never won any fights because he had a bad leg amputation (close to the hip) and serious nerve damage to his left arm. He said he had been knocked unconscious assaulting across a rice paddy and had fallen behind a paddy dike. The only part of him that was exposed was his leg and a sniper had thumped bullets into it until there was nothing left to patch together. Because the one year tour of duty had officially eliminated stress related problems, Joe's behavior was chalked up to a feisty nature.

Adventures in the World could sometimes be exotic. The man across the hall from me, a lieutenant who had lost a foot, returned from a weekend pass with the ominous news that American women now went around with the lower two-thirds of their bodies encased in fine nylon mesh.

"...had me some confused, until she peeled the whole thing off," he explained.

195

Pantyhose, it's called. Strange.

The hospital maintained a "patient club" (i.e., bar) and many men drank with a vengeance. One night at the club, I watched as an amputee spun on his bar stool and attempted to stride off on his missing leg. He fell flat. Someone offered him a hand, but he waved it off and struggled back to his seat. Then he ordered another beer, drank it, hoisted himself on his crutches and left. No one else took any notice of this; apparently it happened all the time.

A variety of charitable organizations, community groups, and television personalities, usually known to us from game shows, prowled the halls. By far the most welcome was the Salvation Army. This chiefly took the form of a black woman of stately bearing and her attractive daughter who pushed a cart of sandwiches, soft drinks and coffee up and down the ward three times a week. I suspect that they did this on their own time. It was appreciated. She would (only if you asked) hand out copies of the Salvation Army magazine. I've forgotten the title but it is pleasant to recall that it contained obituaries under the heading, "Promoted to Glory." Nice touch.

Several times people from God only knows what group came by the ward and insisted that everybody sing. Usually a few men would join them and sing in a halfhearted way. I'm sure these people genuinely wanted to cheer us up but it was also clear that they were reliving their own past good times. So we would go through songs like "Mac-Namara's Band" and (I'm not kidding) "Roll Out the Barrel." Maybe it was some old war movie that inspired them. It was pitiful; they just didn't understand. Just about everyone on that ward was both amazed and delighted to be alive and the problems they did have, which ran deep, no amount of singing would have helped.

After the cast came off my arm for good, my doctor told me to stop "fussing" (a favorite word) and get to work rehabilitating my hand. "If you don't get off your dime, you're going to have a bad hand." He was the enemy of bad hands. In a procedure he developed, or at least refined, the lumpy useless knuckle on my hand was removed and also part of the metacarpal. The result is a fairly normal looking hand and, he claimed, a better hand. He was right.

A few weeks later he came into my room. I was lying on my bed bored stiff. "I notice," he said wryly, "that you don't have many commitments these days. I want you to talk to some guy. He should have your operation but he's afraid of it."

196

So I talked to the guy and showed him my hand. A bullet had gone cleanly through his hand severing the nerves to his middle finger. The finger was useless and only got in the way.

"It's gonna look funny; if they take off that finger, I'm gonna look funny."

"Right now you're giving everybody the finger; you don't want to go through life giving people the finger."

"It's gonna look funny," he moaned. "I don't wanna look funny." There was nothing else wrong with him and how he could give the loss of a finger more than a second thought was beyond imagination. I met no one else at Valley Forge like him.

I wrote a few letters to Second Platoon and sent a package or two—cans of mandarin oranges, a little booze, things like that. I received some letters in return; including one from Gosselin and one from Jerome who I assumed were very close. They were the old hands now, like Ti Ti and Big Man.

Gosselin wrote a sort of collective letter thanking me for the packages. "We thought you would have forgotten us by now." That was not a reproach; they really thought I put them out of my mind. But I had not. "Things are bad where we are now." (The Cav had moved south and was screening Saigon.) I knew that it must be very bad for Gosselin to even mention it. I learned that Ti Ti had made it back to the World and that Sergeant Taliferro, Villareal and Two Six Bandaid never would. They had been killed in an ambush.

Letters written in airport terminals came from men who had finished their tour and were on their way home. What was it like to leave Vietnam after a year in the field and surface a day later in the World? I didn't know, and couldn't imagine, but it was obvious that their minds were still in the field. Bishop wrote to tell me that he had made it back and of the cold, desolate perimeter that night after Second Platoon had killed the men in the bunkers. He had cried, he said. I sometimes thought of Captain Speare who had been left to run the company with two senior NCOs and one green platoon leader. I often thought of Stanhope.

Later, while I was still in the hospital, another letter arrived from Jerome. It was smudged with yellow mud, written in the field. Stubbed would be a better word; in places the black army ballpoint pen had punched through the paper.

He told me that a grenade fragment had caught him in the throat but that by a miracle it had hit no arteries. ("Don't worry, Jon, I guess I can call you Jon now okay, it didn't hit anything. It really had me scared for a while. Ha Ha.") A minor wound officially, so after three weeks at an in-country hospital he had been sent back to the field with little more than a month to go on his tour.

The letter bucked with his thoughts like a runaway gun.

> Gosselin still walks point but Jon he shouldn't do that anymore. We are about the only ones left. Everybody else has gone home somehow. I am real short (37 days!) so maybe I can go home too. I'm more scared than I have ever been before. I don't know why but I guess it's just natural. I sure wish I was home now. I'm pretty homesick. These 37 days should go by slow. I hope not anyway. But I guess I might as well grit my teeth and bear it. About all we get done anymore is fight and patrol. We get out of the field now 7 days before going home. I'm so shaky now it isn't funny. 26 has really changed since you left. I wish this was the same old 26 plat. it was. I don't hardly know anyone here. . . . We have had 3 COs in 6 weeks and the company commander right now is gung ho as hell. All he wants to do is Kill, Kill. It makes me so sick Jon. I wish I could be home right now.

The letter ended there. He had started another paragraph, but lined it out. "Take care!" he closed.

CHAPTER 11

After I was out of the hospital and out of the army I received another letter from Steve Jerome. He was in Germany, assigned to some armored unit and, apart from a lingering case of jungle rot, seemed to be doing well. The infection had left his face and neck deeply scarred and he hoped the dry ice treatments he was getting would finally cure it. "It's got me in real bad pain now."

Steve and Gosselin had kept in touch and planned to tour the country together after Steve was discharged. "Don't be surprised if you see us coming up your driveway someday." But they never came. The last letter from Steve arrived some months later. He had fallen against a window and badly lacerated his arm. He was back in the States. I didn't go to see him. I should have.

I was far luckier than most Vietnam veterans. The long months at Valley Forge Hospital allowed me to move back into the World by stages, by weekend passes. I would take a bus into Philadelphia, see a movie and then get drunk. This seldom varied.

The ride from Valley Forge Hospital to Philadelphia was a passage through a long, serpentine air lock. On the other side I found the World to be a strange place. I can remember standing at the rear of a theatre and having a little boy run up to me to ask where the drinking fountain was. I was in uniform and he had mistaken me for an usher. "Don't bother that man," squeaked the child's mother who was for some inexplicable reason dressed like a mini-skirted Indian.

An afternoon was passed at the Philadelphia Zoo and then I walked back into Center City by way of the ghetto. Five men in their late teens, all wearing black berets, were shooting dice on the sidewalk. Tolerated in good humor, I watched, and later joined the game even though it was expected, and undoubtedly necessary, that I lose money. I did, but not much, and I enjoyed the company. I think they were bemused by the strange, uniformed, left-handed shooter who had dropped in from another world. In the evenings I drank. I was not sparkling company. Usually after an hour or two I would find myself crying. Embarrassed, I would leave and go to another bar so the evening would progress. I went to a college bar once. I was not welcome. I wanted no more than to be ignored, not stared at and avoided.

On leave, I would stand by my son's crib, staring. The Field clanked after me like the chains winding Marley's ghost. That may be overly dramatic but it is true that my social skills were on a par with Marley's ghost. A cousin inquired about the brownies his wife sent to Vietnam. "Moldy," I said, "but we ate the fucking popcorn you packed them in." Marley's ghost never dampened a picnic by blowing a plug of snot into the ground. My fists were clenched, *all* the time. Elsa feared that I had met "otra chinas [girls]" in Vietnam. I said that there weren't any girls in the mountains—just soldiers. "Well," she asked, "what did you do on the weekends?" What I said was brutal and undeserved.

The arguments for and against the war did not interest me; and people ardently supporting either camp I found to be self-serving and distasteful. Both camps regarded soldiers as social residue and those supporting the war, in my small experience, the more so. I suppose that was because the soldiers they saw in airports or on the street—men just back from Vietnam, bewildered and disagreeably drunk, and boys just out of basic training with whitewall haircuts and flaring mastoids—in no way resembled John Wayne or Mrs. Minniver's son.

I went back to college and majored in anthropology because it was the least disreputable form of escapist behavior available to me at the time. I enjoyed archaeology most of all, possibly because of all the social sciences archaeology is the only one that focuses almost exclusively on long-dead people. There are no personalities to deal with, unless you indulge your imagination, and all tragedy is muted. Archaeologists just dig up *things*; they never dig up bodies, just artifacts and skeletons.

Two years before I enrolled at the university the archaeologists there had dug up a very great many skeletons during the excavation of an Indian village and its associated cemetery. The department was lumbered with stone tools, bones and pots and the basement resembled the catacombs of a monastery. The departmental monks, the physical

200

anthropologists, aged the skeletons, sexed them, examined them for evidence of trauma and disease and were well on their way to the discovery that a lot of people died young and a lot of people died violently. I did not find it difficult to accept that conclusion.

But it is an important study, accomplished by careful, exacting people. Of course you have to start somewhere, from *somebody's* skeleton. Now where can you find a large number of skeletons of documented age and sex for comparison? There are two places: charity hospitals and the army. The Quartermaster Corps, of which Graves Registration is a part, has produced an excellent study, *Skeletal Age Changes in Young American Males*, as a serendipitous spinoff of Operation Glory, the "repatriation" (read, "box me up and ship me home") of American soldiers hastily buried in North Korea. Wrapped in rotting shelter halves, their skeletons were still obediently wearing their dog tags. "You realize," said one of the physical anthropologists during a candid moment, "that we're generalizing from bag ladies and infantrymen."

I can remember only once being asked about my experiences in Vietnam. A thin young man who always struck me as unusually placid drew me aside one day.

"You were in Vietnam, right?"

I said, "Yes."

"What did you do with the roots? I hear you guys do something with the roots in Vietnam."

"What roots?"

"Marijuana roots! You bury them somehow and then the stuff, you know, it gets really strong."

The war continued while I was studying stone tools, skeletons, and the decorative motifs the skeletons supposedly used when they made clay pots. I seldom watched the news. The invasion of Cambodia happened to coincide with a warm spring evening. By darkness windows were being broken by a crowd that had gathered along the university town's profitable strip of bars. Toward midnight the damage had already surpassed what normally happened during Homecoming and the mayor ordered the bars closed. This increased the size of the crowd. More windows were broken. A bonfire was kindled in the street and members of a local motorcycle gang rode up and down doing wheelies. When they weren't doing that they stood around urinating into the bonfire.

The following evening, which was a Saturday evening, a mob gathered on campus and by trial and error set fire to an old prefabricated building used by ROTC cadets for marksmanship training (army surplus — it had originally been destined for the invasion of Japan). A shed containing archery equipment was also burned. The National Guard rolled into town before the embers had died and it all looked impressive on TV. Sunday brought a smashed Jeep window and some bayonettings, one serious, a coed, the others (more numerous than officially reported), minor.

As I rode the bus through town on Monday morning I saw boarded up windows along Main Street and spray-painted slogans against Imperialism and also something called "Imperelism." A battalion of guardsmen stood around campus in clusters with their M-1 rifles crooked in their arms.

It was said that during the early morning hours coeds had stood before dormitory windows with their bottoms exposed which the townspeople were quick to say was a scandalously cruel thing to do to men who have been separated from their wives and sweethearts for almost a week (the guardsmen had been called out some days earlier to keep the separate factions in a labor dispute from beating each other up). For some guardsmen, days had passed since their last cheeseburger and many others had missed work. They were angry and long hours spent guarding campus buildings (including the burned out ROTC building), intersections, and in one instance, a water fountain, could not have improved their mood.

I saw no sign whatsoever of anything like an organized guard mount and, in fact, I saw only one National Guard officer that entire morning, a second lieutenant. A short, rather plump man, he was striding toward me on sausage legs that squeezed out of spitshined boots, his face a granite mask of purpose and resolve. This stern appearance was complemented by an old M-3 submachine gun from which two taped-together magazines protruded. He looked like he was about to storm a Bavarian castle.

Classes were mandated but poorly attended. After a few minutes many professors gave up on lecturing. One professor treated us to an impression of the university's small and amazingly hedonistic crop of revolutionaries gathering in an attic. "It's here, it's here. The revolution is here," he intoned, beard uplifted, eyes gleaming in mock excitement.

He thought them delusional and feckless and numbered them among the fringe people who could be found living at the margins of university life, forever on the verge of "taking some classes." You could go away for years and when you came back they would say "haven't seen you around for awhile."

"I've been in the army."

"Oh... Walter's Bar has Heineken now. Did you know that?"

Some were sincere in their detestation of the War, some actually were taking classes—had been for ten years—a few were barking mad. But their pleasures always interfered and any possible conspiracies had long since strayed into a saffron fuddle. So we were all convinced that these vaguely exciting circumstances would soon pass us by; the Guard would pack up and go home and the town's pseudo-revolutionaries would content themselves once again with an occasional graffito.

Over the past several weeks I had been studying the orderly, natural world of Pleistocene man. It may have been violent but it wasn't crazy. Now it was both. Somehow, the world had gone progressively wacky after the last Ice Age and taken a direct path to institutional lunacy. With some difficulty, our professor yanked our attention onto the day's lecture topic which dealt with anatomical changes in the late Pleistocene. He began to discuss the evolution of the mental eminence—the chin. Outside, a Guardsman jacked back the bolt of his M-1 and allowed it to slam forward (they were fond of the noise it made). A hand went up. "Excuse me...what was that? Metal eminence?"

"No, corrected the professor, "men-tal eminence: M-E-N-T-A-L, as in *Mental Hospital.*"

Later I heard someone say that the students who had threatened to assemble on the campus commons at noon believed in Ghost Shirts. I'm not sure, maybe it was intended as a joke, but no one thought it funny. No one thought it prophetic either.

It was much the same in other classes. One professor had served in the British Army. "I've never encountered a soldiery so...quite so.... [long pause] Well, as you see, they handle weapons like rabbit hunters. Aren't they required to undergo any training?" There was some trace of apprehension in his voice but I think he was mostly just puzzled by the Guard. I would not have said so but they reminded me a little of the ARVNs at the bridge. They seemed to have, some of them, that same quality of festering belligerence, just waiting to be lanced. I remembered a Guardsman I had talked to just after I got out of the army. "As long as I make the meetings, I'm set," he crowed. "They can't send me anywhere. And if the niggers in Cleveland get out of hand, we're ready."

You did not see many blacks on campus that day because black student leaders had put out a warning to stay out of sight and if possible to leave campus, which nearly everyone who was not black thought an absurd overreaction. So did I.

Thin clouds of tear gas were drifting around by the time I had walked to the commons and I watched as two groups that shared a common desire to avoid participating in a war, tossed tear gas canisters back and forth. The Guardsmen were plodding heavily, laboring in their gas masks, after a capering mob from which a few golliwog figures would emerge to throw a rock or pitch back a gas canister. In minutes it seemed to be over. The demonstrators fled beyond a rise and I could no longer see them. The Guard, not far behind, stopped and appeared to be about to head back toward the center of campus. Then suddenly they turned and fired, and continued to fire. Immediately a Guardsman, heavier and I thought a little older than the rest, jumped in front of the men who were firing and began whacking at their rifles, slapping them up or aside. The Guard hesitated, then turned away.

"Blanks," said the person beside me, "must be blanks, they're shooting blanks."

I should not have been surprised that people were shot that afternoon. But I was. I thought it murder and said so.

I don't believe that anymore. Kent State was a pitiful, little Wounded Knee and just as predictable. The ill-trained Guard, taunted, ridiculed, pelted now and again by rocks, was spoiling to get even. And, it was true, the demonstrators had their Ghost Shirts on; their white middle class Ghost Shirts which guaranteed that no matter how vile or abusive you become no one will ever shoot you. Few could imagine that the weapons they were confronting were loaded.

Even sadder is the fact that Kent State was a source of entertainment and satisfaction to all those removed from the event. It riled everyone up and people like that. It provoked countless letters to the editor and a lot of bold talk on local newscasts. Deputy sheriffs crouched in the shrubbery and fattened on overtime pay. Television crews stalked the campus. There were many experts. The town of Kent sprouted American flags every 50 feet and its citizens basked in a soul-warming vindication. "Those M-1s sure do hurt." They loved it and would hold up four fingers (four dead and 20,000 to go). A few people sincerely believed that everyone on campus should have been shot and were disappointed that that had not happened.

Nationally there was enough of an uproar to rattle an administration renowned for its political expediency into cutting short the invasion of Cambodia. So in the bitterest irony of all, a battalion of Ohio National Guardsmen had in two days accomplished what the North Vietnamese Army had failed to do in five years: drive American forces from a battlefield. But, after all, that means very little because the decision to pull out of Vietnam was made nearly two years before; it was made about the time I left for Vietnam.

Despite the vigilance of several university administrators, I eventually graduated. Now I teach other people about stone tools, skeletons, and clay pots. I teach people that culture influences what people do and that human institutions are seldom rational and only unreliably kind. Few of my students take those notions very seriously, unless they are welfare mothers, and then I haven't taught them anything they don't already know.

Lately I have been asked to teach a course on the war in Vietnam. "It's a very popular topic these days and our students don't know much about it. There's a lot of meaty stuff in there... popular culture stuff, the first television war, those things." But I can't. Besides, Vietnam was not a "television war" at all, it was a television *show*. The war was something different. This is the best I can do.

EPILOGUE

I kept no journal. The British diarists of the First World War are a source of wonderment to me and so are the innumerable diarists of the North Vietnamese Army. I cannot imagine where they got the will, time, or dry paper.

I have relied on the radio logs (DA form 1594) of the 2nd of the 5th and 1st of the 5th battalions to confirm my recollection of events and to jog my memory. These logs make for stark reading and some of that language has crept unchanged into this narrative. AMS maps (series L7014, 1: 50,000), the same maps we carried in Vietnam, have been used to accurately describe the terrain. Time has softened the Vietnamese landscape. It was more rugged than I had remembered or chose to remember. ("It couldn't have been *that* bad": it was).

It *was* division policy to dig up all graves, or at least it was in the mountains, and the record shows that hundreds were found. The value of this policy was surely nil. I don't recall giving it a thought at the time, or if I did I must have quickly put it out of my mind, but for nearly a year I helped bury young Americans and then I went to Vietnam and helped dig up young Vietnamese.

I do not claim to recall conversations word for word, but I do believe that I have come close to what was said and how people fucking said it. I have changed names. Nicknames (Tex, Ti Ti, Big Man, Home, Ju Ju) and call signs are as I remember them. Two Niner Mike India I knew only as Two Niner Mike India. Two Six Bandaid's name I do not remember. His photograph, among the few I sent home, is of an earnest, red-haired man in his middle twenties who wears glasses. It's the kind of face you would expect to find in the yearbook of a medical school and that is where it should be. I lived with him for months, knew his hometown, the name of his girlfriend, and valued his friendship. He saved my life. But I am unable to remember his name. So, for reasons that I cannot entirely explain, I prefer to identify him in the way that I have.

The ambush at Dong Ha and the attack on the French Fort actually took place about as told to me. Reference to those events can be found in a variety of sources — the radio logs, for example. Shelby Stanton's *Anatomy of a Division* describes the taking of the French Fort as follows: "The 1st Battalion 5th Cavalry was stopped below the fort by heavy mortar fire which caused many casualties and mortally wounded the Battalion Commander. The Battalion was extracted and replaced by the 2nd Battalion of the 5th Cavalry, which flanked the fort from the west." . . . nothing in there about Big Man humping the 90mm for nine clicks and nothing about the junkyard of American equipment found by Delta Company below the fort. Aguirre's version, however narrow the perspective, gives a truer picture, pure butchery. The 1st of the 5th had been inserted into the middle of an NVA mortar range. I should make one correction. The rumor that the NVA battalion trapped "on the beach" had somehow escaped was untrue. It was destroyed.

None of the events I was involved in were important enough to leave deep historical tracks: too few people were killed. Not one of the many accounts of the war in Vietnam contains a map showing the location of LZ Mooney. A map in Del Vecchio's semi-autobiographical *13th Valley* identifies LZ Barbara. It is an interesting map, to me at least, since I was shot somewhere around there during one of the operations by which the division chased after fugitive, TET-mauled NVA battalions in the mountains during the summer and early fall of 1968. That operation had a name, Commanche Falls, but I did not learn that until years later. Commanche Falls involved several battalions (it was far bigger than I thought), lasted for weeks and the body count runs into the many hundreds. It is said to have been a victory but whether or not that is really true is now irrelevant.

No one should suppose that my experience in Vietnam was typical. It was not — except that I was shot. That was typical; indeed, routine. During its time in Vietnam the First Cavalry Division took over 30,000 casualties and most of those were in the infantry.

MILITARY HISTORY

Jon T. Oplinger was born on February 7th, 1944, in Akron, Ohio. He enlisted in the United States Army in April of 1966 and completed basic training at Fort Benning, Georgia. His advanced training (AIT) was at Fort Dix, New Jersey. He graduated from Infantry Officer Candidate School (Fifth Battalion) at Fort Benning in June of 1967 and was subsequently assigned to the Primary Helicopter School at Fort Wolters, Texas, where he served as the executive officer of a Headquarters Company. Immediately after Jungle Training (CZ) he was ordered to Vietnam. While in Vietnam (June through September, 1968) he served as a platoon leader in D Company, Second Battalion, Fifth Cavalry, First Cavalry Division (Air Mobile) and participated in Operation J.E.B. Stuart III and Commanche Falls. Oplinger was discharged from active service at Valley Forge Army Hospital in July of 1969. Thereafter he was assigned to the inactive reserves, which service consisted of receiving letters advising him that he was still in the inactive reserves. In 1983 a computer-generated form arrived notifying Oplinger of his final separation from the United States Army.

INDEX

Cromwell, Oliver, Bde. Commander 30

D Company, Second of the Fifth Cavalry 30–185
Da Nang 189
Dallas, Texas 9
Defoliant 101, 138
Del Vecchio, John M. 208
Demopolis, Alabama 12
Detroit, Michigan, riots 16
Dog tags 163
Dogs, Vietnamese, shot 44; *see also* soupbones
Dong Ha 54, 63, 96; elephants imagined at 102
Dud bombs: advantages of 154
Dust off *see* Medevac
Dysentery 89, 142, 144

Echo Company, Second of the Fifth 120–125, 134
Eisenstein, Sergei 13
Elephants: skeletons of 171

Fake extraction, described 125
Fall, Bernard 54
Fire cracker rounds, described 27; employed 99
First ARVN Division 91
First Cavalry Division 6, 23
First of the Fifth Cavalry: operations with 162–184
First of the Ninth 6, 27, 139, 145, 146, 182–184
Fleet Marines: recreational activities of 17
Flying ants: problems with 105
Flying Leathernecks (film) 13
Fort Benning, Georgia 1; infantry school at 2–4
Fort Gulick, Canal Zone 19
Fort Jackson, South Carolina 16, 20
Fort Wolters, Texas 4–10; Officers Open Mess (FAWOOM) 10
Forward Observer (FO) 28
Frag *see* Grenade, fragmentation

France, State Executioner of 17
Freeze-dried rations 114
French Fort 53; attacked 55, 208
Friendly fire 70
FTA, explained 116
Fuck Book, defined 89
Funeral detail 7, 9

Ghost shirts 203, 204
Gibbons 114
Graves, NVA: disinterment of 78
Graves registration 72, 201
Graves, USA: disinterment of 201
Great Smoky Mountains 14
Green Berets (film) 13, 58
Grenade, fragmentation (M-26): as booby trap 84, 85; as command detonated mine 112; as fishing tackle 41, 42; salvoed 51, 121
Grenade fragmentation, WWII 152
Grenade smoke 52; precautions 68
Grunt humor 44, 116
Guardia Nacíonal, Panama 20
Gun target line, defined 143
Gunships, Cobra *see* AH-1 Helicopter

H-23 helicopter 6
H-34 helicopter 186
Harass and interdict (H and I) 61; comforts of 63; hazards of 117
Heat exhaustion 89, 149, 153
Hia Lang 57
Highway One 35, 39
Ho Chi Minh racing slicks 54
Holes: aesthetics of 66
Homer, Winslow 176
Hospital, NVA 156
Huey *see* UH ID Helicopter

I Corps 24
Ice Cream 75, 112
Insect repellent 18

Jesus nut 69
Jones, James 28
Jungle fatigues: durability of 90, 91
Jungle penetrator 89, 184

213

Quang Tri Hospital 139, 185
Quick Reaction Force 119

Radio, field (PRC-25): importance of
  52
Radio logs (CDA Form, 1594) 207
Ranger training 1, 3
Recoilless rifle, 90 mm 63, 64
Red Splash, described 48
Roman Army: diet of 30

Salvation Army 194
San Francisco, California 21
Scout helicopters *see* OH-6, observa-
  tion helicopter
Search and evade 32; defined 107
Second Battalion Twentieth Aerial
  Rocket Artillery 182–184
Second of the Fifth Cavalry: operations
  of 30–159
Second of the Twelfth Cavalry 55
Sergeant York (film) 12
Shitburners: duties of 28, 29
Simulate, defined 37
*Skeletal Age Changes in Young
  American Males* 201
SKS Carbine 139
Slide for Life 18
Soupbones 95, 96
Special Forces 4
Squad Leaders Course, First Cavalry
  Division 97
Stand to, defined 61
Stanton, Shelby 208
Street Without Joy 54
Stump trained mules 145

Tabasco sauce: necessity of 30, 31
Tableaux Vivant, Methodist 161
Tactical Operations Command (TOC)
  94, 108
Tactical Training Officer (TAC Officer)
  2
Temporarily Disoriented (also Mis-
  oriented): responses to being 74, 75

Tet Offensive 8, 53
Texas Gothic 9
"These Boots Are Made for Walkin'"
  (popular song) 10
Third of the Fifth Armored Cavalry
  129–131
13th Valley 208
Trash dumps, hazards of 53, 93
Travis Air Force Base 21
Trip flares, described 52
Twenty-Fifth Division 4

UH-1 (Huey) helicopters, dependence
  on 69; crash sites 169, 170
U.S. Army Overseas Replacement Station (USAOSREPLSTA), Fort Jackson, South Carolina 16
U.S. Navy, SEALS 19
U.S.S. Repose 186

Valley Forge Army Hospital 193–199
Vancouver, Canada 8
Vicksburg battlefield 11
Vicksburg, Mississippi 11

Wait-a-bit vines 75
War of 1812 16
Warrant officer candidate (WOC) 5
Water buffalo 49, 50
Wayne, John 200
Wayne County, Ohio 15
Weapons cache, NVA 79, 115
West Lebanon, Ohio 14
Wild pigs, attacked 67; uses of 171
Wunder Beach 127

Xa, concept of 49

York, Alvin, Medal of Honor citation
  13
Youngman, Arthur 14–16

Zambar Bar, Colon, Panama 20

214